Translation Practices Explained

Translation Practices Explained is a series of coursebooks designed to help self-learners and teachers of translation. Each volume focuses on a specific aspect of professional translation practice, in many cases corresponding to actual courses available in translator-training institutions. Special volumes are devoted to well consolidated professional areas, such as legal translation or European Union texts; to areas where labour-market demands are currently undergoing considerable growth, such as screen translation in its different forms; and to specific aspects of professional practices on which little teaching and learning material is available, the case of editing and revising, or electronic tools. The authors are practising translators or translator trainers in the fields concerned. Although specialists, they explain their professional insights in a manner accessible to the wider learning public.

These books start from the recognition that professional translation practices require something more than elaborate abstraction or fixed methodologies. They are located close to work on authentic texts, and encourage learners to proceed inductively, solving problems as they arise from examples and case studies.

Each volume includes activities and exercises designed to help self-learners consolidate their knowledge; teachers may also find these useful for direct application in class, or alternatively as the basis for the design and preparation of their own material. Updated reading lists and website addresses will also help individual learners gain further insight into the realities of professional practice.

Sharon O'Brien
Kelly Washbourne
Series Editors

Revising and Editing for Translators

Brian Mossop

Routledge
Taylor & Francis Group

LONDON AND NEW YORK

First published 2001
by St. Jerome Publishing

Second edition published 2007
by St. Jerome Publishing

This edition published 2014
by Routledge
2 Park Square, Milton Park, Abingdon, Oxon OX14 4RN

and by Routledge
711 Third Avenue, New York, NY 10017

Routledge is an imprint of the Taylor & Francis Group, an informa business

© 2001, 2007, 2014 Brian Mossop

British Library Cataloguing in Publication Data
A catalogue record for this book is available from the British Library

Library of Congress Cataloguing in Publication Data
A catalog record for this title has been applied for

ISBN: 978-1-138-78671-4 (hbk)
ISBN: 978-1-909485-01-3 (pbk)
ISBN: 978-1-315-76713-0 (ebk)

Typeset by
Delta Typesetters, Cairo, Egypt

Printed and bound in the United States of America by Edwards Brothers Malloy, Inc.

Contents

Acknowledgements

I would like to acknowledge the following editors, translators, revisers and teachers who commented on various sections of the original manuscript of this book: Louise Brunette, Jane Conway, Sarah Cummins, Albert Daigen, Jacqueline Elton, Anita Kern, Louise Malloch, Ken Popert and Anthony Pym. Special thanks to Anne Schjoldager for her very detailed commentary on the first edition. I have also benefited from comments made during the many revision workshops which I have led in Canada, the US, South Africa and half a dozen European countries since the second edition appeared.

Introduction for Users

This book aims to provide guidance and learning materials for two groups of users: first, professional translators or translation students who wish to improve their ability to revise their own translations ('self-revision') or learn to revise translations prepared by others ('other-revision'); second, translation students who are learning to edit original writing by others. *In this book, revising means reading a translation in order to spot problematic passages, and making any needed corrections or improvements. Editing is this same task applied to texts which are not translations.*

Revising and editing are first and foremost exercises in very careful reading. You can't correct errors until you have found them, and it is very easy to simply not notice problems, or to notice minor problems (a paragraph was not indented) and miss major ones (the word 'not' is missing and the sentence means the opposite of what it is supposed to mean).

Self-revision, other-revision and editing have much in common. They all involve checking linguistic correctness as well as the suitability of a text's style to its future readers and to the use they will make of it. Much of what you do when revising is identical to what you do when editing. Whether you are editing original writing or revising a translation, you may decide to amend an awkward wording, for example. In either case, you have to make sure that you do not change the author's meaning while eliminating the awkwardness. That said, there are of course differences. Revisers will often come across unidiomatic wordings as a result of interference from the source language – a problem which editors will encounter only if the writer is not a native speaker of the language of the text. Revisers must also find and correct mistranslations and omissions – parts of the source text that were overlooked when the translation was drafted.

'Reviser' and 'editor' are not really parallel terms. Both words can be used simply to refer to someone who happens to be checking and amending a text, or someone whose function it is to do so, but 'editor' is more commonly used to name a profession. In many countries, there are editors' associations which are quite separate from writers' associations, but there are no revisers' associations separate from translators' associations. 'Reviser' is not the name of a profession; the activity or function of revising has developed historically as part of the profession of translator, though some translators may spend much or even all of their time revising. The relationship between writer and editor is therefore different from the relationship between translator and reviser, which might perhaps be better described as a relationship between the drafting translator and the revising translator.

In addition, in some countries, translators and editors live in completely separate professional worlds, with little contact between translators' and editors' organizations. In other countries, they have close professional relationships, and translators' and editors' organizations may have overlapping memberships: it may be unusual for someone to be a translator and not also an editor.

As will be seen in Chapter 2, a professional editor may engage in a huge range of tasks, from finding authors to discussing typographical details with printers. An editor may decide to recommend or insist on changes which would fall outside the purview of a translation reviser: delete whole sections, or rewrite them with new content. The treatment of editing in this book, however, is restricted to a fairly narrow range of activities: copyediting, stylistic editing and certain aspects of structural and content editing. The selection of editing topics, and the amount of attention accorded them, is governed by a simple principle: to the extent that an editing skill is also needed by revisers (and self-revisers) of translations, to that extent it is included. This is why the book is entitled Revising and Editing *for Translators*, and it is a feature that distinguishes this book from other treatments of editing.

When translation students graduate, they may find – depending on their language pair and the local translation market – that they cannot earn an adequate income from translation alone. They will be in a better position if they can accept related work such as technical writing or editing. Many people today seek work as translator/revisers and also as editors. A native English speaker resident in the Netherlands may translate from Dutch to English, revise Dutch-English translations, edit material written in English by Dutch speakers, and write original English material for Dutch companies.

Employers often want to hire 'translator-editors', reflecting the fact that in organizations such as corporations and ministries, translation production is integrated into the general process of producing print and electronic documents. Here are descriptions of two translator-editor positions in Canada, the first in a government agency, the second at a science centre:

> Translate, revise, standardize and re-write public and internal documents such as reports, announcements, decisions, ministerial orders, brochures, press releases, memos, etc. for employees and managers of the Agency. Coordinate requests for translation and revision for the Agency. Coordinate the preparation of briefing notes for the Minister and, when the responsible person is absent, of ministerial and executive correspondence.

> Research, write, edit French copy related to scientific technological exhibits and programs for visiting or virtual public. Produce small publications, write for websites, copyedit, translate English material with extensive scientific content into clear, interesting, understandable French copy and meet deadlines.

The editing sections of this book should be of use to anyone who will be doing work of the sort just described. As for the revision sections, they will assist students in degree or diploma translation programs, practising translators who are assigned to revise others, and self-learners who wish to accept freelance revision work. The revision part of the book may also prove instructive to people who manage translation services but are not themselves professional translators.

Professionals who have a degree in translation may recall their teachers telling them how important it is to check their translations, that is, to self-revise. But if they look back at their textbooks, they will see that little or no substantive advice is given about just how to do this. They may never have learned any actual principles or procedures for self-revision. If they have been practising professionals for some time, they will have developed some procedure or other, but they may never have formulated it and looked at it critically. Is it achieving the desired purpose, and just what is that desired purpose?

The same applies to revising others, and to setting up or implementing quality control systems. It is important to think about the concepts involved (Just what *is* quality?) and about the procedures that will be used to achieve quality. New revisers tend to waste a great deal of time making unnecessary changes in texts. If they are to overcome this problem, and be able to decide what is necessary and what is not, they must clearly formulate in their minds the goals of revision.

In day-to-day work, of course, one proceeds to a great degree without conscious thought. As one revises or self-revises, one does not think: now I shall consider point five on my style checklist, and now I shall go on to point six. However, if you have reason to believe that your procedures are not catching errors, or if you think (or your supervisor thinks!) that you are taking too long to quality-control a text, then perhaps you need to bring your procedures to the mental surface – spell them out and then consider them in the light of certain principles. This book is intended to help you do so.

Translating by revising

With the spread of Translation Memory, learning to revise translations by other people is becoming more important than it used to be. Many translators use memories that contain translations done by a large number of other translators. When material from these databases is imported into the translation on which a translator is currently working, he or she must decide to what degree the imported wording is useable in the current context. It may be necessary to make changes for a variety of reasons: the meaning of the imported material is somewhat different from the meaning of the current source text; the imported material is stylistically inconsistent with the translator's own wordings; there is a lack of cohesion between an imported sentence and the previous or following sentence; different imported sentences are not consistent with each other with respect to terminology and phraseology. When a great deal of material is imported from the memory's database, the task of translating becomes, to a great extent, an exercise in revising other people's wordings rather than an exercise in composing sentences in the target language. Translators who use Memory thus need to develop a reviser/editor mentality rather than the mentality of a text composer.

While the above tasks need to be performed even when importing material from a memory that contains nothing but the translator's own previous translations, the revision burden is greater when importing wordings written by others since there is far less certainty about the reliability of the work done by the other translators. There may be pressure on translators to use the imported wordings in order to save time, even though corporate memories (containing translations by large numbers of translators) are notorious disseminators of mistranslations. In any situation where there is a growing volume of material that needs translating, but an insufficient number of translators, there will inevitably be a tendency to modify the concept of what counts as acceptable final quality in order to reflect what the translators are able to achieve with the assistance of the particular technologies they are using.

Aside from memories, translators working in many language pairs and genres now have access to useable machine translation output, and this too calls for people to revise wordings that are not their own.

What this book is not

The book is not intended to form the self-editing component of a writing course. The users of the editing chapters are, after all, students in a professional language programme. Presumably they are already quite good at writing in their own language, and good writing of course requires good self-editing. In the revision part of the book, however, self-revision is included because many working translators are not efficient self-revisers, and also because very little has been written about the practical details of self-revision.

This is not a workbook. Many chapters end with descriptions of exercises, and a few include exercises on short sentences or sentence fragments. However there are no complete texts, for that would have made the book much longer (and more expensive!), and my text selection might not have been found suitable by many if not most course instructors.

The book presumes a basic knowledge of grammar. It does not explain what a subordinate clause is, or give instruction on how to identify the subject of a sentence. When editing and revising the work of others, it is often necessary to explain why a change has been made, and that calls for some knowledge of grammatical structure and terminology. All translation students would be well advised to take an introductory course in linguistics, for this will give them concepts and terms with which to think about and talk about language.

The book is not a guide to writing do's and don'ts. It offers no advice on the correct use of semicolons, on how to avoid sexist language, or on whether a sentence can begin with 'and'. These, and a thousand and one similar issues, are the subject of innumerable writers' handbooks that can be found on the reference shelves of most bookstores. Naturally the exercises in this book call for a knowledge of these substantive matters, but the body of each chapter focuses on principles and procedures.

The book is not a review of the problems of translation. In the course of revising, one is faced with the need not merely to identify errors but also to correct them. To do so, one obviously needs to have the full range of text-interpreting, researching, composing and computer skills that are required of a translator.

These matters are discussed only to the extent that they apply in a special way to the revising process as opposed to the translation drafting process.

The book does not cover the creation of a visual form for the text: desktop publishing and the layout of text and graphics are not discussed. Certain matters of visual presentation are mentioned briefly, such as consistency in typography and in the form and placement of headings and subheadings, but the production of the physical print or on-line document containing the translation is beyond the scope of this book. There is also no coverage of the processes of marking up a manuscript (nowadays usually a Word file) for the printer and checking the printer's output (nowadays often a .pdf file).

The book does not provide a thorough treatment of machine translation post-editing, in part because I have only a small amount of personal experience with it, and in part because most translators I have encountered at recent revision workshops still do not use it. That said, much of what will be found here does apply to post-editing.

The book is not concerned with the editing and revision of literary texts. Literary texts can conveniently be defined as fictional or non-fictional writing in which named individuals engage in self-expression on their own behalf. Part of the value of such texts often lies in the particular linguistic forms selected. A non-literary text by contrast is typically anonymous, or else written by a named individual on behalf of an institution, and the linguistic form is of no value in itself; indeed, in current English, the ideal with such texts is for the linguistic form to be transparent – unnoticed by the reader. The checking and amending of literary translations takes place within a commercial publishing environment that differs from the translation departments and agencies within which non-literary texts are revised. The exception is marketing documents, which have affinities with literary translation in the great importance of the specific linguistic forms selected. A successful translation of such a document (one which helps sell the product) may also need to deviate from the norms of accuracy and completeness that usually govern non-literary translation. Revision of this type of translation work will not be considered here except for a brief mention of adaptation (large-scale adding to and subtracting from the source text).

Finally, the revising and editing work needed for software and webpage localization is not considered since these kinds of translation involve both adaptation and text/graphic/video coordination.

Principles and procedures

Principles versus rules

This book approaches both editing and revising as exercises not in rule-following but in the intelligent application of principles. Neither editing nor revising is straightforward. There are indeed clear-cut cases of right/wrong, but there are many more cases where it is up to you to decide, and for this you will need principles.

Principles are simply guides to action. An example would be the principle of minimizing changes: If in doubt about whether to make a change in the text, don't. You might also think of principles as things you do 'in principle', that is, things you do by default, unless the situation suggests doing something else. 'Follow the paragraphing of the source text' might be a principle in this sense for many language pairs. It is not a 'rule'; when you are revising, you may find that there is a good reason to change the paragraphing.

Formulating procedures

Aside from principles, the main thing you need in order to be a successful editor or reviser is procedures. It is all very well to have a list of error types, but if your procedure does not succeed in finding the errors, the list is not much use. As already mentioned, you cannot correct a problem until you have spotted it! *Editing and revising are both, first and foremost, exercises in very careful reading.*

Eventually, procedures will become second-nature, but the point of studying revision and editing is to formulate them. This book aims to help its readers to answer, or at least think about, questions such as the following: In what *order* should I carry out editing and revising tasks? (What should I do first? Second?) And given that one can go on perfecting a text endlessly, when should I *stop*?

Principles and language pairs

Do the same principles apply to editing in all languages, and to revision in all language pairs? Many do, but editing work in particular will differ from language to language because the linguistic culture of a society will dictate certain emphases; problems of a certain type will be deemed important that may seem quite unimportant in another language community. For example, if one society is moving out from under the influence of a formerly dominating other society, reduction of the linguistic influence of that other society may be seen as an important aspect of editorial work. Also, one linguistic culture may currently be in a phase where a 'plain style' is the ideal in non-literary texts, whereas another culture may currently prefer a more ornate style. This will obviously affect the work of editors; for example, the concept of readability, discussed in Chapter 4, may differ if an ornate style is preferred.

A further important point is that two editors may be working in different linguistic cultures even though both of them use the same name for their language. In other words, the factors affecting editing work may differ depending on whether you are in Dublin or Sydney, in Paris or Montréal, in Lisbon or São Paulo. Obviously if you are editing texts for publication in another country, you will need to make appropriate adjustments. For example, Canadians submitting material to US or British publications may have to edit out Canadian spellings and substitute US or British spellings. To outsiders, the Canadian system looks like a combination of British and American spellings—'honour', not 'honor'; but 'organize', not 'organise'. To Canadians, it is simply the way we learned to spell our language as children. It is also of symbolic importance – one small way in which we English-speaking Canadians distinguish ourselves from the Americans. Defending the local identity of texts is often an important part of the work of editors and revisers.

The editing sections of this book are very heavily oriented toward the linguistic cultures of the countries where the great majority of the population are native speakers of English. For the most part, it is assumed that the texts are written by native speakers and are being edited for reading by native speakers. Much of what is said will be applicable to other cases (texts written in English by non-native speakers or for a multilingual, international audience; texts written in the French-influenced Euro-English of the institutions of the European Union), but the special problems of these cases will be discussed only briefly. Those who will be editing material written in languages other than English may find that some of what is said about English here is relevant to them because English writing habits are increasingly having an effect on how people write in other languages.

The revision sections of the book are probably more universally valid than the editing sections. Again, though, emphases will vary. If translated texts are widely used in a society, an important function of revisers may be to eliminate any traces of foreign influence. In a society where translated texts do not play such a great role, source-language influence on the wording of the translation may be more tolerable.

The revision sections of the book will be applicable when the target language is the self-reviser's second language, or when the source language is the source-text author's second language, or when revising translations of translations. However, little attention will be paid to the special additional problems of these cases, such as the difficulty of assessing idiomaticity when the self-reviser is not a native target-language speaker. For those who are advanced learners or near-native speakers of English, self-revising English is much easier than it used to be because you can check wordings of which you are uncertain in Google (see Chapter 8) or in concordancers and because there are now good Advanced Learner's dictionaries, often on-line or on CD-ROM, which provide vital information that is not given (because it is assumed to be already known) in dictionaries aimed at native speakers.

Outline

The book begins with a consideration of why editing and revising are needed in the first place, and of what quality is (Chapter 1). Chapter 2 concerns the work done by people employed as editors. This is followed by four chapters (3-6) devoted to the various kinds of textual amending work: copyediting, stylistic editing, structural editing and content editing. Chapter 7 is concerned with the question of how much consistency an editor or reviser should seek to achieve, and Chapter 8 with computer aids for editors and revisers. Chapter 9 looks at the work of people who function as revisers. It is followed by three chapters that look at the following questions: What are the features of a draft translation that may require revision (Chapter 10)? To what degree should I revise a translation (Chapter 11)? What procedures should I use to revise (Chapter 12)? Finally, Chapter 13 looks at self-revision, and Chapter 14 at the problems of revising others. The book closes with a list of readings on revision, an index, and six appendixes: a review of the principles of revision, a brief look at systems for assessing the quality of translations, a method for marking exercises, a sample revision, a glossary of editing and revision terms, and an overview of empirical studies of revision.

New in this Edition

For this third edition, aside from checking, improving and updating the entire second edition, and adding more cross-references between chapters, I have placed more emphasis on the reading (as opposed to the writing) aspect of revision and editing. In addition, there is a considerably modified Introduction for Instructors, a greatly expanded section on the vital concept of quality in Chapter 1, a new section on editing non-native English in Chapter 2, additional discussion of quality assurance and a few other topics in Chapter 9, new material on revision policies in Chapter 11, a new presentation of the self-revision process in Chapter 13, a separate section on Translation Memory in Chapter 14, new material on translation assessment in Appendix 2, and a much expanded list of readings.

Introduction for Instructors

This book aims to be of use to three types of instructor:

- those giving courses with an editing or revising component to students at translation schools;

- those leading professional development workshops (PDWs) in revision or self-revision for practising translators;

- those assigned to train junior translators or supervise students doing a practicum at a translation workplace.

The outcomes sought by PDW leaders and workplace trainers are immediately practical: the people they are training want principles and tips which they can immediately put into practice in their professional lives. For those teaching students at translation schools, the situation is different. In some classes, none of the students have practical experience of professional work. Even those who do are not just being trained (prepared for the workplace); they are also being educated in matters linguistic. The course should be an opportunity to acquire an awareness of issues through lecture-discussions, readings, student presentations, and exercises designed to stimulate thought.

Instructors of translation students

Instruction in editing, self-revision and other-revision – whether as a stand-alone course or as a component of another course – is introduced at different stages of learning in different countries and at different schools. Opinions differ as to what is appropriate in this regard, especially since translation degrees may be offered only at the master's level in some countries, but at the undergraduate level as well, or instead, in others. In the two previous editions of this book, I argued that editing can be introduced to senior undergraduates in the classroom, but self-revision should be introduced during practicums (when students work in a translation office for a few weeks), and other-revision should be introduced during PDWs (after a translator has had at least a few months' practice revising others in the workplace) or else in those master's diploma programs in which all students already have professional experience.

One obvious difficulty with this approach is that a great many people do not have access to practicums or PDWs. A second difficulty is that revising others has two aspects – personal interaction with those whose work is being revised, and grappling with other people's wordings. Even undergraduate students need to learn something about this second aspect, because once they enter the work world, they will be faced with revising other people's wordings when using Translation Memory. Revising wordings that are not your own is quite different psychologically from revising wordings that are. Finally, there is no basis in translation pedagogy research for deciding when to introduce self-revision and other-revision. Schools should do what they think best, and see what the results are. The proof of the pudding will be in the eating! That said, I have not written this book with novices such as first-year translation students in mind.

An important distinction when teaching translation students is that between *things they need to know about* and *things they should actually be able to do* upon graduation. For example, students should know *that* a big problem in revising is deciding the extent of revision effort to be applied to a text: should one do both a comparative and a unilingual re-reading or just a single reading? should one read all or just part of the translation? Actually making such decisions is perhaps a matter best left to the workplace or PDWs (see Chapter 11).

A related issue is the connection between *what is to be taught in class* and *what happens in the workplace*. Since different professional editors and revisers work in different ways, there is no point in teaching as if one best way were known. Indeed, there is no particular reason to try to duplicate any of the procedures of professionals. The procedure that is best for learning to edit or revise is not necessarily going to be the procedure that an experienced professional actually uses. This is certainly true of exercises. For example, it is doubtful that anyone in the workplace would ever have occasion to edit a text solely for problems with inter-sentence connector words. But an exercise focused solely on this issue is nevertheless of great pedagogical value.

The two matters just discussed (doing versus knowing and workplace versus classroom) are related to a more general pedagogical issue: achieving results versus internalizing procedures and principles. What students mainly need to do is internalize principles and procedures for editing and revising. They should also become aware of contentious issues and of problems – the things that can make written communication difficult. However, actually becoming good at applying the principles and procedures and at solving the problems (that is, creating high-quality output fairly quickly) takes quite a long time – perhaps five years of full-time professional experience. That is because you cannot revise or edit well until you are familiar with the procedures of a workplace and have had practice interacting with real clients and working under real deadlines.

I strongly suggest, therefore, that instructors use exercises to focus the attention of students on problems, principles and procedures. Do not focus on results ('right' versus 'wrong' answers). Do not get bogged down in substantive details such as whether it is alright to start a sentence with a conjunction. If this latter question arises, just point out that some people allow it, at least in some text types, while others don't. The important thing to learn about such matters is that the answer depends on the particular writing project, on the general approach taken to English usage (see Chapter 3), and on the standards set by employers, publishers and professional associations.

Marking

When it comes to marking, results inevitably take precedence over principles and procedures. The rather obvious reason is that it is hard to grade procedures.

Even if it were practical to watch students doing their assignments, most of the action would be going on unseen in the mind. Empirical studies have been made in which students' translating sessions are recorded and the students are then shown what they did and interviewed about it, but this is far too time-consuming to be practical for everyday marking purposes. Still, one assignment could be the preparation of a diary, which may give the instructor a degree of insight into the student's approach. Each pair of students is given a different text to edit/revise. They make a class presentation, in which they diagnose five or ten problems they experienced while editing/revising the text, and describe the procedure they used (or think they used) to edit/revise it – what they did first, what they did second and so on. (One difficulty here is imperfect recall combined with the natural human tendency to rationalize and prettify what one actually did!) The students then prepare a diary for the instructor, describing how they went about solving problems and taking the class discussion into account.

If you are handing out a text-based assignment on paper, make sure the text to be edited or revised is triple spaced, and that the margins are wide enough for adding annotations or comments. Ask the students to hand-write their changes on the printed text. If the assignment is distributed in electronic form, you might give students a choice between printing it out and handwriting changes or using Track Changes; alternatively you might insist on one or the other of these pos-sibilities. Both are used in the work world (see Chapter 8). However you may find one approach more personally congenial, or one approach better suited to your marking system. If your marking system consists in simply writing comments on the student's work, and then assigning an overall grade, you can do this using the Comments function of your word-processing programs. If on the other hand your system requires positioning a variety of symbols in various locations on the student's text, that may be easier to do on paper.

Students should under no circumstances prepare an edited/revised version on a separate sheet of paper or e-document, first because that will encourage over-editing/over-revising (or worse, complete rewriting/retranslating), second because that is not the way things are done in the work world, and third because the students will not then be able to visualize the relationship between the origin-al and edited/revised versions. (It will also be harder for you to mark!)

Appendix 3 contains a possible marking scheme. It assumes that you have cho-sen to assign marks to the student's treatment of individual words and phrases, rather than simply assign an overall mark based on your general impression.

If you instruct both students who are just beginning a translation program and those near the end of a program, you might consider using two rather dif-ferent approaches to marking. For the junior students, use a more 'humanistic' approach that rewards strengths, rewards good approaches (even if the results are wrong) and gives encouragement on weaknesses. For the senior students, use a more realistic approach focused on penalizing weaknesses. It is not fair to give senior students who will soon be entering the job market an unrealistic view of the quality of their output. They need to know what will be expected of a novice.

Computer aids

If students cannot edit or revise with a pencil, they will not be able to do so with computer tools. By this, I do not mean that students should do all their editing and revision exercises on paper (though a great many professional editors and revisers do still work on paper). I mean that the central skills to be learned are no different whether students are working on screen or on paper: Can they recognize a problem in a text when they see one? Can they decide whether a change is needed? It is important to bear in mind that while professional writing, editing and translating work has become computer-assisted over the past thirty years, it has not become automated. All the knowledge and skills that were needed in the days of manual typewriters are still needed. The existence of Spellcheck does not mean that editors and revisers no longer need an independent knowledge of spelling!

Learning outcomes and exercise types

What are realistic outcomes for a course in revision at a translation school? It is extremely unlikely that after a single semester, students will actually be able to revise well. The most important thing is that they should have a clear awareness of the issues: the need to avoid unnecessary changes so as to get jobs completed as quickly and cheaply as possible, the need to be able to justify changes, the need to develop positive and ethical interactions with other parties involved in translation (original translator, commissioner, source-text author, etc). They should also have tried out various revision procedures (see Chapter 12) and begun to develop a personal systematic approach.

Every in-class exercise and take-home assignment should of course be related to the desired outcomes. Never simply ask students to revise a text. In addition to the revision itself, they should also write out justifications of some of the changes. They should report passages where they considered making a change but then didn't, explaining why not. They should prepare commentaries on pre-revised texts (see Appendix 4 for an example). They should prepare explanations of what they would do in cases where loyalty to one party conflicts with loyalty to another (see the scenario exercise at the end of Chapter 6).

Professional development instructors

The pedagogical approaches suitable for instructing students are quite different from those suitable for professional development sessions with practising translators. Professional translators attending workshops on revision are already producing work for the translation market. The workshop or seminar is about a familiar activity, to which they can mentally refer as the session proceeds. If the workshop deals with other-revision only, it's best that participants already have a few months' experience revising others so that they can refer to that experience during the session.

I have had occasion to lead workshops on revision where all participants had over 15 years' experience. As workshop leader, I was not really teaching revision. Such workshops serve three purposes. First, participants become more self-confident when they discover that others too are having a particular sort of problem, or have not found any better solution to that problem. Sometimes the most important function of a workshop is therapeutic – to relieve participants of a certain burden of anxiety: "Am I the only one having this problem?". Second, since a workshop requires participants to formulate procedures that may have become semi-automated, they may become aware that their revision or self-revision procedure is not as good as some other procedure. Third, workshops are an important social occasion for those participants who spend their days working alone.

In preparing exercises for workshops, remember that an exercise is not a simulation of the workplace. The whole point of a workshop is to look at issues that participants may never have explicitly considered, or matters that remain below the level of consciousness during everyday revision work. Such issues can often be brought out best not through text-based exercises but through scenario exercises (see examples at the end of Chapter 9).

A very important thing to practice in revision workshops is justification of changes, that is, saying why the existing wording was not suitable. It is not sufficient for a reviser to say "It doesn't sound right the way you have it". Justifying changes calls for a fairly high level of awareness about linguistic and textual structure, as well as a set of terms for discussing the changes. This book assumes that users already have an understanding of grammatical concepts and terms (main verb, subject, subordinate clause), but it does introduce terminology for talking about the different kinds of changes which revisers make.

The greatest danger in a revision workshop is that it will turn into a translation workshop. I strongly recommend that during exercises with texts, participants should simply be asked to underline wordings that need change, but *they should not make any changes.* If they make changes, the workshop can easily degenerate into a discussion of what is the best replacement wording. This is not a revision question but rather a translation question. It's true that the correcting work of the reviser is not exactly the same as the work of drafting a translation, in that one is not writing on a blank screen but rather reworking an existing wording. Indeed, given this difference, it may be worth having an exercise on minimizing the extent of rewording (i.e. avoiding out-and-out retranslation unless that's absolutely necessary). Still, going by my own experience, if the instructor asks participants to make changes in every exercise, much time will be wasted discussing competing alternative translations and trying to decide which is the best. The instructor needs to keep the participants focused on *revision issues: finding the passages which might need change, deciding whether they do in fact need change, and stating a justification for making a change.*

Do exercises alone or in groups?

Translation is essentially a solitary occupation. In the workplace, a text may be divided among several translators, or translators may consult each other in person, by telephone or by e-mail. However, the bulk of the work goes on in the individual's mind. Similarly, you cannot efficiently revise a text in a group ('What does everyone think of the first sentence in the second paragraph?').

However, for pedagogical purposes, the situation is quite different. Both professionals and students can learn faster in groups. With students, the situation is complicated by the need to give them marks as individuals. Thus some assignments (both in-class and take-home) must be done alone, in preparation for tests. In workshops for practicing professionals, however, all exercises can be done in groups.

One big advantage of dividing into groups is that each person then spends more time in active rather than passive participation. If each of 15 people gives a 3-minute presentation on their self-revision procedure to the other 14, he or she is passive for 42 minutes out of 45 (93% of the time). If the 15 people are divided into groups of 3, and each group member gives a 3-minute presentation to the other two, he or she is passive for only 6 minutes out of 9 (66% of the time). Also, the exercise will be completed much sooner (in 9 minutes instead of 45!). There is no need for each of the 15 participants to hear all 14 of the other presentations. With some exercises, a plenary session will be needed after the groups have completed their work. Thus each of 5 groups might be assigned one-fifth of a text for a justification-of-changes exercise. When all groups have prepared their justifications, one member presents to the plenary.

Working in groups is important because participants can learn as much from each other as they can from the instructor (perhaps more, according to some). With professional development workshops, only 20-25% of the time should be devoted to a presentation on revision by the instructor; the remainder should be spent on group exercises and discussion. With translation students, the greater difference in knowledge between instructor and learner, especially in introductory courses, will necessitate more direct input from the instructor both before and after exercises. With advanced students, however, some sort of group work should take up much of the classroom time.

Texts for exercises

In selecting exercise materials for editing and revising, an important consideration is the number and type of errors they contain. There are two possibilities: you can find texts with errors, or insert the errors yourself. With the first of these approaches, you will need to find texts of a suitable length that have neither too many errors nor too few. A text with only four errors in thirty pages isn't much use. Neither is a text with five mistakes on every line; as is pointed out in Chapter 1, some texts are so bad that they are not worth editing or revising. Avoid really dreadful pieces of writing or translating.

The big problem with using texts in their natural state is that they will most often contain a wide variety of problems: punctuation errors, idiom errors, poor sentence connectors, mistranslations, errors in level of language and so on. While some exercises should certainly aim at identifying and correcting a wide range of error types, many should focus on a single type of error, or a group of related types of error. To create texts for such exercises, you will need to eliminate all other types of error, and possibly add some errors of the type in question.

Editing instructors may wish to use draft translations for exercises (or published translations of dubious quality), but in order to avoid the above-mentioned danger of retranslation, they should be sure not to distribute the source text. Another type of text worth using is one originally written in the students' first language but by a writer who is not a native speaker of that language. In the case of English in particular, the work of editing such texts is becoming an increasingly common professional assignment (some people now make a living from it). However, once again, avoid using really dreadful writing.

Where can texts be obtained? Leaders of revision workshops can use weak translations by junior translators or freelances. Editing instructors may be able to obtain samples of poor writing from teachers in other departments. Texts written by non-native speakers can be obtained on the Internet, or from teachers in other departments who have foreign students. Newspapers often contain poorly edited articles. Texts selected will of course be anonymous and it is best to select texts that were written a few years earlier, to avoid any possibility that their authors will be present at the session!

On-the-job trainers

The main value of this book for those training junior translators or students doing internships is that it can provide a vocabulary for discussing translation with the trainee.

You will also have to report on the trainee's work, for which you will need some system of diagnosis (see Chapter 14.2). And you will want to offer advice (see Chapter 14.3).

You might want to have the trainee do a few texts with Track Changes turned on so that you can get some idea of how he or she self-revises (see Chapter 13.1), and then perhaps suggest trying out other approaches.

When revising the trainee's texts, it's a good idea to distinguish changes which are necessary before the text can be delivered to the client and on the other hand changes which simply show another way the passage could have been translated. Use pen for the former, pencil for the latter; or if revising on screen, use a Comment box for suggestions about other ways of translating.

Language

The illustrative examples used in this book are for the most part in English. As already mentioned in the Introduction for Users, the editing sections of the book may not be suitable for courses where texts in languages other than English are being edited. As for the revision sections of the book, these should prove useable even by those revising translations into a language other than English, but they may well find that certain problems which are important in their target language are not touched on, or are skimmed over too lightly. For example, the issue of regional varieties of a language is considered here only in passing because it is not a terribly important issue in most parts of the English-speaking world. With languages other than English, this may be an extremely important issue. It will depend on the geographical origin of the participants in your course or workshop, the variety of the language in which they were educated, where they are or will be working, and who their clients are or will be.

In some countries, notably those where 'small' languages are spoken, editors and revisers may find themselves correcting and improving texts written in their second language, often English. Editing instructors in these countries may feel they should be preparing students for such work. However, if this is not the situation in your country, avoid using texts written in the students' second language, since editing issues will then get mixed up with language-learning issues. The same applies to professional development workshops on revision: if you use translations into the second language of all or some of the workshop participants, then revision issues may get mixed up with the problems of working into the second language.

Experience shows that it is perfectly possible to run revision workshops in which different participants work with different language pairs/directions, as long as there is one language which everyone understands fairly well in its spoken form and reads fairly well in its written form. Scenario exercises can be devised which involve no text at all, and some of the text-based exercises can be exercises in unilingual re-reading in the common language (though non-native readers of that language may find the exercise more difficult than native readers). For exercises that involve source/target comparison, if participants work in only a very small number of language pairs, the instructor can prepare several short texts, one for each language pair/direction. With exercises that are very brief (just one or two sentences long), you can try providing a gloss of the source text in the common language. For group work, have each participant sit at a small table with others who can converse in a given language. Plenary discussion will be in the common language of the entire group.

Syllabus suggestions

Some chapters of the book concern revision only (9-14) and some concern editing only (2-6). The remaining chapters (1, 7 and 8), as well as the Introduction for Users, concern both.

Thus for an editing course, use the Introduction for Users and Chapters 1-8. Copyediting, being the easiest type of editing, should be taught first, but of course in the actual process of editing a text, it comes last: there is no point copyediting a passage which will be deleted during content editing.

For a revision course, use the Introduction for Users and Chapters 9-14, plus 1, 7 and 8. You might want to supplement the book with readings on quality assessment (touched on only briefly here, in Appendix 2). When you discuss unilingual re-reading (where the translation is checked without reference to the source text, as described in Chapter 11), you might add materials on editing from Chapters 3-6.

For a professional development workshop on revision, which will typically last just one day, there will be no readings by participants. Rather you, as workshop leader, will prepare speaking notes (drawing on the chapters of this book which you wish to cover), plus exercises, and perhaps a slideshow presentation. A workshop can focus on self-revision, on other-revision, or cover both. However note that text-based exercises on self-revision are very time-consuming because workshop participants first have to prepare a draft translation, and this cannot be done ahead of time because part of the point of such an exercise is to consider the relationship between revising while drafting the translation and revising after drafting is complete (see Chapter 13).

Further Reading

(See the References list near the end of the book for details on these publications.)

Hansen (2009b); Klaudy (1995); Kruger (2008); Künzli (2006a); Mossop (1992); Payne (1987).

1. Why Editing and Revising are Necessary

Why is it necessary for someone other than the writer or translator to check a text, and perhaps make changes, before it is sent off to readers? In this chapter, we'll look at several reasons. First, it is extraordinarily easy to write sentences that are structured in such a way that readers will misunderstand them or have difficulty understanding them. Second, it is easy, while writing, to forget about the future readers and write something which is not suited to them or to the use they will make of the text. Third, a text may fail to conform to society's linguistic rules, or the reigning ideas about the proper way to translate or to write in a particular genre. Finally, what the author or translator has written may conflict with the publisher's goals.

To deal with these problems, revisers and editors amend texts in two ways: they correct and they improve. The editor or reviser is a gatekeeper, who *corrects* the text so that it conforms to society's linguistic and textual rules and achieves the publisher's goals. The editor or reviser is also a language therapist who *improves* the text to ensure ease of mental processing and suitability of the text for its future users. This latter function is certainly important in the English-speaking world, but some language cultures do not value reader-orientation as highly; readers are expected to do more of the work of understanding themselves, bringing their background knowledge to bear on the task. In this kind of lingua-culture, one would not start an article by giving the reader a helpful overview of its structure (first I shall do this, then that); to do so would seem patronizing.

Editors and revisers often find themselves faced with conflicting demands and needs. There are demands from the client – the company, ministry or publishing house which has commissioned a writing or translating job. Then there are standards required by professional associations to which the editor/reviser belongs, and edicts from language-standardization or terminology-standardization bodies. Authors too make certain demands, and finally, editors and revisers must constantly keep in mind the requirements of readers. The need for revisers to deal with conflicting demands is discussed in Chapter 9.10.

Editing or revising is thus not a matter of a vague 'looking over'. There are specific things the editor or reviser is looking for. Here are just a few of the many, many ways in which a text might be defective:

- There are many typographical errors.
- Sometimes the main numbered headings are bolded, and sometimes they are italicized.
- There are unidiomatic word combinations.
- You often have to read a sentence twice to get the point.
- You often come across a word like 'it' or 'they' and you cannot tell what it refers to.
- The text contains a great many words which the readers won't understand because they are not very highly educated, or because they are not experts in the subject matter of the text.

- The text is not written in a way appropriate to the genre. For example, it is a recipe, but it does not begin with a list of ingredients, it is rather vague about how to make the dish, and it is full of commentary on the history of the dish and the chefs who are famous for making it.
- If the text is a narrative, it is hard to follow the sequence of events. If it is an argument, it is hard to follow the steps.
- There are passages which contradict each other.

1.1   The difficulty of writing

In this section, we'll look at why texts need therapy, why they need to be improved to help readers. Writing is difficult work. In this it is quite different from speaking which, while highly complex, is easy: we all learn to converse, without any formal instruction, during infancy. Writing, on the contrary, requires long years of apprenticeship and even then, many people never learn to do it well. Indeed, even the best writers and translators make mistakes – sometimes serious ones. There is no point in seeking out writers and translators who are so good that their work never needs to be checked.

Why is writing so difficult? There are three main reasons. First, there is *no immediate feedback from readers*. If you are conversing, a question from your interlocutor or a puzzled expression on their face will lead you to repeat or rephrase in order to make your message clear. But if you are writing, you may create an ambiguous sentence, or use a word the reader doesn't know, but there is no one there to react to the problem (unless you are engaged in text messaging), so you do not notice the problem. This is part of a larger difference between speech and writing: a conversation is jointly constructed by at least two people who are together in a situation, while in writing the entire burden of successful communication falls on the writer. The writer must imagine the reactions of an often unknown reader in an unknown future situation, anticipate the reader's problems in receiving the intended message and act to forestall them. Poor writers forget this. They treat writing as self-expression rather than communication with others. They seem to operate on the principle that if they have a certain meaning in mind as they write, that meaning will automatically come across to readers.

Second, *written documents tend to be lengthy*. When speaking, you typically need to organize what you are saying over a stretch of a couple of words to a couple of dozen words (the delivery of lengthy monologues such as formal speeches is usually assisted by speakers' notes or scripts). In writing, things are quite different. Unless you are tweeting or sending a very brief email, you typically need to organize a stretch of a few hundred or a few thousand words in the case of a report or article, or a few tens of thousands or hundreds of thousands of words if you are writing a book.

Third, it is easy to forget to *compensate for lack of intonation and gestures*. In conversation, much meaning is conveyed through intonation, and to some extent also by gestures (facial expressions, hand movements such as pointing).

It is very easy to forget to compensate for the lack of intonation in writing, and the result will be ambiguity, or an unclear connection between successive passages. Consider this sentence:

> As these studies tend to show the form translation has taken in Canada, both on an institutional level and on the level of the actual practice of translation, is specific to our particular national context.

Here the reader might wrongly take 'the form' to be the object of 'show', whereas in fact, it is the subject of 'is specific'. In speech, the voice would drop slightly after 'show' and there would be a slight pause. The writer forgot to place a comma after 'show' to ensure a correct reading.

Translational writing, aside from being subject to the three difficulties just described, is also difficult because of the need to convey someone else's meaning. The translator is often not a member of the intended readership of either the source text or the translation. As a result, it's easy to convey to readers a meaning not present in the source text, or to write in a way that will confuse the intended readership. In addition, it is difficult when translating to avoid undesirable linguistic influences seeping in from the source language.

Good writers and translators recognize how easy it is to err. To minimize errors in their final output, they engage in some combination of planning and self-editing. One study of writing strategies (Chandler 1993) found four basic strategies:

Writing strategy	Planning before drafting	Self-editing
Architect	Major	Minimal, after drafting
Bricklayer	Major	Major, during drafting
Watercolourist	Minimal	Minimal, during drafting
Oil painter	Minimal	Major, during & after drafting

Some writers ('architects' and 'bricklayers') forestall error by thinking through their message carefully before they start composing; sometimes they will even prepare a detailed outline. A few of these writers – the 'architects' – are apparently so good at planning that they manage to produce good writing on the first draft, writing that requires only minimal self-editing after they have got the draft down. 'Bricklayers', on the contrary, do major self-editing as they draft.

Quite different are the 'watercolourists' and 'oil painters'. They tend to think *by* writing, so there is little planning. They simply start writing, perhaps with just a theme or a single idea in mind, or a few scribbled notes. Watercolourists, in addition to their minimalist planning, also engage in little self-editing. As a result, watercolourists are generally not very good writers. Oil painters compensate for their lack of planning by engaging in major self-editing both during and after drafting. The book you are now reading was Oil Painted: Planning was limited to preparing a rudimentary outline for the publisher. Then I wrote each chapter quite quickly, though with a fair amount of editing as I went along. After completing a chapter, I made major changes, often completely rearranging the order of presentation of the material, and then I made changes to those changes.

Translators too use different writing strategies, which will be discussed at length in Chapter 13.

Exercise 1. Take a few minutes to consider the following questions and then tell the group about your approach to writing.

a) When you are writing in (not translating into) your own language, which of Chandler's four strategies do you adopt? Are you an architect, bricklayer, watercolourist or oil painter? Or do you use more than one of the strategies, depending on the nature of the writing project?
b) Do you identify with none of the four strategies? Say why not.
c) If you identify yourself as, say, a bricklayer, have you always been a bricklayer? Did you learn one strategy at school and then switch later?
d) Do you use similar strategies when writing and when translating? For example, if you plan your writing extensively, do you also do a lot of preparation before you begin to draft your translations? If you self-edit a lot while writing, do you self-revise a lot while drafting your translations?

1.2   Enforcing rules

In this section, we'll consider why texts need gatekeepers, why they need to be corrected. Writing differs from speech in that it is usually subject to external regulation in a way that conversation is not. This is so in two senses. First, texts are usually written in a standard language, which has more or less clear-cut rules set out in dictionaries, grammars and recognized usage authorities. (Exceptions may be allowed for innovative work, often called 'creative' writing, but the editing of such work will not be considered here.) Publishers of texts may also have special rules about a host of matters such as when to write 'eight' and when to write '8', whether 'he or she' should be replaced by 'they', and whether quotations are to be separated from the main text and indented. In addition, writing in specialized fields is subject to standardized terminology. Finally, every language community or subcommunity has rhetorical habits and genre traditions; there are widely accepted principles for constructing an argument or for writing a recipe.

The second kind of external regulation stems from the fact that writing is often commissioned; that is, there is a publisher who has asked the writer or translator to prepare the text. The publisher has certain goals, and someone has to ensure that these goals are achieved. For example, corrections may be needed to deal with departures from appropriate content, such as political or sexual content. The rules here may be current social conventions (or laws!) or they may be imposed by a particular publisher. Publishers will also want to maintain a certain reputation, and this will require correcting inaccuracies (factual and mathematical errors, erroneous quotations).

A considerable proportion of original writing is not commissioned (diaries, personal email); hence there is no need for an editor to represent the publisher's interest. Also, much commissioned original writing at workplaces (e.g. minutes of meetings, progress reports, emails to colleagues) does not need to be edited because it is ephemeral and circulates within a very restricted group of readers; no great harm is done if no one checks and corrects such writing. Editing by someone acting for the publisher is really vital only when a text bearing a message deemed important by its publisher is being prepared for a large audience of strangers, or for audiences who will be reading it over a long period of time. Editing gives such a text the ability to reach out into space and time, by ensuring that it carries enough contextual information to enable people outside the immediate world of the writer to interpret it in the intended way.

Translations are quite different. Uncommissioned translations are rare, so there is always a client to satisfy. Also, some degree of revision is needed even with ephemeral texts to correct errors which are peculiar to translational writing: mistranslations, omissions, and the strange unidiomatic language which is so hard to avoid when translating (odd word combinations or sentence structures calqued from the source text). Finally, someone is needed to ensure conformance with current norms governing translation: Must the translation reflect the source-text message in tiny detail or only in broad outline? To what extent must the actual wording of the source text be reflected?

1.3   Quality in translation

Translations need to be revised in order to achieve quality. But just what is quality?

Stated and implied needs

The International Organization for Standardization, in its 1994 standard ISO 8402 entitled "Quality Management and Quality Assurance", defines quality in general as the totality of characteristics of an entity that bear on its ability to satisfy stated and implied needs. In the 2000/2005 standard ISO 9000, entitled "Quality management systems: fundamentals and vocabulary", quality was redefined somewhat to mean the degree to which a set of inherent characteristics fulfils requirements, with 'requirements' defined to include needs and expectations. However for our purposes – considering quality in translation rather than quality in general – the earlier definition is better because it includes the important word 'implied'.

There are two important things to note in the original definition. First, quality is always relative to needs. There is no such thing as absolute quality. Different jobs will have different quality criteria because the texts are meeting different needs. In one job, a reviser must improve the readability of the text to a very high level; in another job, a lower degree of readability will suffice. Sometimes several degrees of quality are recognized, sometimes two; in the latter case, a frequent distinction is between information-quality (the document will be used in-house, usually by a small number of people for information only, and then be discarded) and publication-quality (the document will be read by a large number of outside readers over a fairly lengthy period of time).

The second thing to note in the ISO definition is that needs are not just those stated but also those implied. The most important implied need in translation is accuracy. People who use the services of translators don't ask for an accurate translation; they just assume that it will be accurate. Ensuring accuracy is a key task of revisers. Accuracy is discussed in detail in Chapter 10.

Another implied need is successful communication of the text's message to the readers. Achieving this may require an editor or reviser to override the publisher's or client's instructions (sometimes called the brief or commission). This is particularly true in translation, because clients unfamiliar with the target-language community may have a mistaken or incomplete understanding of the cause-and-effect involved. For example, the client asks the translator to follow the paragraphing of the source text, but the paragraphing habits in the target language are quite different for the genre in question. In no profession can one always bow to the client's wishes. Imagine some people who are renovating their house. They tell the architect that they want a certain wall removed. When the plans come back, they see that the wall is still there. Why? Because the architect has determined that it's a bearing wall – the house would fall down without it. Similarly in translation, it is up to the reviser to ensure that communication will not break down when the message is read by members of the target-language community.

In some cases, it may be possible to change the client's stated needs (their expectations) through education. Most clients know next to nothing about what translation involves, how much can be translated in a given time, why translators need documentation, and so on. However, educating clients is not easy, for a variety of reasons (lack of interest, frequent changes in the person who represents the client in dealings with the translator). Consequently, education should probably not be seen, in most instances, as a way of overcoming problems related to clients' stated needs.

Three concepts of quality

There are several broad concepts of quality current in the world of translation, and these lead to differing 'philosophies' of revision. Note that 'quality' here means for the most part linguistic quality. We will not be concerned with visual quality, quality of service or the technical quality of electronic files (these matters are briefly discussed in Chapters 9.15, 10.10, 10.11, 10.12 and 12.6).

Some people say that achieving acceptable quality means satisfying clients. This may lead you to pay most attention, when revising, to finding errors that will be easily noticed by the client, such as typographical errors and client-related terminology. This approach has a contractual version in which an actual agreement is prepared between translation provider and client. The U.S. standardization organization ASTM, in its 2006 document ASTM F2575-06, entitled "Standard Guide for Quality Assurance in Translation" defines translation quality as "the degree to which the characteristics of a translation fulfil the requirements of the agreed-upon specifications".

A second view of quality is that a translation is of acceptable quality if it is 'fit for purpose': it is, in the reviser's view, suited to the people who will be reading it and the reason they will be reading it. A reviser working under this concept of quality will read the draft translation with the purpose in mind, and then make only such changes as are needed to make the translation suitable for that purpose. The translation needs to be 'good enough' to serve its purpose, and no better. The notion of quality as fitness for purpose is endorsed by the European Committee for Standardization in its 2006 standard EN 15038, "Translation Services – Service Requirements", which says that "The reviser shall examine the translation for its suitability for purpose". This is the quality concept on which this book is based.

Third, it may be held that achieving quality means doing what is necessary to protect and promote the target language. This view will typically be found in language communities where translators want to counter the effects of a formerly or currently dominating foreign or majority language – these days very often English. Revision then becomes a quasi-literary writing exercise in language and style improvement. Revisers working under this concept of quality will not limit themselves to changes required to please the client or make the translation fit for purpose. Rather, all texts will be revised until they fit a certain ideal of authentic and excellent writing in the target language, regardless of the time that takes, and thus regardless of the added cost.

Finally, translation companies and the organizations representing them have in recent years advanced a procedural concept of quality that is focused not on the relationship between the source text and the translation, or on the quality of writing in the translation, but on the process used to prepare the translation, the idea being to forestall errors before they are made. This is discussed in Chapter 9.15.

The various quality concepts provide a focus for the reviser's work: will it be on the specifications for the job, on appropriateness for users and use, or on language protection? The chosen focus will dictate what happens during revision. If your focus is language protection, you may make a change which you would not make if your focus were appropriateness or specifications. The concept of quality also has an influence on how you handle 'accuracy' and 'readability' as goals. If you are operating under the concept of language protection, readability may be sacrificed to some degree in order to follow the prescriptions of a conservative language-regulating body. On the other hand, if what you mean by language protection is keeping target-language rhetoric free of English influence, then readability may be your highest value. If you are operating under the concept of fitness for purpose, accuracy may either be extremely important (with legal texts, where extreme accuracy may be required even at the expense of readability) or it may be not so important (with the in-house employee newsletter of a multilingual government ministry, the reviser may well accept wordings where the translator has added to or subtracted from the source text message in order to make it more lively or funnier, if that seems appropriate for target-language readers).

The concept of quality under which revisers work may vary from country to country, or from language pair to language pair. It may even vary by direction. In Canada, for example, English-to-French revisers tend to be quite concerned with the 'language protection' aspect of revision, whereas this is not the case for French-to-English revisers, except perhaps for those who work in Quebec, where English is a minority language influenced by French. Revisers and editors who work in countries where their language of work is not the local language (say, English speakers working in the Netherlands) may also be more concerned with the 'protection' aspect of translation than those who work in majority English-speaking countries.

Note that the 'fit for purpose' concept cannot be expanded to include the other two concepts. Protecting the language and pleasing the client are not 'purposes' in the intended sense because they are not specific to the text at hand. An example of a purpose would be: this translation is to be read by subject-matter experts who are starting a research project and have come across the source text, written in a language they don't know, during their literature search. The question for the reviser then is whether the draft translation is suited to these expert readers and to their need to find out what their colleagues, writing in the source language, have discovered on the subject of the research project.

A difficulty with the fit-for-purpose conception of quality is that it may be hard to determine the purpose. In addition, some readers who are not members of the audience which the reviser had in mind may nevertheless retrieve the translation from an electronic archive, possibly months or years later, and use it in a way which the reviser was not contemplating. However this is simply a risk one takes when using the fit-for-purpose approach. The purpose in question has to be the currently known purpose. One cannot revise a text to be suitable for any possible purpose or readership now or in the distant future.

A final point: it may be psychologically handy, when editing or revising, to think of quality in negative terms: don't ask yourself whether a passage is fit for purpose, for example, but whether it is not fit; does it diverge unacceptably from expectations, however defined?

How important is accuracy?

Aside from different general concepts of quality, there may be differences about which aspect of translation is most important: Is accuracy the prime quality of a good translation, that is, the translation conveys more or less all and only the meaning which the reviser believes to be present, explicitly or implicitly, in the source text? Or is the most important quality of a good translation that it satisfies the agenda of the commissioner, regardless of correspondence to the source text? A rather inaccurate translation of a tourist guide (one with several additions and subtractions) may nevertheless be very well written and be found to be very useful by the tourists who buy it, quite possibly more useful than an 'accurate' translation, because the translator will have a good idea of the culture-based interests of target-language readers who are visiting the country or city in question. Some people refuse to call such texts translations, and insist they be called adaptations, but since many translators produce them, the distinction seems pointless in the world of translation practice (though it may be useful in theoretical writing). An 'accurate' translation can be of high quality, and so can an 'agenda-based' one.

Quality and computer tools

It should be mentioned that the advent of computer tools may be having an effect on the notion of what counts as acceptable quality. That is, once a freelance translator, translation company or organization with a translation department has committed to using such tools, and invested money in them, the concept of quality will tend to be drawn toward what can feasibly be produced with the tools. The result may be either 'higher' or 'lower' expectations by comparison to a previous period of time. For example, expectations about subject-matter research are now much, much higher than they were in the pre-search-engine era, when translators had to depend on telephoning experts and on the very slow process of reading paper documents in libraries or the occasional document sent by the client to the translator by traditional stamped mail or (at considerable expense) by courier or fax. On the other hand, it's possible that expectations about inter-sentence cohesion and consistency in level of language are declining because Translation Memory by its nature tends to generate problems in these areas to an extent previously unknown (see Chapter 14.5). And if Machine Translation continues to spread, it may become acceptable to eliminate only the worst instances of wrong collocations, wrong prepositions and other unidiomatic expressions, because MT still has considerable difficulty with such matters.

Today many people who are not professional translators are revising machine outputs or translating and self-revising on a volunteer basis. It is worth noting that concepts of quality that reign among professional translators may differ from those found among non-professionals. For example, non-translators (along with many of their readers who are aware they are reading a translation) may expect the final result to 'sound like a translation' and be suspicious if it does not.

1.4   Limits to editing and revision

Theoretically one could edit or revise any text until it fits a given quality ideal. However, from a business point of view, some texts are not worth editing or revising. They are so badly written or translated that it would take a very long time to edit or revise them and, consequently, it would cost too much. Consider this badly written version of a passage near the beginning of the section entitled "The difficulty of writing" in this chapter:

> Its hard to write but speaking is very easy even though its complicated, we all learned to speak as children without any insrtuction. But it takes a very long time to learn to write and many people's writing is still awful.

If an entire article of this quality were submitted for publication in a magazine, it would probably be rejected. The problem is not so much the mechanical errors (its, insrtuction, the comma after 'complicated'); even large numbers of mechanical errors can be corrected easily and fairly quickly. The problem lies in the lack of flow and poor focus – an ordering of words that does not bring out the logic of the argument. A few such problems scattered through a long text are fixable, but if almost every sentence needs recasting, then it simply would not be economical to proceed. The above passage does not call for editing; it calls for rewriting – preferably by a different writer.

Some clients may wish to proceed with the editing of bad writing despite economic considerations. Perhaps some political or ideological concern is more important than cost. Or perhaps the author is an Important Person. You may therefore find yourself editing the work of people who need help writing: learners of English as a second language; people who had insufficient or ineffective schooling and have still not mastered the differences between speech and writing; or people who think that they will impress readers if they write in very long sentences chock full of subordinate clauses, clauses within clauses, and parenthetical expressions.

Just as editing is not rewriting, so revising is not retranslating. If a translation is full of unidiomatic word combinations, if the sentence structures are so influenced by the source text that the result is unreadable, and of course, if the translator has clearly misunderstood numerous passages of the original text, the solution is to retranslate, not revise.

Exercise 2. Machine translation (MT) output is often unrevisable. Create your own example by pasting a paragraph from an online news article (written in your second or third language) into the source-text box at www.babelfish.altavista. com, translate.google.com or any other site you can reach by entering "machine translation sites" in your search engine. Ask for a translation into your first language. Does the output seem revisable? Try to actually revise it, removing only the worst mistakes. Does this confirm your initial impression about its revisability?

1.5   The proper role of revision

Revising is necessary because translators make mistakes, but it is important not to place too great a burden on it. It should not be the main way of ensuring quality. Quality is best ensured by *preventive* action: using properly trained translators, using the right translator for a given job, making sure the specifications for the job are known to the translator, passing on any client feedback from previous translations, making sure the translator has access to appropriate technological tools and to the necessary documentation, terminology resources, previous translations on the subject and subject-matter experts.

When working with a new translator, the reviser should forestall predictable errors. For example, if the text is a set of instructions, point out that the source language may convey instructions with the passive (the green button should now be pressed), but in the target language, the imperative is probably best (press the green button).

Revision should be seen as a necessary final resort to clean up the inevitable errors that will occur despite such precautions. Unfortunately revision is often – perhaps increasingly – used as a way of dealing with the problems that arise when translation is outsourced to cheap but unqualified contractors.

Summary

1. It is very easy for things to go wrong during writing, and there are a great many different kinds of things that can go wrong.
2. Editors and revisers make corrections so that the text conforms to the rules governing writing, and so that the writing project achieves the publisher's goals.
3. Editors and revisers make improvements to fix problems that will hinder mental processing of the text, and to tailor the writing to its future readers and the use they will make of it.
4. Editors and revisers must somehow resolve any conflicts among the needs or interests of clients, readers, source-text authors and other parties.
5. Revisers work with a variety of concepts of translation quality.
6. Some original writing and translating is so bad that it is not worth fixing.

Further reading

(See the References list near the end of the book for details on these publications.)

Speech versus writing: Halliday (1989); Baron (2000); Hirsch (1977: chs. 1 and 3).
Norms governing language and translation: Chesterman (1997: ch. 3).
Quality: Chakhachiro (2005); Hansen (2009a); Künzli (2009); Martin (2007); Morin-Hernández (2009).
EN 15038: Biel (2011); Parra Galiano (2011); Schopp (2007).

2.   The Work of an Editor

In this chapter, we'll look briefly at the jobs of people who work as editors. We'll then distinguish editing from adapting and rewriting, and look at the editing work done mentally by translators when their source texts are poorly written, as well as the editing of non-native English. By way of introduction to editing exercises, the chapter concludes with a discussion of degrees of editing.

In this book, editing means reading a text which is not a translation in order to spot problematic passages, and making any needed corrections or improvements. In some cases, the text may just happen to be a translation but the editor either does not know this or does know it but treats the text as if it were not a translation. (The activity in which a reviser of translations reads a draft translation without reference to the source text is here called unilingual re-reading, not editing.)

2.1   Tasks of editors

Dictionary definitions of the verb 'edit' present a considerable variety of meanings. Here is a sample, culled from various dictionaries:

- assemble, prepare or adapt (an article, a book) so that it is suitable for publication;
- prepare an edition of (a literary author's work), especially by researching manuscripts;
- be in overall charge of the content and arrangement (of a newspaper, journal, etc);
- reword, revise or alter (a text) to correct, alter the emphasis, etc.

As for the occupation 'editor', here is what we find in the 2011 National Occupational Classification published by Canada's employment ministry:

> Editors review, evaluate and edit manuscripts, articles, news reports and other material for publication, broadcast or interactive media and co-ordinate the activities of writers, journalists and other staff. They are employed by publishing firms, magazines, journals, newspapers, radio and television networks and stations, and by companies and government departments that produce publications such as newsletters, handbooks, manuals and Web sites. Editors may also work on a freelance basis.

Editors have many duties, and different editors have different duties. An editor's daily routine will be rather different at a newspaper from what it will be at the office of a firm publishing a medical journal. The description of a particular editor's job might include one or more of the following:

- finding or assigning writers and handling relations with them;
- evaluating the suitability of manuscripts and recommending changes in content, style or organization;
- dealing with reviewers (subject-matter experts who comment on the content of specialized writing);
- scheduling the publication process;
- designing page layouts, with incorporation of graphics;
- marking up manuscripts with instructions for printers;
- obtaining permission to use copyrighted material, and dealing with other legal concerns such as libel;
- managing the financial and material resources, and the employees, of a publishing enterprise or department;
- amending the text submitted by a writer.

In a one-person publications department, the editor will either have to do all the above tasks – perhaps even pack and ship the final product – or else farm out tasks to freelance editors.

An editor's work will also vary greatly with the type of writer being edited; editing the work of professional writers is quite different from editing the writing efforts of, for example, scientists writing articles for a journal or employees who are required to prepare reports as part of their job but do not actually like writing or are not very good at it. For many editors, relations with professional writers may be the most difficult feature of their work.

In translation, the situation is rather different. While literary translators must often negotiate rather carefully with source-text authors, non-literary translators – the great majority – are usually dealing with non-professional writers. The translator is therefore the writing expert in the relationship, and in addition, often enjoys the advantage of being a native speaker of the target language. In non-literary translation, difficulties tend to arise in the relationship between translator and reviser, or translator and client, and not so much in the relationship between translator and author.

Types of amending work

Notable in the job description for editors near the beginning of this chapter is that editing in the sense of checking and amending a text is mentioned as just one among many tasks. In this book, we will not be looking at the full range of editors' duties or the various situations in which they work. Instead, we will be concerned almost entirely with the task of textual amendment – a task some people with the job title Editor do not perform at all. There are four broad types of amending work, which will be considered in the next four chapters:

- *Copyediting* (Chapter 3). This is the work of correcting a manuscript to bring it into conformance with pre-set rules – the generally recognized grammar and spelling rules of a language community, rules of 'good usage', and the publisher's 'house style'. The copyeditor must also ensure a degree of consistency in such matters as terminology and the positioning, numbering and appearance of section headings and subheadings. Consistency is considered as a separate topic in Chapter 7.

- *Stylistic editing* (Chapter 4). This is work done to improve rather than correct the text. It involves tailoring vocabulary and sentence structure to the readership, and creating a readable text by making sentences more concise, positioning the main verb near the subject, and so on.
- *Structural editing* (Chapter 5). This is the work of reorganizing the text to achieve a better order of presentation of the material, or to help the readers by signalling the relationships among the parts of the message.
- *Content editing* (Chapter 6). This is the work of suggesting additions to or subtractions from the coverage of the topic. The editor may (perhaps with the assistance of a researcher) personally have to write the additions if the author for some reason cannot or will not do so. Aside from such 'macro-level' work, content editing also includes the 'micro-level' tasks of correcting factual, mathematical and logical errors.

In this book, most attention will be given to copyediting and stylistic editing, since these are the tasks translators are most likely to be asked to perform.

If you have simply been asked to 'edit', you should inquire about what is wanted: stylistic editing, copyediting, or both? The former is much, much more time-consuming. It's also a good idea to know where you fit into the overall scheme of preparation of a document for publication. Perhaps structural editing has already been done, in which case decisions about combining or splitting paragraphs, or other matters discussed in Chapter 5, may already have been made. Perhaps a copyeditor will be working on the text after you, in which case you do not need to worry about things like consistency or compliance with house style.

Note that in some editing situations, changes are made without consulting the author; in others, the text is sent back to the author with suggested amendments and perhaps comments next to certain passages (either handwritten or made with the Comment function of a word processor), or separate sheets are sent containing specific or general suggestions and questions.

One final type of amending work is making changes of all kinds to produce a new edition of a previously published work. Somewhat confusingly for our purposes in this book, the term 'revise' is sometimes used to refer to the process of reviewing the original edition with an eye to such amendments, or to refer to both the reviewing and the consequent amending, the final result being a 're-vised edition'. Occasionally, 'revise' is used in this sense for translations, usually when someone makes amendments to a previously published translation of a literary work.

In large organizations, a similar process may go on *before* a document is published: a draft is prepared and sent out for comment; amendments are made on the basis of the comments, the outcome being labelled 'version 2'. The process repeats until a satisfactory result is achieved. 'Version', like 'revision', is a term which has a different meaning in the worlds of editors and translators; for the latter, it is a synonym of 'translation', mostly used in combination with a language name ('the German version').

Division of labour

In large publishing companies, and in corporations or government ministries that have a publications department, there may be a considerable division of labour – a hierarchy of employees working under a variety of titles such as senior editor, assignment editor, editorial assistant, copyeditor, production editor, fact-checker or proofreader. The title Editor is often used just to designate the person in charge of some area of work, such as the photo editor or the sports editor at a newspaper. Also, titles do not necessarily reflect tasks: a copyeditor may also do stylistic editing and micro-level content editing. This may happen unofficially: an editor's official task may be copyediting, but in practice, they may see that other types of editing have not been done and will intervene.

Senior editors

A senior editor will oversee a publishing project, deal with authors and reviewers, and suggest macro-level content changes in the text. All the more detailed textual work, as well as the layout and printing work, will be left to others. Senior editors at publishing companies and newspapers often find themselves at the interface between the creative and the commercial aspects of publishing; they may want to promote a certain writing style or certain innovative ideas, but the marketing department may not be supportive, or the budget for hiring a sufficient number of good editors and writers may not be available.

Senior editors in the publication departments of government ministries, churches or other institutions may often not be bothered by such commercial considerations, but like newspaper editors they will be responsible for ensur-ing that the final version of a text is consistent with, or actively promotes, the political or ideological goals of the organization. As a result, the editor may be in the position of having to negotiate with or exclude authors whose ideas are not ideologically acceptable to the publisher.

Thus, far from simply dealing with words on a page, the editor becomes the focal point of negotiation among the sometimes conflicting interests of publisher, writer, marketers and buyers (readers).

Subject-matter reviewers

When it comes to highly specialized documents, some publishers will draw on the services of experts; for example a manuscript in the field of atmospheric physics will be looked at by a meteorologist. Such an expert may review the manuscript, prior to acceptance for publication, in order to determine whether it is original work and represents a contribution to the field, point out gaps in the argument, and so on. Experts may also be employed to do content editing for factual and conceptual accuracy and any other matters calling for specialist knowledge. Alternatively, such a text may be edited by someone who specializes in editing scientific texts. 'Scientific and technical editor' and 'medical editor' are now occupations engaged in by people who are not themselves technicians, engineers, scientists or doctors. This is less often the case with other specialized areas: people who edit specialized works in law or music will usually be subject-matter experts themselves.

Proofreaders

After a manuscript (usually in the form of a Word document) has been edited, it goes to the publisher's production department for page design and typesetting (the old term is still used, though nowadays literal setting of metal type is an artisanal pursuit; typographical decisions are made on a computer screen). The outcome of this process (often in the form of a .pdf file) then has to be compared with the original Word document in order to catch any remaining errors, or errors introduced during design and typesetting. This task, known as proofreading, may be assigned to the author, the editor, or a specialized proofreader employed by the publisher.

Proofreaders use special paired marks to indicate errors: one mark appears within the text itself (the copymark) and the other in the margin, to draw the printer's attention to the change. Note that not all proofreaders in the English-speaking world use the same set of marks. For exercises, use the copymarks your instructor recommends. Proofreading per se lies outside the scope of this book.

> *Terminology note:* The term *proofreading* is sometimes used by translators to mean copyediting, the topic of the next chapter. It is also used by some translators to refer to the procedure called *unilingual re-reading* in Chapter 11. It is even used as a synonym of *revision*.

2.2   Editing, rewriting and adapting

Editing needs to be distinguished from rewriting and adapting. When editing, you start from an existing text and make changes in its wording. Sometimes, however, the existing text is so badly written that it is easier to abandon the existing wording and re-express the text's content with newly composed sentences and possibly a new text structure. This is rewriting. In *Complete Plain Words*, Ernest Gowers provides a treasure trove of real examples of bad bureaucratic writing, and discusses the principles that should be used in rewriting them. Here's an example that illustrates the single greatest problem with such writing – overuse of nouns and sequences of nouns:

> This compulsion is much regretted, but a large vehicle fleet operator restriction in mileage has now been made imperative in meeting the demand for petrol economy.

This sentence may not pose a problem for specialists in road transportation, but non-specialists will find the following easier to read:

> We much regret having to do this but we have been obliged to greatly reduce the use of our fleet of large vehicles in order to meet the demand that we economize on petrol.

Clearly this second sentence was not created by adding, subtracting and moving words in the first sentence. Sometimes such rewriting is needed only in the occasional sentence; sometimes most of a text has to be overhauled in this way.

Now, both editing and rewriting aim to create a text that is maximally suitable for the *original* intended audience. Sometimes, however, people don't want to replace the old poorly written document with one that is better written; instead, they want to prepare an *additional* document for a *new* audience. In this case we'll call the activity adaptation. This may involve either complete recomposition (as in the above example of rewriting) or relatively minor rewording of the existing sentences (as in editing).

First, let's look at a case where adaptation will typically require complete recomposition. English legal documents traditionally address an audience of lawyers and judges; a legal editor would check that such documents were suited to that readership. However in recent years the English-speaking world has seen a movement demanding 'plain writing' of legal documents so that they can be read by non-lawyers. In some jurisdictions, there has even been 'plain writing' legislation, requiring for example that consumer financial documents such as mortgages be in readily understandable language. This will generally call for complete recomposition of sentences in order to achieve a high level of readability, perhaps at the expense of precision. Legal language is often hard to read because the writer was trying to be extremely precise, eliminating as much vagueness and ambiguity as possible; often this cannot be accomplished without sacrificing ease of reading.

Now, let's look at two cases where minor rewording would probably suffice to adapt a text:

- Start from a document originally written for a British audience and adjust it for an American audience (e.g. make adjustments in vocabulary and spelling).
- Start from a document originally written for an audience of native readers and adjust it for an international audience that includes mainly (or even mostly) non-native readers.

These cases exemplify two common procedures for document adaptation: localization and internationalization. In the former, features are added to a document that are specific to a local readership, while features specific to other localities are subtracted. In the latter, all local features are subtracted, in order to address the broadest possible, international audience. Preparing a document for such a broad audience is especially difficult for adapters who are native speakers of the language in which the text is written and members of the culture from which it originates. That is because they must have a knowledge of what others do *not* know, whether it be difficult aspects of the language or local history. Thus a reference to the "44th president" (of the United States) is likely to be obscure to readers in other countries.

A final case of preparing a supplementary document through adjustment of an existing one is repurposing. Here material is adjusted for use with a new medium. For example, text might be adjusted for use in a printed brochure, on a Web page, or in a slideshow presentation. The adjustments might include changes to the wording but also to visual appearance (e.g. some fonts work better on paper, others on screen).

> *Terminology Note:* The terms *adapt* and *rewrite* have been used here to denote activities within a single language. The terms are also used, with a variety of meanings, by translation theorists.

2.3   Mental editing during translation

Another activity which is similar to editing is a regular feature of professional translation. It is often noted that translations are easier to read than their sources. That is because experienced translators of non-literary texts tend to produce translations whose writing quality is much superior to that of the source text. To accomplish this, they do not actually prepare an edited version of the source text; instead, they engage in what might be called mental stylistic editing and mental structure/content editing *while they translate*. Three examples (with an English gloss of the source text):

- If the source text has 'necessary pre-requisites', the translator will just write 'pre-requisites', eliminating the redundancy.
- If the source text has 'fish and animals', the translator will write 'fish and other animals', since fish are themselves animals.
- If the source text has 'with a view to the need for a clear definition of the concept of violence at the very outset of the preventive work, an inclusive definition is to be preferred', the translator will write something much simpler, such as 'the first step in prevention is to define violence clearly, and the definition should be an inclusive one'.

In each of Chapters 4 to 6, there is a short section devoted to this quasi-editing work. Just how much such cleaning up is permissible? It's not possible to formulate any precise answer. There is a permissible range: some translators do more cleaning up than others, just as some translate more freely than others. You learn the permissible range by working under the supervision of experienced translators. The most common type of improvement is paring down the convo-luted, verbose sentences and eliminating the high-flown vocabulary or jargon commonly used in bureaucratic writing to express rather simple ideas. The obvious limitation here is that clients might wonder about a translation that is only half the length of the source text!

One view often voiced is that the burden of mental editing should not be placed on the translator. That is, the source text should be edited before submission for translation. In some cases, this is just a matter of timing. The source text is going to be published and does have to be edited; the only question is whether this will occur before or after translation. In other cases, the situation is quite different. Within a multilingual bureaucracy, someone who is either a poor writer, or not a native speaker, writes a document which will be circulated as a draft rather than a final version. Spending time and money to edit it is not thought worthwhile by the powers that be. In these cases, the translator's desire for a well written source text is likely to remain a dream.

> *Terminology Note:* Mental editing while translating is sometimes called *transediting* or *trediting*. This term is also used to refer to adapting a text to a new audience while translating it.

2.4   Editing non-native English

In many organizations and countries, texts are very frequently written in English by people who are not native speakers. For example, as the website of the South African Translators' Institute mentions in its definition of editing: "In a country like South Africa, where many people are forced to write in a language that is not their mother tongue, the work of editors is extremely important." (This is a reference to speakers of Afrikaans and of the indigenous languages such as Xhosa and Zulu, who find themselves having to write in English.)

More often than not, texts written in English within the European Union bureaucracy are written by non-native speakers; the Directorate General for Translation at the European Commission has a unit to edit these writings before they are sent for translation into other EU languages.

Then there is the case of science writing. These days, scientists very often write directly in English rather than in their own language. Many scientific and other scholarly publications insist that such writers have their work edited by a native speaker of English prior to submission. Here is a sentence from an article written in English by a French-speaking scientist:

> Activity levels were not correlated to brains or bodies mass.

A native speaker would never use the plurals 'brains' and 'bodies' here. One has to write 'brain or body mass', even though the meaning is 'the mass of brains or bodies'.

People who attempt to write in English as a second language are often quite good or even excellent *speakers* of English, but poor *writers* of the language. Their justified confidence in their speaking ability may lead them to overestimate their writing ability. They make all sorts of elementary errors (they fail to capitalize the days of the week if their native language is one which does not capitalize week days) as well as errors in such matters as language level (they use overly informal language that is acceptable in speech but not in writing, or odd mixtures of formal and informal language). Also, if their native language is historically related to English in some way (Dutch or French for example), they may frequently use 'false friends': a French speaker might use 'library' to mean 'bookshop' because in French 'librairie' means 'bookshop'.

The biggest problems seen in non-native English are not micro-errors such as failure to capitalize or a wrong lexical choice. The biggest problems are failures in English composition: since the writers were not educated in English, they may never have learned how to organize sentences in the English manner, using English methods of ensuring inter-sentence cohesion and positioning of focused information (see Chapters 4.2 and 4.4 for examples of cohesion and focus problems). They may also not have learned how to organize paragraphs, or entire arguments or narratives, in the English manner. Instead they will inappropriately use the sentence-organizing, text-composing and rhetorical devices of their own language which they learned as children at school.

If you edit non-native English, you may be employed directly by the author of the text, not by the publisher. You are acting as an 'author's editor' rather than a 'publisher's editor', but you will still want to know about the intended publisher's requirements, since your task is to increase the likelihood that the manuscript will be accepted for publication.

Ideally, editors of non-native English should be native speakers who were educated in English. However in many countries, it is not always practical to find such a person, and the editor may be someone with near-native ability. It is also a good idea if the editor knows the native language of the writer, since it will then be easier to reconstruct what the writer had in mind in passages which are obscure (the writer may have been engaging in literal mental translation from his or her own language). Translators who work from that language are obviously well positioned to accept such editing work. Thus a translator who works from German to English, or at least has some knowledge of German, will have an easier time with a passage such as the following, taken from a text written by a German speaker about how to design roads in a way that will reduce accidents:

> Some new opened roads unfortunately show accident concentrations (black spots) in a short time. In these road sections have to be done a Road Safety Inspection to detect the deficiencies causing accidents.

In the first sentence, a native English reader who knows no German might think that the writer is talking about new roads, but that is not the intended meaning. They can also be old roads that have been closed for modifications or repairs and have now been newly opened. 'New' needs to be understood as an adverb modifying 'opened', not as an adjective modifying 'roads'. The German word 'neu' (new) can function either as an adverb or an adjective, whereas in English, the adverb form 'newly' is needed to make the meaning immediately clear. The second sentence manifests the so-called 'verb second' construction that is compulsory in main clauses in all the Germanic languages except English. In the other Germanic languages, one says 'yesterday saw she an elephant': since 'yesterday' is occupying the first structural position in the sentence, the next position must be occupied by the verb ('saw'). An editor who does not know another Germanic language may well become confused upon reading this sentence, especially since the verb 'have' does not agree in number with 'inspection' (this is not an influence of German but just a plain old mistake on the writer's part). The sentence needs to be edited to read '...a road safety inspection has to be done in these...'. In this particular case, an editor will probably be able to deduce the meaning from world knowledge, that is, by relating the words 'sections', 'inspection', 'deficiencies' and 'accidents' to what he or she already knows about road safety. But that will not always be the case, either because the editor does not have the requisite world knowledge, or because he or she makes an incorrect deduction from world knowledge. At any rate, the failure of syntax to signal the meaning in this sentence will slow down the editing process for editors unfamiliar with German word order.

Here is a case where the editor will probably not be able to work properly unless he or she knows the writer's native language:

> To be effective, the committee should be subjected to the support of local management.

The ideas expressed by 'subjected to' and 'support' do not fit together. However if you know the writer's native language, French, you will recognize a word that may have inspired the English, namely 'assujetti'. This word is indeed often translated by 'subject(ed) to'. However it also has the sense 'secured', as when a boat is secured to a dock. By extension then, the committee here can only be effective if it has a secure tie to management, which supports its work. Unfortunately this meaning cannot be borne by English 'subjected to'. Even if 'subjected to' is changed to 'subject to', it still sounds like local management is constraining rather than assisting the work of the committee.

If as the editor you are not familiar with the writer's native language (and sometimes even if you are), there is an important technique you can use to identify the meaning of obscure passages. Consider this baffling passage from a text about weather observations in developing countries:

> ..the difficulty of maintaining observation sites with recordings homogeneous with development

What does 'recordings homogenous with development' mean? In such cases, the best approach is to hope that the writer repeats the point using a different wording later in the text. You should therefore keep an eye out for such wordings. In the case under consideration, a later passage reads:

> With economic and social development, it is difficult to maintain obser-
> vation sites in operation, protect them from deterioration and maintain
> homogeneous data series.

Here are some general things to watch for in non-native writing. The writers may not know that a word or turn of phrase is very formal, very informal,
old-fashioned or infrequent. They may not know that a certain phrasing may be
viewed as impolite or, conversely, overly polite. Languages differ in how direct
one can be: in the writer's language, one might need to write 'we wonder if you
might not possibly send us a letter' whereas in English that seems overdone;
'send us a letter' would be normal, or at most 'please send us a letter'. In a text
that praises an individual (an announcement of a promotion for example), it may
be customary in the writer's language to keep repeating praise expressions like
'absolutely outstanding' and 'incomparable'. In English, such effusiveness will
seem insincere, defeating the purpose of the text. Non-native writers may also
not know about genre conventions: a French speaker writing up the minutes
of a meeting may use the present tense, not knowing that minutes are written
in the past tense in English (not "Mary suggests postponing the decision" but
"Mary suggested...").

Like any other text, one written by a non-native can be stylistically edited
or simply copyedited (see Chapters 3 and 4). In some cases, non-native English
which is very badly written may be treated like the output of machine translation
(even though the types of error will be quite different); the text will be edited
just enough to make it intelligible (see Chapters 14.4 and 11.2).

2.5   Degrees of editing and editing procedure

Professional editors do not apply equal editing effort to every text. In the first
place, an editor may only have time to go through a particular text once, doing
all four kinds of editing simultaneously, or perhaps just copyediting to eliminate
the most obvious errors. With other texts, it may be possible to perform two or
more separate edits. Additional factors are the nature of the publication and the
reputation of the publisher: the editors of a scientific journal whose publisher
wishes to be known internationally for readability and freedom from factual
error will need to edit very carefully.

Since editors may well have several jobs going at once, they need to consider
whether all merit equal attention; there is not much point in spending vast
amounts of time on the stylistic editing of a text which is relatively ephemeral,
like a report which only a limited number of people within an organization will
look over, fairly quickly, and then discard. Readers will likely have higher tolerance for uncaught errors in this type of text.

Another important consideration is the reaction of writers. If an editor hopes
to work for a writer at some time in the future, it will be a good idea to keep

changes to a minimum. The editor may have thought of a brilliant new wording for a sentence, but if the writer's sentence is satisfactory, it may be best to leave it. Writers will be more inclined to work with an editor who appears to be helping them get their message across, and less inclined to work with one who appears to be competing with them as a substitute writer.

Some books on editing refer to a specific number of degrees of editing. For example, a distinction may be made between light, medium and heavy editing, each being appropriate to a particular type of job. As many as nine degrees may be distinguished, with particular tasks specified for each degree. This approach is a kind of summary of the experience of people who have been editing for a long time. If you want to read more about the factors involved in selecting a degree of editing, see the Further Reading section at the end of this chapter, or read Chapter 11 on degrees of revision. Terms such as 'light' and 'heavy' are a bit misleading since they may seem to refer to the number of changes the editor makes – something which of course depends on the quality of the text submitted for editing. The actual intent of the terms is to refer to the number of aspects of a text which are checked: in a light edit, you might just check for grammar, spelling and punctuation errors.

When you are just learning, the first step is to master each of the types of editing. This will be done here through exercises in individual aspects of copyediting, stylistic editing, structural editing, content editing and consistency checking. Thus in Chapter 3, you will be practising punctuation editing in one exercise and grammar editing in another; then you will practise doing all aspects of copyediting at once.

The next step is to do a full edit of a text several pages long. Do this in separate run-throughs of the entire text. Begin with the structural editing of the whole text, then proceed to check the content for factual, mathematical and logical errors, then do the stylistic editing, then the copyediting and then a consistency check. At the very end, run Spellcheck to catch any typographical errors you may have missed (or introduced yourself while editing!).

The third step might be to try a combined edit in which you correct errors of all types as you come to them. Move back and forth in the text as necessary. When you've finished, put the result aside. Then a few days later, correct the same text using separate edits. Compare the results. Look in particular for the following in your combined edit:

- errors you missed;
- wasted work: copyediting changes that were overridden by stylistic or structural changes;
- errors you introduced.

Alternatively, work with a partner. You do a combined edit while your partner does separate edits. Exchange copies of your edited texts and compare the results.

Practice

Exercise: Copyediting non-native writers
Your instructor will give you a document written in English by someone who is not a native speaker of English, but whose native language you know. Find and correct linguistic errors.

Further reading

(See the References list near the end of the book for details on these publications.)

At the websites of the Society for Editors and Proofreaders (UK) and the European Association of Science Editors, you'll find links to editors' associations elsewhere in the world.

At the website of the Editors' Association of Canada, you can download the document *Professional Editorial Standards,* which describes the various kinds of text-amending work.

Also of interest is the Mediterranean Editors and Translators website.

Proofreading: Samson (1993: chs. 3 and 9) gives editing and proofreading marks and sample texts, as do Dragga and Gong (1989: ch. 3), Judd (2001: ch. 2) and O'Connor (1986: ch. 9).

Degrees of editing: Samson (1993: ch. 6); Rude and Eaton (2011).

Editing at newspapers: Bell (1991).

Manipulative rewriting and translating at newspapers: Vuorinen (1997).

Plain language: Steinberg (1991: pp 59-80 and 148-203).

Writing for an international audience: Kirkman (2005: ch. 21-24).

Typography: Dragga and Gong (1989: ch. 5).

Samples of editing: Almost every chapter of Samson (1993) and of Dragga and Gong (1989) contains samples of various kinds of editing.

Editing non-native writers: Burrough-Boenisch (2003) and (2013b); Van de Poel *et al.* (2012); Ventola and Mauranen (1991).

Authors' editors: Burrough-Boenisch (2013a).

Transediting: Stetting (1989).

3. Copyediting

In this chapter, we'll look at copyediting under five headings: 'house style', spelling, syntax and idiom, punctuation and correct usage. Checking for consistency, which is also an aspect of copyediting, will be considered separately, in Chapter 7.

3.1 Rules

Copyediting may be defined as checking and correcting a document to bring it into conformance with pre-set rules. The second last word of the sentence you are now reading must be 'says', not 'say', because there is a rule in the grammar of standard written English that says so. (Several forms of spoken English omit this –s.) In the case of correct usage, the rules to be enforced are controversial, and involve matters of authority, ideology and tradition. In the case of punctuation, the rules are often not clear-cut. The sections dealing with these two topics are therefore rather lengthy.

Copyediting requires close attention to small details; you can't do it properly if your mind is on other things. Sometimes you may find it a relief from the more demanding (less clear-cut) aspects of writing and translating work, and sometimes you may get satisfaction from those copyediting decisions that do require some thought. But unless you derive pleasure from correcting other people's errors, or creating 'order' out of untidiness, you may find this necessary task somewhat unattractive.

Ultimately, you may discover that you can combine copyediting with stylistic, structural and content editing, but at this stage, while you are still learning, you should do it separately. Perhaps try thinking of it as a game: How many mistakes can I find? Can I score better than last time?

Copyediting is line-by-line, 'micro-level' work. It is therefore done after the author and editor have completed 'macro-level' changes to the content and structure of the text. There is no point copyediting a paragraph which will later be deleted.

Copyeditors also check certain typographical and layout features, especially for consistency: Are all paragraphs indented? Are all headings bolded? However, some of these features are really a matter of stylistic editing or structural editing. For example, italics are commonly used to indicate to the reader that mental stress should be placed on a particular word. This is a matter of readability, and more specifically, smoothing – a style matter which is dealt with in Chapter 4. Similarly, headings may be underlined and indented as a way of signalling the structure of an argument to readers – a subject discussed in Chapter 5.

Terminology notes: The term *copyediting* is used by some editors to include stylistic editing in the sense of Chapter 4. Indeed, some editors use *copyediting* to include fact-checking (see Chapter 6) as well as any other tasks which are performed on a 'line-by-line' basis. These are all 'micro-editing' tasks, as opposed to such 'macro-editing' tasks as rearranging the order of presentation of topics in a document.

Where British and US terminology differ, this book uses the US term: 'period' instead of 'full stop'; 'parenthesis' instead of 'bracket'; 'typo' instead of 'literal'.

3.2 House style

Editors sometimes provide writers with a one- or two-page set of instructions known as a style sheet. The word 'style' is unfortunate in that style sheets deal with mechanical matters, whereas 'stylistic editing', to be discussed in the next chapter, refers to matters which are very far from mechanical.

Here are some of the instructions from the style sheet that can be found at the website of St. Jerome Publishing (https://www.stjerome.co.uk/about/authors), the publisher of this book:

- Use -ize rather than -ise except for standard spellings such as 'advertise' and 'televise'.
- Quotations longer than forty words should be taken out of the text and indented, with an extra space above and one below the quotation. Do not use quotation marks with indented quotations.
- Number all illustrations consecutively, using Arabic numerals. In the body of the text, refer to illustrations by their number (for example: Figure 1; Table 2); do not use expressions such as 'the following table'.

In addition to (or instead of) a style sheet, editors will often direct writers to follow a particular style manual or guide, which may be hundreds of pages long. A style manual gives instructions on a wide variety of matters, including spelling (advertise or advertize?), capitalization, hyphenation, numerals (eight days or 8 days?), Latin or English plurals (fungi or funguses?), acronyms, use of italicization and bolding, presentation of quotations, footnotes and reference works, treatment of place names (Montreal or Montréal?), transliteration of names from languages that use a different script, what if anything to do about non-gender-neutral language, and much more. Sometimes style manuals give a choice of approach, and simply demand consistency (e.g. spell numbers up to nine, then use figures from 10; or spell up to ninety-nine, then use figures from 100). Note, by the way, that if you follow the first of these two rules about numbers blindly, you may end up writing sentences like:

There was one case of 11 people in a car and 12 cases of nine in a car.

where form does not match meaning: the number of people should be either '11...9' or 'eleven...nine'.

Style manuals are published by governments, newspapers, university presses and editors' associations. A few are listed at the end of the chapter. You may find it useful to compare manuals for English with manuals for your other languages, noting differences in matters such as comma use or hyphenation.

Style manuals and style sheets help create a distinctive institutional voice and visual image for a publication – a 'house style'. They also create consistency among all the texts produced by a given publisher. This is especially important in journals, magazines and collections of articles, where several different authors are contributing to a single issue or book. Once the contribution arrives, it is up to the copyeditor to check that the instructions have been followed.

3.3   Spelling and typographical errors

Why should a text be correctly spelled and be free of typographical errors? Even asking this question may seem odd. The need for correct spelling was drummed into us at elementary school, and we may never have given a moment's thought to its rationale.

Spelling errors are bad because of the effect on the reader. Mispelings and typograhpical errors produce a very bad impression. They suggest that the author and editor are sloppy thinkers, and that the publisher tolerates carelessness. As a result, readers may lose confidence in the actual content of the work. Of course, it does not follow logically that if there are spelling errors, there must also be errors in the facts or arguments presented, but subconsciously at least, that is what readers will suspect. Misspellings and typos are also distracting, and therefore they slow down the reading process. Finally, typos can directly affect meaning, both when keys get pressed in the wrong order (have you read about the artist who fearlessly attacked scared cows?) and when the wrong word is transmitted from the mind to the fingers: there is a big difference between adopting a plan and adapting one, between having an aptitude and having an attitude.

The work of searching for misspellings and typos is greatly facilitated by the Spellcheck utilities included with word processing software. If you are not already in the habit of using Spellcheck, then get into the habit immediately. There can be no excuse for htis tpye of mistake. Run Spellcheck after all other changes have been made.

Spellcheckers do have weaknesses and pitfalls, which are discussed in Chapter 8. One of the most notable weaknesses is proper names; you will need to independently verify that the names of people and places are properly spelled. Consider this sentence from a funding proposal:

> Our health centre is working in partnership with Merck Frost.

Since 'frost' is a correctly spelled English word, it would be easy to let this sentence slip by unchecked. In fact, the correct spelling of the name of this pharmaceutical corporation is Merck Frosst. You could easily find this spelling by entering 'Merck' in your web search engine and then consulting one of the documents you find.

One aspect of English spelling is highly variable. Which is correct: life style, life-style or lifestyle? The answer is: all three, depending on which dictionary you consult. Also, usage may vary with the field; for example, the Canadian Government's terminology bank Termium says that 'caseworker' (one word) is correct in the field of social services but 'case worker' (two words) is correct for the person who works with inmates in a penitentiary. If you are doing freelance editing for a corporation or government ministry, documents on the subject of your text may reveal your client's practices regarding common compounds.

If your style sheet prescribes a particular dictionary, then the compounding problem will most often be solved. However compounding is a highly productive process in English; that is, writers can make up new compounds at the drop of a hat, and these will not appear in your prescribed dictionary. The easiest principle to follow here is consistency: make your choice for each compound, and then make sure you stick to it throughout the text. You can also try using Google to investigate the relative frequency of the two-word versus one-word treatment of a compound. See Chapter 8 for a discussion of problems in the use of Google for such purposes.

In general, there is a progression over time from open spelling (two words) when a compound is first introduced, through hyphenation, to solid spelling (one word) as a compound becomes established in the language. The Americans tend to move through this progression more quickly than the British. Hyphens are less common in US English; words written with a hyphen in Britain will tend to be written solid in the United States or (less often) as two words. (There is also a trend, more advanced in the US, toward omitting the hyphen in prefixed words like 'coordinate', 'cooperate' and 'preeminent'.)

A final point, concerning another use of hyphens: if your style sheet calls for breaking long words at the ends of lines, note that American practice is to break at phonetically natural points ('trium-phant') whereas British practice tends to draw on morphological considerations ('triumph-ant'). Check to see which principle the automatic hyphenator in your word processor follows. Note that some automatic hyphenating utilities may produce wrong or even bizarre results (bat-hroom).

3.4   Syntax and idiom

If the text you are editing is written by a reasonably well educated native speaker of English, and is not a translation, there is a good chance that it will be syntactically correct and idiomatic. That is, it will not contain sentences like

> He washes frequently his teeth, sometimes after every dining.

in which the adverb 'frequently' is in a position it cannot occupy, the word combination 'wash teeth' is unidiomatic, and the word 'dining' is used in a meaning it does not have. These are errors of a kind which native speakers normally do not make. However there are several exceptions:

1. People attempting to write in fields with which they are not familiar may have problems with the specialized phraseology of that field. Similarly, if you are just beginning to edit in a field with which you are not yet familiar, you must be careful not to replace the customary phrasings of that field with more universal ones. For example, when editing a work in the field of meteorology, you might come across the term 'summer severe weather' and you might be tempted to normalize the word order to 'severe summer weather'. That would be a mistake; the phrase is correct as it stands, 'severe weather' being a defined concept in this field. When a severe weather event occurs in summer, it is 'summer severe winter'; when it occurs in winter, it is 'winter severe weather'.

2. Since the advent of word processors, mechanical slips during composition often create serious errors in sentence structure.
   (a) There may be word missing (or an unwanted extra word) if during self-editing the writer pressed the delete key once too often (or not often enough). Did you notice the missing word in the previous sentence?
   (b) Cut-and-paste or click-and-drag operations, during which a passage is moved within a document or pasted in from another document, often produce imperfect transitions between the pasted passage and what surrounds it. The structure of the pasted portion may not fit into the sentence properly, or there may be a word missing at the boundary of the pasted portion, or there may be an extra word – commonly a double double word. (Spellcheckers catch double words, but be careful not to automatically delete the sequence 'had had'; 'he had had a bad time' may be an incorrect doubling, or it may be correct if the sentence calls for the pluperfect tense of 'have'.)
   (c) Partly amended sentences such as the following are now common:

   > It would be appropriate for computational terminology researchers would do well to investigate the potential usefulness of existing knowledge-engineering technology.

   The writer decided to add 'would do well' but forgot to delete 'it would be appropriate for'. In the days of typewriters, such sentences were hardly ever produced. Changing the structure of a sentence once it was down was a very time-consuming (and messy) operation. As a result, people either spent more timing planning their sentences, or else they made changes in handwriting during a separate self-editing phase, at which time their attention would be on the sentence as a whole. (Then someone else – a typist – would prepare an entirely fresh copy.) Nowadays, it is very easy to make changes as you write, and there is a tendency to focus only on the bit you are changing.

3. There is a tendency to make present-tense verbs agree in number with the nearest noun whose combination with the verb makes sense:

The legacy of the social service cutbacks of previous governments remain with us.

4. The mind sometimes retrieves the wrong word or phrase from the mental store:

Bank machines, photocopiers and central heating are a few examples from an almost infinite list of technologies and products that are an indelible component of modern life.

Here 'indelible' was retrieved instead of 'permanent' or some such word. Another possibility is that the mind will retrieve two expressions at once:

Beyond a question of a doubt, this enhanced our cynicism in parliament as an effective instrument of government.

Here 'beyond any question' and 'beyond a shadow of a doubt' have been retrieved together.

5. When people are translating into their native language, they often write ungrammatical and especially unidiomatic sentences, under the influence of the source text. When the source language is one whose vocabulary includes many cognates of words in their native language (e.g. any Romance or Germanic language in the case of translation into English), translators may use words in meanings they do not have ('he was invited to give a conference' for French 'conférence', which often means 'lecture' or 'talk'). Such unidiomatic usages may also appear in the original writing of people who work in a multilingual environment. If the readers also operate in such an environment, there may be no problem. But if they do not, then the editor must take action.

These then are the syntax and idiom problems found in the work of well educated native speakers. But you may also find yourself having to edit writing by people who are not well educated or not native speakers. The problems found in the work of non-native speakers were discussed in Chapter 2.4. A syntax-related problem in the writing of less well educated people is discussed briefly in connection with punctuation in Chapter 3.5.

Terminology note: The word *idiomatic* is used in this book to cover a variety of phenomena which are sometimes distinguished: collocations such as 'brush one's teeth', prepositional idioms such as 'depend on' and phrasal verbs such as 'put up with'; set phrases such as 'not on your life'; or clichés such as 'please be advised that'. Similarly, expressions like 'wash one's teeth' or 'depend from' are all described as *unidiomatic*. The term *idiomatic* is also sometimes used in a broader sense to refer to 'the way we say things in our language', that is, to refer to stylistic/rhetorical preferences such as the English preference for the plural rather than the singular in generic statements ('students must have obtained a mark of C in order to pass' rather than 'the student must...'). Here copyediting shades into stylistic editing.

Syntactic change and variability

Syntax and idiom are not eternal; they change as the generations pass. As a result, what older editors see as a clear error may be perfectly acceptable to educated younger speakers. Once innovations have begun to spread, editors have to decide whether they are now acceptable or still have to be edited out. A common type of innovation in English is the conversion of adjectives and nouns to verbs: 'pockets of downtown that are *resurging* as fashionable addresses'; 'an escaped convict *upheaves* the lives of a businessman and his wife'. These are probably one-off innovations by the writer, but you may want to check the most recent edition of your dictionary. Some publications insist on removing anything that is not recognized in an authoritative dictionary (unless it's in a quotation); others take a more relaxed attitude and allow considerable room for authors to innovate.

Bear in mind that syntax and idiom vary somewhat from person to person. The syntactic structures and word combinations felt to be natural by other speakers may not coincide exactly with those which you find natural. As a result, a writer may have used a structure or word combination which you find odd or impossible; but that does not mean it is wrong. I once discovered, through a Google search, that one can say 'underhand deal'; previously I thought it had to be 'underhand*ed*', though the two forms do seem to vary with geography, with most hits for 'underhand' coming from the UK, Africa, India and Pakistan, and most hits for 'underhanded' coming from the U.S. and Canada.

A further danger with using yourself as an authority is that you may end up introducing your own personal linguistic idiosyncrasies into a text. A few years ago, I discovered to my surprise that the expression 'she favours her right arm' does not at all mean 'she tends to use her right arm rather than her left' but rather the exact opposite: 'she avoids putting too much strain on her right arm, by using her left arm instead'; her right arm is 'favoured' by being given a rest! A further discovery: I had always thought that 'fulsome praise' means abundant praise, but recently I discovered that for many people it means excessive praise.

Acceptable syntax also varies with genre. For example, in cook books, ellipsis of articles and pronouns is common: 'Slice onions. Then saute on high heat' rather than 'Slice the onions. Then saute them on high heat'. Such ellipsis is also often accepted in lists of points, which may diverge in other ways as well from the rules that apply to full sentences (e.g. no capital letter at the beginning or period at the end).

To check idiomaticity, consult the combinatory dictionaries listed at the end of this chapter. For example, if the text you are editing has the phrase 'sorry choice', and you are uncertain whether this is an idiomatic word combination, the Benson dictionary will confirm that it is (you will learn that a choice can be bad, sorry, wrong, careful, difficult, good, happy, intelligent, judicious, wise, random or wide). The dictionaries by Wood and by Cowie and Mackin are entirely devoted to prepositional idioms, which often pose problems even for educated native speakers (report *to* or *for* work? compared *to* or *with* Paris?). To check the syntactic structure used with a word, try the *Collins Cobuild English Dictionary*, which always gives a full-sentence example for each sense of a word. To check whether a word has a particular sense, or can be used in a certain syntactic structure, or in combination with a certain other word, you can also try on-line concordances, some of which are free or have free versions, such as the American National Corpus at www.anc.org or the British National Corpus and Corpus of Contemporary American English at corpus.byu.edu. Be aware however that a corpus does not tell you what is 'correct', only what is actually in use by native speakers and writers. On concordances and on grammar-checking software, see Chapter 8.

A final type of variability that may be important for editors in some geographical areas is dialect differences. Standard languages are historically based in certain local forms of speech as opposed to other local forms, which are deemed 'non-standard'. As a result, some people's natural syntax and idiom may be unacceptable in writing, and children are taught to avoid using them. Thus, to many native speakers of English in Ireland, the following are all perfectly natural sentences, inherent in their language: 'Is this car belonging to you?', 'They were after leaving a gym across the street', 'It does be colder at nights'. Such syntax is not currently acceptable in formal writing, but that could change. In a given geographical area, it may happen that people who use a non-standard dialect in their everyday speech decide they want to start using that dialect in books and newspapers (and not just in quotations for 'local colour'). At that point, editors have to decide what to do.

3.5   Punctuation

Punctuation, in a narrow sense, includes the familiar marks: the comma, the period, the quotation mark, the dash and so on. In a broader sense, punctuation includes a variety of other indicators that provide guidance to readers: the linespace or indentation between paragraphs, the capital letter that begins a sentence. A few aspects of punctuation (paragraph divisions, some uses of the comma) are really stylistic or structural matters, and will be considered in the next two chapters.

Some very common errors are opening a parenthetical remark but forgetting the closing parenthesis, and inconsistent punctuation in point-form presentation.

The rules governing punctuation are not as clear-cut as those governing spelling. Also, the British and US rules differ somewhat, for example in the positioning of closing quotation marks. With respect to point form, it is worth noting that while sentences inside paragraphs have a highly standardized punctuation regime (initial capital; period or question mark or exclamation mark at the end), words in other parts of texts do not. Section headings, points in lists, captions of graphics and column titles on tables may take a wide variety of regimes: all keywords capitalized, first word capitalized or no words capitalized; various punctuation marks or no punctuation mark at the end.

Most uses of the English comma are not bound by rules at all. Using commas well calls for thought. There are two main types of variation:

- Some writers use many commas, some few.
- Some writers use commas to mark speech features such as pauses and emphasis, others to mark the boundaries of syntactic structures.

Regarding the second of these differences, it seems that there are three principles upon which comma use in English has historically been based:

(A) When writing a sentence, use commas to indicate where someone should pause when reading the text aloud.
(B) Place commas at the boundaries of the syntactic constituents of the sentence.
(C) Imagine the sentence being spoken, then place commas to reflect your mental pauses or emphases (which may or may not occur at syntactic boundaries).

Approach (A) was historically first. Until a couple of hundred years ago, most literate people did not read silently. Aside from documents such as records (tax lists, property titles and so on), writing was a sort of script for reading aloud, either to oneself or to others. Punctuation indicated places to breathe, or to pause for rhetorical effect. Commas, colons and periods seem to have indicated increasing lengths of pause.

During the late 18th century and throughout the 19th century, approach (B) was widely advocated, though the older rhetorical tradition never died out. In this approach, thought to be suited to silent reading at great speed, commas help the eye by picking out syntactic structure, and thus clarify meaning. Finally, during the 20th century, approach (C) grew in importance, though it has not yet displaced the syntactic principle. The upshot is that people often use a combination of approaches (B) and (C).

Here's a very simple example of the difference between the two approaches:

approach (B):
Marilyn was the best translator available and, as soon as she returned from holiday, she was chosen to head up the prestigious project.

approach (C):
Marilyn was the best translator available, and as soon as she returned from holiday she was chosen to head up a prestigious project.

In the first sentence, the commas visually mark off 'as soon as she returned from holiday' as a clause interrupting the conjoined structure 'Mary was...and...she was...'. In the second sentence, the comma reflects how someone might have mentally imagined speaking the sentence. A further point of interest here: if you ever had occasion to read the first of these two sentences aloud, you might revert to approach (A) and use the commas as indicators of when to pause, or perhaps lower the voice. However this would be a case of 'pronouncing the commas', as opposed to using them to reflect a prior imagined speaking, for the position after 'and' is just not a natural place to pause during speech.

An important point about approach (C) is that sometimes the addition of a comma to indicate a mental pause has the effect of adding attitudinal meaning. Consider:

He was apparently willing to support you.

He was, apparently, willing to support you.

The second sentence expresses a bit of surprise, or casts doubt either on 'his' motive for supporting 'you' or on whether 'he' really was willing, as 'you' have alleged.

More generally, the choice of a comma rather than some other punctuation mark (or no mark) can be used to reflect varying degrees of some attitudinal feature:

I went to his house and I found him there.

I went to his house, and I found him there.

I went to his house. And I found him there.

As we move from the first sentence to the third, an increasing degree of surprise at 'his' presence 'there' is expressed. Now, according to some versions of punctuation rules (perhaps those you learned at school), the last two of the above sentences are impermissible. However if you rigidly exclude sentences beginning with 'and', you will not be able to obtain the effect achieved in the third sentence. Indeed you will often find that if you follow the most rigid version of rules, in any area of language, you will reduce the number of semantic options open to you. Worse than that, if you try to implement rigid rules with word processor tools, you may create a disaster. One editor decided that the word 'however' must always be followed by a comma, and implemented this decision using the Search & Replace All function. The result, in one passage, was a sentence which began 'However, much you enjoy translating...'.

A final important point about the two conflicting principles (B) and (C): some uses of the comma to reflect mental pauses are still quite strictly prohibited despite the rise of approach (C). If you are editing the work of people with relatively poor education in the standard written language, you may find such sentences as the following, from a report written by a health and safety officer:

The beeping of the alarm at an interval of thirty seconds or a minute, is a warning you should attend to. It means the batteries are dying, you need to replace them with fresh batteries.

The first sentence has a comma functioning to separate the subject of the sentence from the predicate. Although people do often pause at the subject-predicate boundary in speech, this use of commas ceased to be permissible in the written language during the 19th century. The second sentence has a comma where there should be a period or semi-colon. This usage is particularly common in the writing of less well educated people. The sentence is not a natural unit corresponding to a segment of the spoken language, and as a result it takes children some time to learn where to place periods. Some people never succeed and you may find yourself having to correct their errors.

Turning now to the second type of variation in comma use, let's look briefly at heavy versus light punctuation. The heavy punctuation of the 19th century was associated with the use of commas to mark grammatical boundaries. Over the course of the 20th century, punctuation became lighter, especially in the US. This was partly because sentences became shorter; obviously, shorter sentences don't need as many internal boundary markers. But in addition, commas became optional at many boundaries. In the lightest use, a comma will only appear when absolutely necessary to avoid misunderstanding. Four of the six commas in this paragraph you are now reading could be eliminated.

When you are not sure whether to use a comma, do not agonize. Avoid the situation Oscar Wilde describes: "I was working on the proof of one of my poems all morning, and took out a comma. In the afternoon, I put it back." Instead, follow this handy rule of thumb: *If in doubt, take it out.*

3.6   Usage

Copyeditors are widely expected to make texts conform to something variously called 'correct usage', 'good grammar', 'correct English' or 'proper English'. This is something quite different from the problems of Syntax and Idiom discussed earlier. There, the task was to make sure the text conforms to rules which are inherent in the spoken language, and don't need to be stated or taught to children (e.g. the possible positions in a sentence of an adverb like 'frequently'). Occasionally people fail to observe these rules (for example in long sentences with complicated structures, or when translating) but there is no debate about them; as soon as an error is pointed out, people immediately recognize it as an error. No native speaker, of any educational level, thinks 'he washes frequently his teeth' is acceptable English.

Correct usage, on the contrary, is a matter of debate. It is overtly prescribed in publications by various 'authorities' as well as in angry letters to the editor by private individuals. These prescriptivists, as I will call them, condemn certain usages as wrong, but many people do not agree and simply ignore the various prescriptions in their own writing.

Webster's Dictionary of English Usage defines usage as 'a collection of opin-ions about what English grammar is or should be, about the propriety of using certain words and phrases, and about the social status of those who use certain words and constructions'. These opinions are voiced with a view to standard-ization, that is, the elimination of variants. If some people write 'it's me' and others write 'it's I', only one – in this approach – can be right; the other must be proscribed. It's worth noting that this idea – there is only one right way – is not as widely accepted in the English-speaking world as it is in some other language communities. A common view among English-speaking writers is that one should certainly consider all opinions regarding a point of usage, but each person should then decide for themselves what is best.

Now in every speech community, variants are constantly appearing in the spoken language. People in one geographical area start to pronounce a word differently; members of the younger generation start to give a word a slightly changed meaning. Obviously there are limits to such variation if communication is to be maintained. As a result, every language community has a process, operat-ing below the level of consciousness, whereby some variant usages are rejected and others accepted. However, greater variation can be tolerated in speech than in writing. Written language needs a higher level of standardization so that texts written at one time and place will be understandable at other times and places, possibly by readers not known to the author.

The question is: what degree of standardization should be enforced and on what principle should a proposed standard be accepted or rejected? More specifically for our concerns in this book: what should be the attitude of editors to matters of correct usage?

Consider the following sentences and ask yourself whether you would make any corrections in them:

(1) If everybody minded their own business, the world would go round a good deal faster than it does.
(2) A flock of birds were alighting here and there around the field.
(3) Hopefully this text will be translated by tomorrow.
(4) The volume can be increased by turning the blue knob.
(5) Their mission is to boldly translate what no one has translated before.

There is nothing in any of these sentences that violates any syntactic rule inher-ent in the English language. Yet they all contain features that continue to be condemned in angry letters to the editor. According to some people:

In (1), *their* is wrong because *everybody* is singular; it has to be *his*.
In (2), *were* is wrong because *flock* is singular; it has to be *was*.
In (3), *hopefully* cannot be used as a disjunctive adverb; it's always a manner adverb, as in 'he looked at me hopefully'; the sentence should read 'it is to be hoped that this text...'.

> In (4) the subject of *turning* must be the same as the subject of *can,* but it is not the volume that will be turning the knob; the sentence must be reworded to 'You can increase the volume by turning...' or 'The volume can be increased if you turn...'.
> In (5) *boldly* must be moved because it is 'splitting' the infinitive 'to translate'.

For an editor, the first thing to notice about all these complaints is that they have little to do with successful communication. None of these sentences are hard to read and none will be misunderstood.

A second point worth noticing is that prescriptions sometimes mask ideological agendas. Consider sentence (1). Those who demand 'everybody minded *his* own business' instead of '*their* own business' claim that this is a matter of grammar ('everybody' is grammatically singular), but there is obviously an ideological agenda at work as well – a resistance to gender-neutral language. In fact, the use of *their* as a gender-neutral pronoun that can have a singular antecedent goes back many hundreds of years in English. It was not proscribed until the 18th century. You may have noticed that 'they' and 'their' are used with singular antecedents throughout this book.

The 18th century was a time when many notions of correct usage were first formulated, and Latin was often used as the model for what proper English should be. This is the origin for example of the rule prohibiting so-called split infinitives (see sentence 5 above). If a Latin sentence containing an infinitive is turned into English:

> Nec quicquam est philosophia, si *interpretari* velis, quam studium sapientiae. (Cicero)
> Philosophy is nothing other – if you wanted *to translate* – than the study of wisdom.

the part of the English corresponding to the italicized Latin infinitive has two words (*to translate*). Grammarians therefore decided, taking Latin as a universally valid model, that in English the infinitive is two words long ('to X'). Since obviously no adverb can be placed in the middle of the Latin infinitive, it 'followed' that no adverb should be placed between the two parts of the English infinitive. Expressions like 'to boldly go' were proscribed, even though they had been in use for centuries. Split infinitives have in fact never ceased to be in widespread use; most people simply ignore the proscription, probably because it has no bearing whatsoever on the successful communication of ideas. Moreover, many sentences read awkwardly if the adverb is moved from its position between *to* and the verb: 'You can choose to cooperate always with colleagues inside and also outside your work unit' ('you can always choose to cooperate...' is not awkward, but it has a different meaning). Overly zealous avoidance of split infinitives can even create ambiguity: 'He asked us clearly to underline the main points'; this could mean either 'ask clearly' or 'underline clearly'.

Prescriptions sometimes actually create 'incorrect' usage through a process known as hypercorrection. This occurs in particular when they are taught in primary and secondary school classrooms, but not fully understood. You may recall being told not to write 'Gwendolyn and me translated this text together'; it should be 'Gwendolyn and I....' because 'I' is the proper form for the subject of a finite verb. Many people have taken in the injunction itself (don't use 'Gwendolyn and me') but not the explanation. As a result, one now frequently comes across sentences such as 'This text was translated by Gwendolyn and I'. The 'correct' usage is in fact 'Gwendolyn and me' because 'me' is the correct form for the object of a preposition; you wouldn't say '...translated by I'.

Not only do prescriptions sometimes create error, and not only do they have next to nothing to do with effective communication, but also they may actually hinder communication, by reducing the semantic options available to writers. Consider the rule that requires present-tense verbs to agree in number with their subject. Purveyors of correctness insist on a very rigid application of this rule. They prescribe 'A flock of birds *was* alighting' and rule out '*were* alighting'. This makes it impossible (without expanding the sentence) to distinguish two different situations: the ducks all alighted together at one spot ('flock...was alighting') as opposed to the situation where some alighted here and others there, at different times ('birds were alighting'). If as editor you change 'were alighting' to 'was alighting', you may well be preventing the writer from saying what they want to say. More generally, usage 'rules' can become a crutch for editors. It is so much easier to mechanically apply pseudo-rules like 'never start a sentence with a conjunction' than to ask whether starting a particular sentence with 'but' is communicatively effective.

Another criticism one can make of the prescriptivists is their arbitrariness. For example, they rule out the use of 'hopefully' as a disjunctive adverb – see sentence (3) above – but they do not criticize other such adverbs. They have nothing to say about a sentence like 'Frankly, this text will not be translated by tomorrow'. Yet the sentences are exactly parallel in meaning: I tell you hopefully/frankly that this text...

The prescriptivists also distinguish themselves by not being there when you need them. They complain about usages which do not impede effective communication, but fail to complain about usages which do impede it. For example they do not draw attention to a use of 'may' which is often ambiguous, even in context: 'Helicopters may be used to fly heart attack victims to hospital' can mean either that it is permitted to so use the helicopters or that it is possible that they will be so used.

A final criticism is that sometimes prescriptivists do manage to pick out a point that really can lead to misunderstanding, but their recommendations are not helpful. An example is the position of the word 'only'. The written sentence 'His condition can only be alleviated by surgery' is ambiguous; it can mean either that his condition can be alleviated but not cured by surgery, or it can mean that the alleviation can be accomplished through surgery but not by any other means. In speech, this distinction is made by placing stress on *alleviated* for the former meaning and on *surgery* for the latter. The prescriptivists correctly say that in writing, ambiguity can be avoided if 'only' is always placed directly before the expression it modifies: 'only be alleviated' for the first meaning, 'only by surgery' for the second. The problem is that if we followed this rule all the time, we would be forced to write awkward and unnatural sentences; instead of 'I only wanted to talk to her', we would have to write 'I wanted only to talk to her'. There is simply no easy way to avoid ambiguity with 'only'; you need to think about the possibility of misinterpretation every time.

Now prescriptivists often say that a certain usage should be followed because it was observed by the best writers of the past. Such references to writers of the past lend a patina of objectivity to their claims, but in reality, the prescriptivists do not do any research to determine the usage of 'the best writers'. Sentence (1), for example, is by Lewis Carroll – surely a good writer – and many usages condemned by prescriptivists can be found in Milton and Shakespeare. In practice, the 'best writers' turn out to be those who follow the critic's prescriptions.

Why do some people get angry about what they perceive as incorrect usage? For some, the motivation is social liberalism; they believe that if the children of poorly educated parents, or parents educated outside the English-speaking world, could learn a certain version of Standard English usage, this would help pave the way for their social advancement. Indeed, it may have been a political concern to eliminate differences among immigrants and among social classes that originally led to a much greater interest in prescriptive grammar in the United States than in Britain. There continues to be much greater resistance in the US to the idea that dictionaries and grammars simply describe the language. There is a demand – both from the linguistically insecure and from the self-appointed saviours of the language – that such publications serve as sources of authority, that they prescribe what is right. Quite different are British authorities such as Henry Fowler and Ernest Gowers, who tend to take a relatively moderate and reasoned approach; they do not rule out split infinitives, for example. They tend to be more focused on effective communication than on correctness.

American linguistic conservatives like John Simon, on the other hand, tend to ban certain usages outright and fail to give reasons for their prescriptions; such and such a usage is just wrong, indeed barbaric, and shame on you for not knowing so! There is often a strong moralizing tone in their writings, suggesting that incorrect usage is on a par with sexual permissiveness and other conservative bugbears. English, in this view, is not merely changing; it is in decline and needs to be saved. Linguistic conservatives are motivated by various combinations of snobbery (any cultured person would know that you don't start a sentence with 'but') and despair that the younger generation is not emulating the older.

All these criticisms of the prescriptivists are not meant to suggest that there are no problems standing in the way of effective communication. Of course such problems exist; indeed, that is why editors are needed. As we saw in Chapter 1, writing lends itself much more than speech to misunderstanding. The problem with the prescriptivists is that they generally do not draw attention to the prob-lems that hinder effective communication. In the next chapter, we'll be looking at features of writing which really do cause readers problems, features which prescriptivists practically never mention, such as poor inter-sentence connections.

Does all this mean that editors can ignore the prescriptivists? Definitely not. The reason is that many people think 'correct' usage is important and they expect editors to serve as sources of authority, defending the language against 'incorrect' usage. Also, many readers of your edited text will be displeased by 'incorrect' usages. They may very well make the condemned errors themselves, in their own writing, but they believe in the idea of maintaining the standard.

How far should you go, as an editor, in enforcing 'correct' usage? Since the various published authorities often do not agree on particular points of usage, you will need to adopt an approach to each contentious point. Sometimes your employer's style guide, or a senior editor, will decide the matter for you, but more often you will have to decide yourself. You must bear in mind that if you adopt a conservative position, you risk being branded as out of touch with the younger generation, with current social movements, and other sources of linguistic innovation; on the other hand, if you adopt a more liberal position, you risk annoying conservative readers and being branded as an agent of declining standards. You won't be able to satisfy everyone.

A point to bear in mind in this regard is that translators and editors, by virtue of their self-image as 'servants', or by virtue of demands made on them to be 'language guardians', probably have a tendency to lean unconsciously toward a conservative approach to usage. A special effort will be needed if you want to counteract this and take a more liberal or even innovating approach to language when appropriate.

One possibly comforting thought is that as the number of people who write in English as their second language increases, editors may become less fussy about correctness because these writers, being members of other cultures, will not have any particular allegiance to traditions of correctness; they will be concerned only with communicative effectiveness. This will of course also be true of the constantly increasing number of *readers* of English who are not native speakers. They will in all likelihood never have heard of split infinitives, and be blissfully unaware of their incorrectness. On the other hand, the situation may be quite different with those non-native users of English who have spent long years studying the language and have achieved a very high level of mastery. They may have been taught a rather rigid and conservative version of English, and may be shocked at the 'laxness' of many native users. As a result, they may provide added support for native-speaker traditionalists.

To make usage decisions, rely on sources whose judgments are based on actual investigations of what appears to be acceptable and what not. If you are wondering, for example, whether 'they substituted x with y' is acceptable, Webster's Dictionary of English Usage will tell you that 'substitute with' is standard but that one may wish to avoid it because of the potential for negative reaction. The Canadian Oxford Dictionary is somewhat more negative, saying that this is a disputed usage and should be avoided in standard English: use 'they substituted y for x' or 'they replaced x with y'. The New Oxford Dictionary of English, on the other hand, says that despite the potential for confusion, 'substitute with' is well established, especially in some scientific contexts, and though still disapproved of by traditionalists, is now generally regarded as part of normal standard English. This suggests that an editor who wishes to appeal to either a traditionalist or a Canadian audience will avoid 'substitute with', but that otherwise a writer's 'substitute with' need not be altered.

Practice

In copyediting, there are a great many different kinds of error to catch, and you may find it difficult to attend to them all at once. In particular, you may find it hard to pay attention to errors that affect word-level units and at the same time to pay attention to errors that affect larger units. For example, if you are attending to individual words, you may not notice that a lengthy parenthetical expression has no closing parenthesis, or that some paragraphs in the text are indented whereas others are not. Sometimes your attention may be so focused on individual words that you do not even notice errors such as 'funds to assist towns rebuild their sewers', where 'help' was changed to 'assist' but the needed accompanying syntax change was not made ('to rebuild' or 'in rebuilding'). This problem – 'micro-attention' versus 'macro-attention' – affects all types of editing (and revision), not just copyediting.

You may find it easier, at first, to work through a text twice: once paying attention to micro-level problems and once to macro-level problems. Some of the exercises suggested below go even further: you will be asked to copyedit for just one feature, such as specific punctuation marks, ignoring all other problems.

Later, when you are practising 'full' copyediting (that is, for all types of error), count the number of problems of each type which you missed: typos, inconsistency of format, closing parentheses and so on. It may be that mere awareness of your problem will correct it; subconsciously, you will start paying more attention to that type of problem. If this does not help, and you continue to miss a significant number of errors, you should make a practice of going through a text more than once.

Regarding the speed with which you move through the text, your instructor will give you some time-limited exercises to do in class. However, you may also find it useful to experiment with speed at home. For example, before you prepare the final version of an assignment, work very quickly through the first half of a text and much more slowly through the second half. Then, when the class goes over the text, see whether you caught more errors when working slowly.

A tip on micro-editing: you may find it useful to place a ruler or sheet of paper under the line you are working on. This will direct your attention to the words on that line, and ensure that your eye does not skip lines. By the way, it is much easier for the eye to miss problems if you work on screen (see Chapter 8), so for now, do all your copyediting work on paper.

Exercises can be speeded up if you simply underline places in the text where a change is needed, without actually making the change. Remember that the difficult thing in editing is finding the problems. Correcting copyediting problems, once you have found them, is usually fairly easy.

Exercise 1. *Following style sheets*
Using the style sheet your instructor gives you, find (but don't correct) the places in the practice text that deviate from the style sheet.

Exercise 2. *Punctuation – commas*
Your instructor will give you a text from which all the commas have been stripped. Add just those commas which are necessary for clarity.

   You will then receive a text that does contain commas. Remove all those not necessary for clarity. If necessary, reword sentences to reduce the number of commas if you feel there are too many.

Exercise 3. *Punctuation – paired marks*
Your instructor will give you a text containing many paired punctuation marks (parentheses, quotation marks, dashes, delimiting commas). Be sure the closing mark is not omitted, that the paired marks are not overused, and that there is some principle behind the use of, say, a dash as opposed to a parenthesis.

Exercise 4. *Spelling – spotting the errors*
Your instructor will give you a text containing spelling and typographical errors that would not be detected by Spellcheck. Find them but don't correct them.

Exercise 5. *Spelling – frequently confused words*
Some of the following sentences contain the wrong word; for example, sentence (a) should read 'dispersed the crowd', not 'disbursed the crowd'. First find and correct the errors. Then, regardless of whether a sentence contains an erroneous word, identify the frequently confused pair, and state the meaning of each of the words. (Note that this is a type of error which Spellcheck will not detect. Grammar checkers have a 'confused words' option, but they do not include all common confusions.)

(a) The police disbursed the crowd.
(b) You should be more discreet about what you say.
(c) Her grandmother gave her a broach for Christmas.
(d) His tie doesn't compliment his suit.
(e) City councillors voted 5-3 against the motion.
(f) She was censored for failing to report a conflict of interest
(g) ... (Your instructor will provide further examples.)

Exercise 6. *Syntax – word-processing errors*
Read through several articles in a newspaper and try to find some examples of syntactic errors arising from word-processing slips (deletions not made; too many words deleted, etc).

Exercise 7. *Syntax – structure and meaning*
Consider this sentence:

> While few would argue that nuclear weapons are a great evil, one can't
> help but wonder about the state of the world had Hitler or the Soviets
> acquired such weapons and the US not.

Clearly, 'argue' here is intended to mean 'dispute' in the sense of 'disagree with
the proposition that' (as opposed to 'engage in an argument about' or 'give reasons for something'). Consult a variety of sources to determine whether 'argue'
can have this meaning when it appears in this particular syntactic structure (i.e.
followed by a *that*-clause).

Exercise 8. *Usage*
Between about 1970 and 1985, social conservatives battled unsuccessfully to
prevent 'sexually attracted to members of the same sex' from becoming an
accepted meaning of the word 'gay' in standard written English. They claimed
that there was already a perfectly acceptable word, namely 'homosexual'. Their
opponents said that 'homosexual' was a medical label imposed by those who
thought same-sex attraction was a sickness, and that the self-description 'gay',
which had a long history in spoken English, should be used instead. Imagine you
are an editor in the late 1970s. Will you replace 'homosexual' with 'gay'? Or will
you replace 'gay' with 'homosexual'? If the latter, what will you do with proper
names such as 'Gay Liberation League'? How will the following factors bear on
your decision: the publication? its readers? the writer whose work you are editing? style sheets? dictionary entries? your own views on sexual orientation? Try
to find some documents from the period (dictionaries, style manuals published
by newspapers, letters to the editor) that bear on the question.

Exercise 9. Usage
What policy would you as an editor adopt toward a writer's use of 'he' to refer
to any human being, as opposed to 'he or she' (i.e. overtly non-sexist), or 'they'.
(For the purpose of this exercise 'they' covers all such neutral solutions to the
problem of avoiding either 'he' or 'he or she'.)

Would you (i) always leave whatever the writer uses? (ii) always replace
'he' with 'he or she'? (iii) always replace 'he' with 'they' but leave 'he or she'
(iv) always replace both 'he' and 'he or she' (whichever the writer uses) with
'they'? If you would sometimes use one approach, sometimes another, state
the circumstances.

Find out what two or three of the guides listed at the end of this chapter
have to say on the subject.

If you would always use the neutralizing strategy (iv), how would you respond
to the argument that you are engaging in censorship, that is, preventing the
writer from expressing the message (whatever that may be) which is conveyed
by using 'he' or 'he or she'?

Suppose you are editing a translation into English, and you find that the translator has not used an 'equivalent' strategy (i.e. has changed the 'degree of gender neutrality' in one direction or the other). What would you do: create 'equivalence' with the source text? adopt one of the above strategies (ii) to (iv) regardless of what is in the source text? sometimes adopt one approach, sometimes another?

Exercise 10. *Usage*

Many usage authorities require the so-called 'serial comma' (use of a comma before the final 'and' or 'or' of a list, as in "height, width, or depth"). Others disapprove of it, while still others allow or recommend it under certain circumstances. Read the Wikipedia article 'Serial comma', which lists the views of a considerable number of style guides. What is your opinion?

Further reading

(See the References list near the end of the book for details on these publications.)

Copyediting guides: Butcher (2009); Judd (2001); O'Connor (1986); Rude and Eaton (2011 Part 3).
About style sheets and manuals: Samson (1993: ch. 7).

Style manuals:

The Chicago Manual of Style, 16th edition, 2011. University of Chicago Press.
Wikipedia Manual of Style
Scientific Style and Format: the CSE Manual for Authors, Editors, and Publishers, 7th edition, 2006. Council of Science Editors.
European Commission Directorate General for Translation English Style Guide. 7th edition, June 2011. http://ec.europa.eu/translation/english/guidelines/documents/styleguide_english_dgt_en.pdf
European Union *Interinstitutional Style Guide,* 2011 edition: http://publications.europa.eu/code/en/en-000100.htm (From this page you can select English or any of 23 other EU languages.)
United Nations Editorial Manual: http://dd.dgacm.org/editorialmanual/
The Canadian Style: http://www.btb.termiumplus.gc.ca/tpv2guides/guides/tcdnstyl/index-eng.html?lang=eng
List of dictionaries, grammars, style manuals and usage guides: Dragga and Gong (1989: 101-106).
Both native and non-native speakers will benefit from the *Collins Cobuild Advanced Learner's English Dictionary* (5th edition 2006), which is available in paper and as an e-dictionary.
Combinatory dictionaries: Benson *et al* (2010); Cowie and Mackin (1975); Rodale (1947); Wood (1967). Or enter "combinatory dictionary" or "collocation finder" in your search engine.
Usage: Milroy and Milroy (1999); Bodine (1974); Hirsch (1977: ch. 2); Crystal (2007).

Diversity of English, Standard English: McArthur (1998); Greenbaum (1996: ch. 1).
Punctuation: Baron (2000: ch. 6); Halliday (1989: 32-39); Gowers (1987: ch. 14);
    Samson (1993: ch. 12); Greenbaum (1996: ch. 11).
Spelling: Greenbaum (1996: ch. 12); Baron (2000: ch. 4).
Copyediting at newspapers: Westley (1972: ch. 3).

4.   Stylistic Editing

In the last chapter, we looked at corrections that bring the text into conformance with pre-set rules. In this chapter we will look at two types of editing work that are more difficult because they do not involve applying rules:

- Tailoring vocabulary and sentence structure to the particular readers of a text and to the use they will make of it.
- Creating a smooth-flowing text by fixing problems such as poor inter-sentence connections, wrong focus within sentences, confusing verbosity, and awkward (difficult-to-follow) sentence structures.

Bear in mind that the style improvement principles described in this chapter pertain to English and may have no application to other languages.

4.1   Tailoring language to readers

The readers of a text may be identified in two ways. They may be projected, that is, the author imagines (or is asked to imagine) a certain type of reader and then the editor ensures that the book is suited to this ideal reader (e.g. a middle-aged reader interested in exotic holidays, in the case of a travel book). Alternatively, the document may be aimed at a known set of real readers (e.g. the book-keepers in a company's accounting department, in the case of a financial manual). Tailoring for real readers is easier since more is known about their characteristics, which we'll now look at.

Motivation

The intended readers of a document may or may not have a prior motivation to read it. If they are motivated (as when they are extremely interested in the topic), they will have greater tolerance for poorly edited text, though obviously there are limits beyond which they will be left with an unfavourable impression of writer and publisher. If the intended readers are not already motivated, then one task of the editor may be to liven up the writing in order to make the reading experience more enjoyable, to make the document physically more attractive, in short, to make the message more 'receivable'.

Knowledgeability

To what extent are the readers familiar with the concepts, terms and phrases of the particular field with which the text is concerned? Texts written by and for specialists in a field must contain the 'hard words', peculiar usages and odd turns of phrase specialists use, or else the readers will wonder if the author is really one of them. Also, texts aimed at specialists should be less redundant and less explicit than a text aimed at a non-specialist readership. Specialists will not feel they are being addressed if concepts familiar to them are repeated and spelled out.

Redundancy – the repetition of concepts – is important to make a text readable by people with no specialized knowledge of a subject. It will often be helpful to repeat concepts using synonyms and paraphrases; that way, a reader who did not understand the first wording may understand the second one. The same applies to explicitness; with a general readership, you need to make sure concepts are spelled out the first time they are invoked: not 'document readability checker' but 'software for assigning a score to documents in order to indicate how easy they are to read', or more briefly 'utility for checking the readability of a document'.

Where the readership needs a high level of redundancy and explicitness, that will obviously place a limit on conciseness. We often hear that texts should be concise, the implication being that editors should remove excess verbiage. But the shortest way will not always be the best, in particular for non-specialist readers.

Some documents will be for a mixed readership – both specialists and non-specialists will read them. For example, an engineering project document may have an executive summary, a section on financing and a scheduling section aimed at non-engineers, as well as several much more technical sections aimed at engineers. Alternatively, all parts of the document may be aimed at both specialists and non-specialists. For example, this chapter you are now reading was written mainly for translation students who are learning to edit, but it may also be read by experienced translators who have never actually formulated their ideas about stylistic editing, and may find something of interest here as well.

Generally speaking, editing for non-expert readers is much harder than editing for experts, who because of their subject-matter knowledge will often be able to puzzle out the meaning of poor writing.

Editing for the knowledgeability factor overlaps with content editing, i.e. not just the language but the coverage of the topic needs to be suited to the knowledge of the readers.

Education

Readers without post-secondary education will generally find it harder to read texts full of very long sentences with many subordinate clauses (and clauses within clauses); nominal structures ('in the event of your being evicted' instead of the verbal structure 'if you are evicted'), and words derived from Latin and Greek (e.g. 'cognition' rather than 'thought'). This factor is to be distinguished from the knowledgeability factor discussed above. People without higher education who are specialists in their field (a trade such as plumbing for example) will know its terms even if they are derived from Latin and Greek.

If the text will have a mass readership – one that includes people with relatively low literacy – the editor must ensure that all intended readers will in fact be able to read it, especially if it contains crucial information (e.g. public health documents). It might be useful to test the edited version on some members of the intended readership.

Language

If a text is intended for an audience that includes recent immigrants who are not yet good readers of the language in which the text is written, then editors may want to seek advice from specialists in second-language learning, who will know which sorts of wordings in a text are likely to prove difficult. An English example would be phrasal verbs, the meaning of which is not predictable from the meanings of the parts: "She ran into Professor Plum on campus yesterday" does not mean that she was running across the campus and crashed into Professor Plum. This could be changed to "She met Professor Plum...", or (since 'ran into' implies that the meeting was accidental rather than by appointment) "She happened to meet Professor Plum...".

Other texts are for international audiences who have a very good reading knowledge of the language but may not be familiar with the informal spoken language, recent expressions, or local culture. For this type of readership, editors will want to eliminate, for example, metaphors that draw on local sports: 'those suggestions are really out in left field' (baseball); 'she got knocked for six at the supermarket' (cricket); 'they stickhandled their way out of a situation that could have been disastrous' (hockey).

Time and place

The geographical location of readers may differ from the geographical location of the author you are editing. As a result, it may be necessary to eliminate Australianisms, Americanisms, Britishisms, and so on. Thus a non-Canadian reader may be at least momentarily puzzled by a reference to 'the government's inaction on the Aboriginal land claims file'; perhaps you should change 'file' (which originated in this meaning as a literal translation of French 'dossier') to 'issue'. Or you might want to replace a British usage with an American one: 'revise', meaning go over course materials in preparation for an examination, would become 'review'.

Turning from place to time, you may be editing material that was written decades ago and contains obsolete words that readers will not know. Perhaps you need to make the language more contemporary so that the readers will understand, or so that they do not have the perhaps unconscious reaction 'old language - old ideas - not interesting'. Another possibility is that a present-day writer is using old-fashioned language (e.g. 'moving pictures' instead of 'films' or 'movies'; 'I shall' in cases where almost everyone now uses 'I will'). You may want to eliminate such wordings if you think the effect is unintentionally or inappropriately pompous or comic, though you might retain them if they seem intentional or appropriate in context.

Writer-reader relationship

The formality of the language needs to reflect the relationship between writer and reader. For example, with an in-house employee newsletter, the relationship is taken to be one of equality and familiarity. This calls for chatty language with direct address ('take a look at the bulletin board', not 'employees should consult the bulletin board'), contractions ('isn't' rather than 'is not'), and, more generally, features of spoken conversation.

When the writer is not known to the readers except through the wording of the text, it is especially important to attend to the impression this wording creates. Let me illustrate with a feature of my own writing which I find I often have to correct while self-editing, namely my tendency to overuse the expression 'of course', as in "Split infinitives have of course never ceased to be in widespread use" – the original form of a sentence which you will, of course, recall from Chapter 3. 'Of course' implies that readers are simply being reminded of something they already know. If in fact they do not already know, they may have one of two opposite but equally undesirable reactions: they may feel intimidated (why didn't I know that? maybe this book is too advanced for me) or angry (this guy seems to think I'm an ignoramus because I don't know the history of split infinitives). Such an emotional reaction will (of course) distract the reader from the message.

Reader's use of the text

So far, the discussion has been about characteristics of the reader, such as knowledgeability and education. Also important is the text's use: how, where and why it will be read.

- How: Will the document be read aloud or silently? Will the readers be reading the document through from start to finish, or will they be consulting sections of it?
- Where: Will the reader be walking past a sign that provides information they need? Watching a slide presentation? Referring to a document while installing newly purchased electronic equipment? Sitting in a coffee shop or on a bus reading a Web page on a handheld device?
- Why: For enjoyment? To pass the time while commuting to work? To make a decision? To obtain instructions?

The how, where and why are mainly important for content and structural editing, and for page layout and typography decisions. However these factors may also bear on style. Take instruction manuals. These may occasionally be read aloud, by one employee to another who is engaged in the activity the manual describes. The instructions should therefore be given in sentences which are short and addressed directly to the reader/listener ('press the button', not 'the button should be pressed' or 'the operator will press the button').

4.2 Smoothing

Readers need to be able to process a text easily. They should not find the wordings getting in the way of the meanings. To put this in negative terms, the sequence of words must not give rise to the 'huh?' reaction. Readers should not have to go over a sentence two or three times just to see how the parts of the sentence are connected to each other and to get the basic point. And they should not be distracted or misled by unintended ambiguities.

Features that make for a smooth-reading text are:

(a)   It is clear what-goes-with-what within each sentence

It is generally a good idea to put a modifier next to what it modifies. Consider:

> Parents with children who want to be at the front should arrive at the parade early.

The writer may have meant 'parents who want to be at the front' but the reader may take it to mean 'children who want to be at the front'. More often, it is not a matter of two completely different interpretations; rather, careless positioning simply makes mental processing more difficult than it needs to be. Consider this passage from a text about paroled offenders who are not sent back to prison even though there is a risk they will commit a fresh offence:

> ... keep individuals in the community whose risk calls for special supervision.

This should be changed to 'keep in the community individuals whose risk calls for special supervision', so that in processing the sentence, the reader's mind does not waste time considering (and rejecting) the possibility that 'risk' goes with 'community' rather than 'individuals'. The sentence should not be changed to 'keep individuals whose risk calls for special supervision in the community', since this may lead to a wrong interpretation (supervision in the community as opposed to somewhere else).

However the principle of putting modifier next to modified does not always work. You would not want to change 'legislation on the meat industry that comes into effect on December 31' to 'legislation that comes into effect on December 31 on the meat industry'. After moving a phrase, re-read the sentence to ensure you have not made it worse.

Indicating what-goes-with-what is the single most important function of punctuation, especially the comma. didyouknowthatatonetimetextswereunpunctuatedtherewerenodemarcationsbetweenwordssentencespartsofsentences orparagraphs Consider these two sentences:

> (1) Frequently bored translators need to be given other assignments.
> (2) Frequently, bored translators need to be given other assignments.

(1) says something about translators who are frequently bored; (2) says that bored translators frequently need to be given other assignments. A common error here would be to write (1) when the author is in fact thinking of the meaning which is properly expressed by (2).

Here is a case where adding commas solves a what-goes-with-what problem:

> The effects on virtuous insect species such as bees of plants that have had natural pesticides engineered into them should continually be monitored.

The reader is liable to become puzzled upon reaching 'of plants'. Inserting commas after 'effects' and 'bees' clears up the difficulty.

Here is a somewhat different case:

> (3) In addition to the fact that more than 30 percent of immigrants speak English, when they reach Canada 95 percent of those who are not of British or French origin show a marked preference for English as their home language.

> (4) In addition to the fact that more than 30 percent of immigrants speak English when they reach Canada, 95 percent of those who are not of British or French origin show a marked preference for English as their home language.

In (3), 'when they reach Canada' means 'after they reach Canada'; in (4), it means 'before they reach Canada'. It is unlikely that a writer would err in placing the comma during the original drafting of such a sentence. However, the comma might well get moved to the wrong position during self-editing, when attention is often parcelized – the self-editor focuses on one part of a sentence rather than on overall meaning.

Sometimes commas prevent misreadings; in many other cases, they simply prevent stumbling by the reader and the need to re-read. For example, readers will stumble when they come across a 'garden path' sentence such as the following, already seen in another connection in Chapter 1:

> As these studies tend to show the form translation has taken in Canada, both on an institutional level and on the level of the actual practice of translation, is specific to our particular national context.

At the beginning of this sentence, the reader is 'led up the garden path' to the incorrect interpretation that the studies show the form which translation has taken.

(b)   The subject and verb of the main clause are easily located, and are also fairly close to each other

Generally speaking, the easiest sentences to read are those which start with the subject and verb of the main clause. The later the main clause comes, and the further apart its subject and verb are, the harder the reader's task will be. Actually, to be more accurate, the real problem is not so much the number of words preceding the main-clause subject, or intervening between subject and verb, as the structural complexity of these preceding and interceding passages. Here is an example of a grammatically perfect sentence which is extremely difficult to read:

> Although the procedure provides that at all times when the inmate is being escorted outside the custodial unit, from the time he is taken out of the escort van to the time he is locked in the custodial unit, or during the time he is escorted within the other areas of the hospital, he is always to be taken in a wheelchair with his hands and feet restrained, the officer-in-charge is indeed alone with the inmate outside the custodial unit while proceeding through the foyer of the emergency wing which leads to the custodial unit.

Readers may have lost track of the structure of this sentence by the time they reach 'he is always to be taken...' (the subject and verb of the clause beginning 'that at all times...'). They will almost certainly be baffled by 'the officer-in-charge is alone...' (the main clause of the sentence). Here is an edited version that solves the problem by splitting the sentence in two, moving 'he is always to be taken...' to a position near the beginning of the first sentence, and replacing two of the commas with parentheses:

> The procedure does provide that the inmate is always to be taken in a wheelchair with his hands and feet restrained when he is being escorted outside the hospital's custodial unit (from the time he is taken out of the escort van to the time he is locked in the custodial unit, or when he is being escorted within the other areas of the hospital). Nevertheless, the officer-in-charge is indeed alone with the inmate, outside the custodial unit, while they are proceeding through the foyer of the emergency wing which leads to the custodial unit.

(c)   *Each sentence is properly related to the preceding one in terms of information flow and focus*

Consider the first two sentences of the section in this chapter headed "Reader's use of the text":

> So far, the discussion has been about characteristics of the reader, such as knowledgeability and education. Also important is the text's use: how, where and why it will be read.

Originally there was no comma after 'reader'. As a result, the focus was on 'knowledgeability and education'. This is undesirable because the next sentence does not go on to discuss some new category of reader characteristics (the first category being one that includes knowledgeability and education). Rather, the next sentence introduces a contrasting topic – the use of a text as opposed to its readers. The comma after 'reader' keeps the focus on that word, in preparation for the contrast with 'use' in the next sentence.

Now consider the following passage from a text on acid precipitation; it appears at the transition between a discussion of sulphur dioxide and a discussion of carbon dioxide:

> This study has begun to give us a good idea of the extent of transport of fossil sulphur put into circulation by human activity, but there has been little advance in our understanding of the relationship between sulphur and free acids in rainfall.
> It is also difficult to tell whether carbon dioxide is or is not a pollutant.

The last sentence would normally be read with the following mental stress:

> It is ALso difficult to tell whether carbon dioxide IS or is NOT a pollUTant.

Now, the argument here is 'as with sulphur dioxide (just discussed), so with carbon dioxide'. For the reader to get this meaning, the word 'also' would have to be read as going with 'carbon dioxide' only, not with the entire expression 'difficult to tell whether carbon dioxide is or is not a pollutant'. To obtain this result, the sentence would have to be read:

> It is ALso difficult to tell whether carbon diOXide is or is not a pollutant.

But that is not the stress pattern which a first-time reader will use. So the sentence has to be reworded to move 'carbon dioxide' into focus:

> Another substance which may or may not be a pollutant is carbon dioxide.

Simplifying somewhat, the focus position in English comes at the end of a sentence.

(d)   Connector words (but, therefore, etc) are not misleading

It is very important that readers be able to see how each sentence is functioning with respect to the previous sentence. The connection may be left for the reader to fill in or it may be signalled by a special connector word. Among the possible functions are: restating in a more elaborate way what has just been said; saying what happened next; giving evidence for what has just been said; saying something that contrasts with what came previously; giving the cause, purpose or result of what has just been said (it must be clear which). Here's an example where the second sentence is giving the cause, but this will not be immediately apparent to the reader:

> The dominant natural disturbance in most Canadian forests is wildfires, whose frequency in the past three decades has increased markedly. Longer and warmer summers, a phenomenon that has been exacerbated by human-induced climate change, are widely thought to be the reason.

The second sentence should be changed to:

> The increase is widely thought to be due to longer and warmer summers,...

Here the word 'increase' creates an immediate connection to the 'increased' which appears near the end of the first sentence, and 'due to' informs the reader that this sentence is explaining the increase.

(e) *Parallel ideas are expressed through parallel forms*

If the text has parallel inserted comments, make sure the punctuation marks are parallel. Watch for sentences like 'The boys – whether or not they exercised regularly – had similar percentage weight increases, whereas the girls (whatever their diet) did not'.

In point-form writing, watch for instances where points lower in the list do not have the same form as the earlier points:

> The incumbent of this position must be able to:
> * translate difficult texts rapidly;
> * carry out terminological research on the Internet;
> * have a sound knowledge of editorial practices;
> * good relationships with clients.

The third and fourth items in the list do not fit into the sentence structure: 'must be able to have a sound knowledge...', 'must be able to good relationships'. Perhaps the last two items were pasted in from another document, and the writer did not think to check for parallelism of form.

(f) *The antecedents of pronouns are immediately clear*

A sentence which appeared in an earlier version of this chapter read as follows:

> It is also important to anticipate reader reactions to the person addressing them, their entire knowledge of whom may well arise from the wording of the text.

Who is 'them' and 'their'? The only preceding plural noun is 'reactions', and that cannot very well be the antecedent, since reactions don't have knowledge. Mental processing of the sentence will be made easier if 'reader reactions' is changed to 'the reactions of readers'. In passing, note here the danger of the editor introducing an error in the opposite case, where the writer has correctly used 'the reactions of readers' but the editor wrongly decides to 'tighten the sentence up' by substituting 'reader reactions'.

(g)   The correct interpretation of noun sequences and other ambiguous structures is clear from context

Consider 'check the translation against customer specifications'. Is it clear from context whether 'customer specifications' means specifications *from* the customer (e.g. use British spelling) or specifications *about* the customer (e.g. this is a Class A customer – one who gives us a lot of work)? If not, insert the appropriate preposition.

This may be especially a problem in the elliptical style which omits words like 'the' (as in point-form writing):

> Voltage values are seen through small windows in panel. Switch ranges from 100 to 240 in six steps, and is positioned by turning...

The reader, having seen that 'the' has been omitted in front of 'panel', may well assume that it has similarly been omitted in front of 'ranges'. That is, the reader will take 'switch' to be an imperative verb: you should switch the ranges. However, upon arriving at 'and is positioned', the reader sees that this interpretation is wrong, and must reinterpret with 'ranges' as the verb: 'the switch ranges... and is positioned'.

Every language has its common ambiguities that must be watched. In English, the structure exemplified in 'more structured supervision' is often not disambiguated by context: more supervision that is structured, or supervision that is more structured?

4.3   Readability versus clarity

Readability must be distinguished from clarity. Clarity is a feature of the meaning of a text, rather than its wording. A text may be readable in both the senses we have discussed – its language may be smooth-flowing and it may be suited to the intended readers – but it may still be unclear. A text is unclear if its message contains some slip in logic, for example it is self-contradictory, or effects precede causes. The sentence 'Your wait between planes will last up to an hour or more' is unclear: at first we seem to be told that our wait will be an hour or less ('up to'), but then we learn that it may be more than hour. The sentence is both contradictory and uninformative: the wait could be any length of time. Perhaps the writer was trying to say that the wait will most likely be under an hour, but may be over.

Clarity should not be confused with simplicity or familiarity. A document may seem 'clear' because its ideas are simple or because it contains nothing but familiar notions. Notoriously, simple and familiar ideas sometimes turn out to be laden with obscurity when subjected to closer inspection. Conversely, a text which contains complex or challenging new ideas will not necessarily be unclear, in the sense of containing slips of logic. It may be perfectly clear even though it has to be read slowly, or re-read with considerable thought, as long as this need to re-read is due to the inherent complexity of the thought, not to a lack of smooth sentence structure, or to language that is unsuited to the readers, or to unnecessary terminological innovation. A legal text may require several readings because the writer's aim was not to lighten the reader's task but to state things in a completely unambiguous way.

4.4   Stylistic editing during translation

Translators often engage in smoothing and tailoring work as they translate. Consider the following extract from an annual report on forest pests and other sources of damage to timber; (5) gives the translation as it might appear if the source-text phrase order were to be observed, while (6) gives the translation as it might appear if the translator engaged in mental editing while translating:

> (5) The spruce budworm and the hemlock looper were the principal insects defoliating evergreen forests in 1999. In deciduous forests, the main problem was the tent caterpillar. The pine shoot beetle became a major concern at plantations. Several severe wind storms also caused heavy damage in the summer of 1999.

> (6) In 1999, the principal insects defoliating evergreen forests were the spruce budworm and the hemlock looper. In deciduous forests, the main problem was the tent caterpillar, while at plantations a major concern was the pine shoot beetle. In the summer, there was also heavy damage due to severe wind storms.

We'll assume here, for the sake of argument, that this is not a case where rearrangement is needed despite a well written source text; that is, the changes shown in the mentally edited version (6) are not a result of the normal differences between the ways the two languages organize the information in a sentence.

Note how sentence constituents have been positioned in (6) so that the entities causing damage are at the ends of sentences and clauses. Such a change is definitely necessary in the last sentence: in the unedited version (5), the last sentence does not flow on at all well from what precedes. In the first and third sentences of the unedited version, repositionings make for a minor but definite improvement because all sentences then have the same structure (place followed by cause of damage to trees), and the new information in each sentence (the names of the insects causing the damage) is in focus position at the end of each sentence. Note too how the year number has been deleted in the last sentence: placing it in a high-focus position (at the end of a sentence) is confusing because it suggests that the year is of some special importance (perhaps as contrasted with another year), whereas in fact it is understood throughout the text that we are talking about events during 1999.

Another important type of stylistic editing during translation is elimination of verbosity. Some people appear to delight in saying simple things in a complicated way. Consider the following sentence from a translated job description, where (7) follows the wording of the source text but (8) is the result of mental editing while translating:

> (7) Adapt technical issues and complex regulations and information in order to present these issues and this information in a way that is at the same time simple, accurate and comprehensible.

> (8) Explain technical issues, complex regulations and other information in a way that is accurate but comprehensible.

Aside from reducing verbosity, the translator has also made explicit the logic of the message, by bringing out the nature of the problem which confronts the incumbent of this job: when addressing non-experts, there is a conflict between being accurate and being comprehensible (hence 'but' rather than 'and'). 'Simple' does not add anything to what is already expressed by 'comprehensible'.

4.5   Some traps to avoid

There is a great temptation when engaged in stylistic editing to rewrite sentences, that is, to compose a completely new sentence with different vocabulary and sentence structure. You may find that such a new sentence is what comes to mind first, once you have spotted a stylistic problem. However, you should resist rewriting and instead ask yourself whether the sentence can be fixed by a much smaller alteration (change a word here, move a phrase there). At first, this may take more time than complete rewriting, but once you become good at making minimal changes, you will be able to edit much faster. Consider:

> The abundance of overmature black spruce stands leads to an increase in logging costs because the trees are often small and the merchantable volumes are low.

The logical structure of this sentence is "X causes Y because Z", which is confusing. You could completely rewrite the sentence:

> In the many overmature black spruce stands, trees are often small and merchantable volumes low; logging costs are consequently higher.

But the problem can be fixed much more simply:

> Given the abundance of overmature black spruce stands, there is an increase in logging costs because the trees are often small and the merchantable volumes are low.

This is perhaps not quite as good as the complete rewrite, but it does eliminate the confusion.

A second danger when editing style is paying exclusive attention to very small bits of language and losing track of meaning. Consider this sentence fragment from a text on operations in a port:

Original:
...the relationship between freight unloaded and operating time...

Edited version:
...the relationship between unloaded freight and operating time...

The editor perhaps thought that 'unloaded freight' is easier to read than 'freight unloaded'. However context makes clear that the author meant 'freight that has already been unloaded'. Unfortunately the edited version, 'unloaded freight', is more likely to be interpreted as 'freight that has not yet been loaded' – a very different idea.

Here's another example:

Original:
Government health inspectors must be able to explain the rationale for inspecting establishments registered under the Act and specific foods.

Edited version:
...must be able to explain the rationale for inspecting specific foods and establishments registered under the Act.

In the original, 'specific foods', the second of the two phrases joined by 'and', is hanging awkwardly at the end of the sentence. Usually if there are two conjoined phrases, one long and one short, it is best to have the short one first. The edited version clears up this problem but creates a worse one: the change in order means that 'specific' now applies to both 'foods' and 'establishments'. The edited sentence seems to suggest that inspectors need to justify their habit of picking on certain establishments rather than dealing even-handedly with all establishments. A further change is needed: '...for inspecting specific foods and for inspecting establishments...'.

And a final example: perhaps you think that 'obtain documents required for clearance' can be shortened to 'obtain clearance documents', but is the meaning the same? In one text it may be, but in another text it may not; perhaps one needs certain documents (which are not themselves clearance documents) in order to apply for a clearance document.

Practice

Since stylistic editing is not as cut and dried as copyediting, there is a danger of making too many changes. Do not make a change simply because you would have expressed an idea differently had you been the author. You are not the author. You are editing someone else's work, and you must respect their individual style of writing. So whenever you make a change, be sure you can justify it. "It sounds better" does not count as a justification. You must be specific: this word is too informal; there is a confusing ambiguity in the structure of this sentence. Exercise 1 is explicitly an exercise in justification, but you should always be able to justify your changes.

Exercises can be speeded up if you simply underline places in the text where a change is needed, without actually making the change. Remember that the difficult thing in editing is finding the problems. Correcting stylistic problems, once you have found them, can be quite time-consuming.

Exercise 1. *Justifying changes*
Your instructor will give you a printed text, with a variety of handwritten stylistic changes. For each change, say whether you think it is justified, and if so, why. If the editor has completely rewritten a sentence that needed changing, try to think of a smaller change that would suffice.

Exercise 2. *Verbosity*
Reduce the verbosity of two samples of bureaucratic prose which you have found or which your instructor has given you. The first sample should be addressed to a reader outside the bureaucracy, the second to a reader inside. See how few words you can use to express the ideas, bearing in mind the needs of the two types of reader.

Exercise 3. *Smoothing*
Newspaper articles are often insufficiently edited for smoothness. Find some examples of unsmooth sentences or paragraphs in a newspaper and smooth them, paying special attention to pronouns and intersentence connecting words (this, they, also, but etc).

Exercise 4. *Tailoring*
Your instructor will give you a text and a description of the intended readers (in terms of their knowledge, education etc). Tailor the text to the readers.

Further reading

(See the References list near the end of the book for details on these publications.)

Inter-sentence connections: Halliday and Hasan (1976); Dragga and Gong (1989: ch. 3); Greenbaum (1996: ch. 7).
Readership analysis: Dragga and Gong (1989: ch. 2); Samson (1993: ch. 4); Bell (1991: ch. 6).
Readability: Gopen and Swan (1990); Hirsch (1977: chs. 4 and 5); Kirkman (2005: ch. 2).

5. Structural Editing

Texts have two types of structure: conceptual structure and physical structure. An example of the former would be an argument structure: presentation of problem, tentative solution, arguments for, arguments against, conclusion. An example of physical structure would be the parts of an article: title, summary, section head, sequence of paragraphs, inserted table, next section head, and so on. The structural editor's job is to help the reader follow the conceptual structure by making adjustments in the physical structure. This may involve large-scale work rearranging paragraphs, sections and chapters. However, in this chapter we will be concerned with smaller scale changes, because that is the kind of work translators most often need to do.

5.1 Physical structure of a text

Documents typically have several physically distinct structural parts:

- Prose: a continuous sequence of sentences and paragraphs. Words in e-texts may be clickable, that is, linked electronically to other parts of the text or to other texts.
- Headings, often hierarchical and sometimes numbered: chapter titles, sections heads, subsection heads, and so on.
- Lists: the main types are point-form lists, which may be numbered or let-tered (or bulleted like the list you are reading now), and tables (a table is a series of parallel lists, usually called columns). The boxes of which tables are composed may themselves contain prose sequences. There may also be locator lists to help readers move to specific places within the document: the table of contents at the front, and one or more al-phabetical indexes at the back listing topics dealt with in the document, names of people mentioned, and the like. Finally there may be linking lists to help readers move outward toward other relevant works: a list of references (works referred to in the document); sometimes a separate list of readings (works of interest on the subject of the document).
- Graphics: diagrams, photographs, drawings, maps, embedded videos and other such entities, usually referred to in the consecutive prose. These are often intermixed with the consecutive prose but sometimes they are located in a separate part of the document devoted specifically to graphics.
- Isolated items: footnotes, endnotes, captions of graphics and tables, la-bels on diagrams, column or row titles on tables, etc.

In the remainder of the chapter, we'll look at several problems that may arise with the prose and with the headings.

5.2   Problems with prose

Missing markers

A paragraph begins 'There are four factors that lead parolees to re-offend. First....'. The reader continues and then realizes, a few paragraphs later, that he is now reading about a second factor. The writer forgot to insert the important structural marker 'second'.

A related error is a sequence like 'There are four factors...first,...second,... third,... lastly,... finally'. When the writer had completed her rather lengthy discussion of the fourth factor, she thought of a further factor meriting mention. Having lost track of the numbering, however, she introduced her discussion with 'finally'. The editor will make the required changes: 'There are five factors: first...fourth...finally'.

Unfulfilled announcements

The writer announces 'Let us first look at the arguments in favour of this view, and then at the arguments against'. A couple of pages later, the arguments in favour terminate, and so does the section; the author moves on to another matter, and the arguments against appear 10 or 15 pages later in another section of the document. The editor will have to either amend the introductory sentence ('Here we will look at the arguments in favour; the arguments against will be discussed in section 9') or else move the material from section 9 back to the earlier section.

Empty backward references

In the 4th paragraph of the text, there is a reference to 'this committee', but no committee has been mentioned in the text so far. Perhaps there used to be such a reference, but it was deleted. The editor should amend to 'a committee'.

False backward or forward references

A sentence refers the reader to the 'fifth paragraph on page 27' for more information on the matter under discussion. But that paragraph contains no such additional information. The information in question is in the first paragraph on page 28. This is because the document is being circulated in electronic form, not just in final printed form. When the reader prints out the electronic form, some factor such as a larger default font or wider margins results in the paragraph appearing on page 28 rather than page 27. Solution: avoid referring to page numbers in such documents.

Unexplained acronyms

In the 3rd paragraph of the text, the reader learns that the NBRS will be disbanding. What, the reader wonders, is the NBRS? Three pages later there is a reference to the North Bambridge Roselovers Society, which the reader may or may not connect with the mysterious acronym earlier in the text. The writer forgot that not all readers would be familiar with North Bambridge and its renowned rose gardens. The editor will adjust the first mention to 'North Bambridge Roselovers Society (NBRS)', and then adjust later uses to 'the NBRS' or 'the Society'.

However, if several pages go by with no mention of the Society, it may be best to revert to the full name. This is especially important if chunks of the document are likely to be consulted independently of the rest of the text, as with reference works. In such cases, the reader may not have looked at the first occurrence of the acronym in the work as a whole. There are two solutions: spell out the acronym on its first occurrence in each section, or append a list of acronyms for ready reference.

References to graphics and tables

The editor will often need to eliminate expressions like 'the following table' or 'the chart opposite' because page designers will want to have flexibility in placing graphics and tables. Instead, tables and graphics should be numbered and referred to in the consecutive prose by those numbers: 'Table 14 shows...'; '... as seen in Figure 5'.

Poor paragraphing

Paragraph divisions are important markers that guide the reader through the text's structure. Suppose you find an extremely long paragraph followed by a rather short one. On inspection of the content, you notice that the last third of the long paragraph discusses the same topic as the short paragraph. The writer was working along, decided that the paragraph was getting too long, and simply started a new one at an arbitrary point. You should divide the long paragraph at the point where the topic changes, and then adjoin the short paragraph to the new second paragraph.

Quite independently of the unity of a paragraph's content, the length of paragraphs appears to have an effect on ease of reading. Readers who are less educated, or less knowledgeable about the text's subject matter, find shorter paragraphs easier to handle. On the other hand, a long sequence of short paragraphs (especially one-sentence paragraphs) is not optimal; rather a mixture of long and short paragraphs appears to be best.

Ideally, the length of paragraphs should be correlated with topic: use a short paragraph, for example, to sum up at the end of one phase of an argument. However, there are no natural places to end paragraphs. It is more a matter of what the writer wants the reader to consider as going together. For example, I could have combined this present paragraph with the preceding one. By not doing so, I have separated the question of ease of reading from the question of the relationship between meaning and paragraphing. I could have pointed to this distinction even more clearly by turning the first sentence of the previous paragraph (which mentions both content and ease of reading) into a paragraph of its own. Finally, I could have moved the first sentence of this present paragraph to the previous paragraph, and deleted 'however' from the second sentence. That would have given more prominence to the sentence 'There are no natural places to end paragraphs', and made it a fresh topic rather than a contrast with the thought in the previous sentence.

5.3 Problems with headings

Misconceived headings

The heading of a subsection reads 'implementation of the guidelines', but the material in the body of the subsection only mentions the guidelines in passing at the outset, and then moves on to some other topic. The writer wrote the heading, then got off-topic and forgot to amend the heading to suit the section.

Confusing heading system

On one page the main headings are numbered and bolded while the subheadings are indented and underlined. Two pages later, a main heading has been indented and a subheading has been italicized. Consistency in the positioning, numbering/lettering and formatting (bolding, underlining, italicizing) of headings is important because these features are visual signals of the structure of an argument.

Readers may also be confused by a many-layered system of headings, one with sub-subheadings and sub-sub-subheadings. Such a system is appropriate for manuals and other documents that are not meant to be read from start to finish, because it assists quick referencing ('see section III.A.5.b)ii of the Manual on Administrative Policy'). However, if your author has used an elaborate system in a document which is not a manual, try to reduce the number of layers in an article or chapter to one or two. Also, signal these layers by position and formatting (e.g. the italicization used in this book) rather than by numbers or letters unless the Style Sheet for a publication requires sections of articles to be numbered, or there is considerable cross-referencing ('see section 2 below').

Lack of subheadings

It is easier to read a text in which subheadings appear every few paragraphs. Subheadings signal a change of topic and also remind the reader of the structure of an argument: 'we are now moving on to the next factor in the list which appeared a few pages back'. The reader is relieved of the task of trying to relate the first sentence of a new paragraph to what precedes; the subheading makes the relationship explicit.

Headings that do not match the table of contents

If the numbering of headings within the consecutive prose differs from the numbering in the Table of Contents, or if the wording of a heading differs significantly from the Table of Contents wording, the reader may be misled or become confused. Ideally, the writer has used the word processor's automatic Table of Contents generator, but many people find this hard to use. Consequently, you as the editor must check that the section 6.7 mentioned in the Table of Contents really exists, that it does indeed start on page 94, and that it is in fact entitled 'How to Fire Employees', not 'The Human Aspect of Downsizing'.

5.4   Structural editing during translation

Some people new to translation think that the structure of the text has already been created by the source-text author, and that there is therefore no work for them to do in this respect. That is not the case. During translation, you may sometimes find that you need to make structural adjustments: change the order of sentences for example to bring out the argument; change the paragraph or sentence divisions; turn a point-form list into consecutive prose or vice versa. The reason may be poor writing in the source text, or simply different rhetorical habits in the target language. For example, English tends to avoid the rather lengthy headings sometimes seen in French writing, so as the editor you might replace a lengthy translated heading with a two-word or three-word heading that is appropriate for the section that follows.

The case of paragraphing is of special interest, since many people ignore this. Clients sometimes ask to have the paragraphing of the source text imitated, but that is not always advisable. For example, there is a style of writing in French in which the last sentence of a paragraph needs to be turned into the first sentence of the next paragraph in English, because it introduces a new topic. Also, paragraphing habits may differ in the corresponding target-language genre. For example, if you are translating English newspaper articles for a corporate or ministerial clipping service, you may want to eliminate the one-sentence paragraphs which are common in English journalism. Conversely, if translating a news story from another language into English, for publication in a newspaper (not just for information), you may want to split long paragraphs, and even create some one-sentence paragraphs.

Practice

Exercise

Your instructor will give you a text in which the paragraph divisions and any headings have been eliminated. First, divide the text into paragraphs. Then add headings and possibly subheadings.

Compare your paragraphing with that of other members of the class. Are the differences small or large? Do there seem to be differing principles at work? Do the paragraphing differences affect meaning?

Compare the positioning and wording of the headings added by various class members. Do some heading decisions make it easier to follow the chain of thought? Do some heading decisions focus the reader's attention differently from others?

Further reading

(See the References list near the end of the book for details on these publications.)

Dragga and Gong (1989: ch. 3); Van de Poel (2012: ch. 7).

6.   Content Editing

Content editing is checking and amending a text for its ideas. As with structural editing, content editing takes place both on the large scale (the macro-level) and the small scale (the micro-level). Since macro-level content editing is generally not a concern for translators, this chapter will be principally concerned with those micro-level tasks which translators may be called upon to perform, namely the correction of factual, logical and mathematical errors. No hard and fast boundary can be drawn between outright errors of fact on the one hand and problems such as obscure passages or confused theoretical notions on the other; these will all be discussed together under the heading 'factual errors'.

6.1   Macro-level content editing

Editors may suggest or require major changes in the coverage of a document's topic. Additions or subtractions may be requested in order to make the text suitable for the audience, in order to include the latest developments in the subject, or in order to distinguish a book from others on the same topic. Sometimes subtractions will be needed in order to make the text fit the available space.

With some texts, macro-level content editing is closely tied to the social gatekeeper function of editors. That is, the editor may be acting on behalf of an institution with an ideological purpose. Newspapers of particular political complexions come to mind in this connection; governments too may employ editors to cover unpleasant facts with euphemism or vagueness. More insidiously, editors may be employed to censor written materials before publication, by removing passages that are ideologically unacceptable.

Editors have even engaged in deliberate falsification on behalf of their employers. In his novel *Nineteen Eighty-Four*, George Orwell takes this to its logical extreme: the central character, Winston Smith, is a content editor at the Ministry of Truth who edits texts *after* publication. As chapter 4 opens, we find him 'editing' the already published *Times* account of a speech by Big Brother promising an increase in the chocolate ration. After the destruction of all existing copies of that issue of the newspaper, the historical record will show that the great leader in fact announced a considerable *de*crease in the ration. Interestingly, fiction has now become reality: with the advent of pure e-publishing (i.e. there are no paper copies of a publication), it *is* now possible to engage in post-publication content editing. Archives are available of earlier states of Web sites, but most people will never bother to look at these or are unaware of their existence.

The ethical content editor has a professional commitment to truth. There are two aspects to this. One is the avoidance of unintentional falsehoods. For this purpose, many publishing organizations employ special fact-checkers. The second aspect is the avoidance of deception, by ensuring that the published item tells 'the whole truth and nothing but the truth'. Also, if there are certain well-known objections to the author's arguments, these are at least admitted, if not answered.

It should be borne in mind that the selecting function of editors (accepting or rejecting whole texts, or parts of texts) is a two-edged sword. On the one hand, the editor may select in order to conceal truths (which may be deemed danger-ous or simply offensive); on the other hand, the selection may be made in the service of quality. For example, many people prefer to join Internet discussion forums which have a moderator (i.e. a content editor) because they do not want to spend huge amounts of time wading through material of no interest. They trust the moderator to select well written and well thought out contributions, representing a diversity of views. Thus another characteristic of the ethical con-tent editor will be trustworthiness.

6.2   Factual errors

One reason specialized texts need to be content-edited by subject-matter special-ists is that others may not recognize factual errors. But factual errors may also come up in otherwise unspecialized texts, and it will not always be obvious (for example through self-contradiction) that there is an error.

Read the following passage and decide whether, if you had not read it in a chap-ter about correcting content errors, you would have recognized the problem:

> In a plain-looking shop in the untouristy 19th arrondissement, a 1930 second edition of George Orwell's Nineteen Eighty-Four in dust jacket recently sold for $10.

This certainly was an unusual find, since the first edition of Orwell's novel was not published until 1949.

Factual errors also include more mundane things such as incorrect street addresses; incorrect website addresses; not-quite-right book titles or names of organizations (North Bumbridge Roselovers Society instead of Roselovers Association of North Bambridge), and incorrect references (the quoted mater-ial was on page 406, not page 306 of vol 3 no 2 of the Journal of Xology). Such fact-checking used to involve some rather tedious searches through almanacs, yearbooks, telephone directories and other reference works, but nowadays much of the information is available on the Internet. To check that a Web address is correct, try to go to the site using your browser. If the text is a translation posted at a website, links should lead readers to a target-language site, if possible and appropriate.

A final and very important type of fact that has to be checked is the accu-racy of quotations. If the source of a quotation cannot be tracked down, then the quotation marks should be removed, and indirect speech used instead. If the quoted material was spoken rather than written, the quotation does not normally need to be a verbatim transcript: hesitations (....um...) and false starts can be cleaned up, and some publications replace professional jargon or dialect with more readily understandable wordings. Sometimes awkward wordings are improved to spare the quoted speaker embarrassment: 'The architecture down there is some of the best in the city. A greater degree of people are wanting to be down there' might be changed to read '...More people want to live there'.

Conceptual errors and obscure passages

Non-expert popularizers frequently make conceptual errors. For example, science columnists in newspapers often discuss evolution in non-Darwinian, teleological language: giraffes developed long necks 'in order to' reach leaves higher up on the trees. Normally, people writing in their own field of expertise do not make errors in field-specific concepts, though sometimes experts writing for lay audiences do not express concepts as well as they might. Thus "greenhouse gases absorb heat and then radiate it back to the Earth" should perhaps be changed to "absorb heat emitted by the Earth which would normally go into space, and then send it back to Earth". Here we see content editing overlapping with the audience-related concerns of stylistic editing.

Some conceptual errors are quite subtle. Consider the sentence 'Ms. J. denies the historical fact of the massacre'. Imagine it in an article whose author, like Ms. J., does not believe the massacre occurred. Unfortunately the sentence means: 'the massacre is a historical fact but Ms. J. denies it'. The author has inadvertently attributed to himself a belief which he does not hold. What he wanted to say was: 'Ms. J. denies the massacre as a historical fact'. With this wording, the author avoids attributing to himself any belief about the massacre; he expresses only a belief about what Ms. J. thinks concerning it. It is very easy to miss such errors if your attention is on linguistic form. A content editor must follow an argument very closely.

Another common problem is passages where, as a result of poor writing, it is hard to see what the author is trying to say. In some editing situations, the author may not be reachable for clarification, and you must then decide on a course of action. Consider the word 'restive' in the following sentence from the gardening column of a community newspaper, discussing ornamental grasses:

> The varied colours and textures of their foliages and swaying flower spikes offer a colourful and restive scene which can rival any field of golden wheat or waving green oats.

What has happened here? Does the writer think 'restive' means restful? Is there a misprint: 'restive' for 'festive'? Perhaps the best thing would be to delete 'and restive'.

A final problem is apparently odd passages which turn out to be correct after all. In one case, a text on naval architecture mentioned that the water which is used to cool machinery had to be heated. This does not seem to make sense: why heat water that is to be used for cooling? In such specialized texts, the non-expert editor must not rely on logic; research on the Internet or consultation with an expert is essential. It turns out that in winter, there is a danger that the water will freeze, thus rendering it useless for the purpose of cooling machinery, so it must be heated just enough to keep it liquid.

Introducing errors

Worse than failing to see an error is introducing error where none existed. At the end of Chapter 4, we saw two cases where a conceptual error was introduced in the course of stylistic editing. Conceptual error may also be introduced if you fail to take the author's wording seriously. Consider a text in which a prisoner is described as doing something 'for fear of being congratulated by the warden'. An editor unthinkingly assumed this was an error and changed 'congratulated' to 'punished'. But the text made perfect sense as it stood: the prisoner did not want to be seen by other prisoners as the warden's pet.

6.3   Logical errors

This category of error includes contradictions, nonsense, tautologies, impossible time sequences, and confusions of cause and effect. Sometimes these errors can only be fixed by asking the author what was meant. In other cases, you may be able to resolve the problem yourself.
    Here's an example of nonsense:

> The mother tongue of nearly 650,000 Canadians of English ethnic origin is English, and this represents more than 10% of Canadians of French origin.

The meaning is easily recovered from context: 'the mother tongue of nearly 650,000 Canadians of French ethnic origin is English'.
    Tautologies are quite common in careless writing:

> Parole supervisors give offenders instructions, monitor their behaviour, and give them assistance and supervision.

The final phrase tells us that one thing supervisors do is....supervise – a not very informative statement.
    Here's an example of a contradictory time sequence:

> At a news conference today in San Francisco, IBM and Apple said they will disclose further details about their plans for linking computers, creating new software and advancing computer chip technology. The news conference will be held at the Fairmont Hotel.

In the first sentence, it appears that the news conference has already occurred; in the second sentence, the conference seems to be in the future. A little thought shows the problem can be solved by placing a comma after the word 'said'.
    Once again, you need to be alert to notice the errors exemplified above. It's very easy to skip past them if your attention is not on meaning.

6.4   Mathematical errors

Editors and translators are language people, who perhaps thought that they would never have to deal with math again after graduating from secondary school. They avoid scientific and technical translation, but in fact mathematical issues arise in many texts which are not scientific, technical or financial.

Sometimes a mathematical error just arises from carelessness. For example, the decimal point is in the wrong place, or the addition is wrong: 68% of the respondents to a survey were men and 42% were women! Harder to spot are cases where writers who are not mathematically inclined have tripped up conceptually, like the journalist who wrote:

> Today the Canadian dollar was worth 66 cents US. That means a $100 hotel room in the US will cost you $133 Canadian.

Wrong. This is a ratio problem: $US 0.66 is to $CAN 1.00 as $US 100 is to $CAN x. Solution: 66 cents is two-thirds of 100 cents; $100 is two-thirds of $150. The room will cost $150.

Very common are problems with percentages: An increase in weight from 2 grams to 7 grams is a 250% increase but a drop in weight from 7 grams to 2 grams is not, as one writer seems to have thought, a 250% decrease; it's a decrease of 5 out of 7, which is approximately 70%. Another example:

> The number of errors in transactions improved by 23%, dropping from 37% of sample transactions in April to 14% in May.

This is actually an improvement not of 23% but of 23 percentage points. If there were 200 sample transactions in each month, then the improvement was from 74 erroneous transactions in April (37% of the sample) to 28 in May (14% of the sample), and this is an improvement of about 62%: ((74-28) / 74) x 100.

Precision is another problem area. If the text has "7.0 cm", this can't be edited to or translated as "7 cm" because there is a difference in the fineness of measurement. With 7 cm, measurement is to the nearest whole centimetre (the actual length would between 6.5 and 7.4 cm), but with 7.0 cm, measurement is to the nearest tenth of a centimetre (i.e. the true value lies somewhere between 6.95 and 7.04 cm).

Here are two further common errors, the first related to time, the second to space. When clocks go *back* an hour from summer time to standard time in the autumn, you *gain* rather than lose an hour. If a map's resolution has been changed from 15 km per cm to 10 km per cm, then the resolution has gone *up,* not down. Each centimetre of the map now represents a *smaller* real geographical area, and hence *greater* detail can be seen.

Life expectancy figures are frequently misunderstood. If the life expectancy of women in a certain country is 48 years, it does not follow that a woman of 45 has only 3 years to live, or even that the average 45-year-old woman will live for only another 3 years. Life expectancies for countries are averages *at birth*. In countries with high infant mortality, the life expectancy at birth may be 48 years, but the life expectancy of 4-year-olds (i.e. those who survived infancy) may be to live, on average, a further 60 years.

Finally, unawareness of the difference between inclusive and exclusive counting can lead to problems. If the source language (unlike English) counts inclusively, then the source text is not wrong when it says *On Tuesday, she bought a sweater; three days later, on Thursday, she returned it.* With inclusive counting, Thursday is three days after Tuesday, because Tuesday is included in the count. But if your target language counts exclusively, then this same span of time will be *two* days, not three!

6.5   Content editing during translation

The factual, logical and mathematical errors discussed above may of course be present in your source text when you are translating. Unless instructed otherwise, you should correct logical and mathematical errors in the translation and append a note to the client pointing them out so that action can be taken to correct the source text. Factual errors should be corrected if they seem to be inadvertent but not if they are important as indicators of the author's ignorance of the facts. In the latter case, you may want to indicate that the error is due to the author, not the translator, by writing [sic—Tr] in the body of the text.

Sample correction of a logical error: the source text has 'we evaluated, analyzed and gathered the data'; the temporal sequence here makes no sense, so mentally edit to 'we gathered, evaluated and analyzed the data' before translating.

Translators may have to subtract material from the source text in order to make the translation fit into the available space. Sometimes it's possible to avoid this by typographical means, by eliminating redundancies in the translation, or by leaving meaning implicit, but on other occasions actual eliminations of content may be required.

Translators may also deliberately change the meaning of the source text as they translate, adding and subtracting material. For example, at newspapers, stories taken from international wire services may be translated with a different slant. Lu and Chen (2011: 56) give the following example of soft news reporting:

> [English source] Last month, Mr. Lindbergh stirred the pot by creating a series of covers for French Elle that showed stars like Monica Bellucci, Eva Herzigova and Sophie Marceau without makeup or retouching.

> [backtranslation of Chinese version] Mr. Lindbergh shot the covers of the April issue for French Elle, featuring eight European female celebrities without makeup. What's even more shocking is that the photos were not at all processed or altered, emphasising natural and real.

Here, the elimination of the names of the stars (because they are not familiar to Chinese readers) is run-of-the-mill adaptation, but notice that the single word 'retouching' in the source has been turned into an entire sentence which does much more than simply explain what retouching is.

6.6   Content editing after translation

Unfortunately, when translations of scientific and technical texts are published, the task of content editing may be omitted. The source text may be sent for translation before content editing, and then no one thinks to have the translation edited for content. Alternatively, if the source text *has* been content edited before translation, it may be assumed that there is then no *need* to content edit the translation: it will automatically be correct. This assumption is wrong since translators often do not have the relevant scientific/technical education and are prone to inadvertently introducing factual or conceptual errors.

Where scientific editors do not know the source language, they should work with the translator so that when they have queries about some point in the translation, the translator will be able to tell them whether the query pertains to some feature of the source text or to the translator's interpretation. (Editors, like most people, tend to be somewhat naive about translation; they think they are reading some sort of direct transcript of the source text, not realizing how much transformation is involved.)

Practice

1.   **Discussion:** Leaving aside the correction of unintended factual errors, do translators (as opposed to editors) have any obligations regarding truthfulness? Is it alright to pass on an untruth (intentional or not) without comment? Is it alright to omit a truth while translating, on the ground that it may give offence?

2.   **Scenario:** In the course of revising a translation, you discover that the author of an application for research funding has made a serious mistake in reporting the results of a previous study. Do you help the funding body by pointing out the mistake, or do you help the researcher by correcting the error or asking the researcher whether a change is needed? Or do you leave the error and not mention it to anyone? Assume that the translation has been commissioned by the funding body.

3.   **Exercise:** Your instructor will give you a text containing factual, logical and possibly mathematical errors. Find them and correct them, doing any necessary research in the case of factual errors.

7.   Checking for Consistency

The American essayist Ralph Waldo Emerson wrote in 1841 that "a foolish consistency is the hobgoblin of little minds". In 1923, US newspaper editor William Allen White delivered a similar opinion: "Consistency is a paste jewel that only cheap men cherish". Now, Emerson was talking about consistency of opinion: if you change your mind, say so; there is no virtue in keeping to the same view. However the sentiment he expresses is to some degree applicable to an insistence on consistency when editing and revising. We need to ask whether consistency is always necessary, and how much effort should be put into it. Creating consistency is a purely mechanical task that requires little thought, yet gives a feeling of accomplishment. As a result, some editors and revisers are tempted to devote considerable time to it.

Achieving total consistency in translation work would mean: (i) never translating a given source-text expression in one way in one passage and in another way in another passage (assuming the concept is the same in both passages), and (ii) always translating differing terms or phrasings in the source text in different ways (even if they are being used as synonyms or paraphrases by the source-text author). Spelled out in this way, the notion that consistency per se is a good thing seems extremely dubious. Probably no one would seriously advocate it in this extreme form; for one thing, that would prevent authentic translation from a language which often repeats noun phrases over the course of a paragraph ('the instruction manual... the instruction manual...the instruction manual') to one that does not ('the instruction manual...the manual...it'). But that leaves a reviser who is seeking some principle regarding consistency with the question: what departures from the extreme form will I allow?

This chapter will focus on consistency in the sense just described. There will be only passing mention of consistency in matters such as page layout or the treatment of numerals. Achieving this type of consistency is the chief purpose of the house style sheets and style manuals already discussed in Chapter 3, and once again, editors can waste a great deal of time if they try to achieve complete consistency, especially with long texts. Just how much does it matter if a text has "eight" on page 5 but "8" on page 39? Who will notice? Even if someone does notice, will communication be impeded? And might it not have been more worthwhile to devote the available editing/revising time to something else?

7.1   Degrees of consistency

You should not try to achieve 'consistency in general'. Instead, ask yourself the following pair of questions:

- What features of the text need to be consistent: terminology? page layout? manner of addressing the reader?
- Over what range of texts is consistency required: consistency within this

text only? consistency with previous texts you have done for a given client? consistency with colleagues also working for that client? consistency among texts for all clients from the same organization? consistency with other documents that can be found on the client's intranet?

Obviously the more text features you choose, and the greater the range of texts you choose, the more checking you will have to do. With long texts, achieving even text-internal consistency for terminology and layout can be *very* time-consuming, even with computer aids.

One important factor for revisers and editors to consider is whether someone else will be reviewing the text after them. If a proofreader or copyeditor will be going over the text, then it would be a duplication of effort to seek a high degree of consistency in the matters covered by style sheets.

A consistency problem unique to translation is recurring wordings in different source texts. If you work for a corporation or government ministry, documents such as successive annual reports or descriptions of similar jobs will contain passages of identical or almost identical wording. When you come to revise such a document, the question will arise: does this passage occur in a previous source-language document and if so, how was it translated last time? If a previous source-translation pair is available in an easily searchable database, the problem is solved. If not, do not unthinkingly initiate an exhaustive search in order to check whether the draft wording is consistent with previous translations. Instead, ask yourself how much effort it is worth devoting to this task. It may be very important to use the same wording this time, or it may be quite unimportant. For example, if the document is a contract, and the translation will have legal force, then it may be very important. But in others cases, it may not matter.

The same applies to consistency of the translation with existing documents originally written in the target language. Sometimes the source text contains passages that are themselves translations of original target-language material. Such passages may or may not be identified in the source text as translations (i.e. there may or may not be quotation marks or references). The translator whose work you are revising may have backtranslated this material rather than searching for the original target-language wording. You must now decide whether it's worth spending the time to locate this original wording. The mere fact that you *can* search documentary databases for this purpose is not a reason to do so. (For more on the drawbacks of such searches, see Chapter 8.)

One final point: consistency should never take priority over accuracy. If you see that the previous translation of a passage contains an error, do not reproduce the error for the sake of consistency, even if the client has given you the earlier translation as a reference.

7.2 Pre-arranging consistency

The ideal approach to consistency, for both editors and revisers, is to arrange for texts to be consistent ahead of time, before the writing or translating begins.

Regarding layout and typography, a certain amount of editing/revising effort can be avoided if the writer or translator is given either an electronic template or specific settings for use with the Styles option of their word processors. In the case of translation, if a client wants the layout to be consistent with that of the source text, the translator can simply be instructed to enter the translation on top of the source text, using the word processor's Typeover feature. Of course this will only work if the source wording is available as editable e-text (not for example, an uneditable .pdf document, or a .jpeg image with captions).

Regarding terminology, consistency is a problem when several writers or translators are working on a single document. Some decisions can be made before the project starts; in other cases, one member of the writing/translating team can carry out research while the others start writing, and that person can then enunciate terminology decisions as the work proceeds.

When a text is divided in this way, questions of style arise as well. For example, how will the reader of the text be addressed: in the second person (press the green button)? the third person (the user will press the green button)? the passive (the green button must be pressed)? the impersonal active (it is necessary to press/one must press the green button)? or the first person plural (we then press/let's now press the green button)? One option will give the text a certain tone, another option quite a different tone. It is important to decide this sort of thing ahead of time; achieving consistency at the editing or revision stage will be very time-consuming.

Translation software suites typically contain a terminology-management component that can help ensure consistency in the translation of terminology at the start of a project. It can also check, at the revision stage, that each target-language term is one of the members of a pre-approved list of allowable equivalents for the source-language term in question.

7.3   Translation databases and consistency

With the advent of databases of previously completed translations, whether stand-alone concordancers or databases available within Translation Memory (see Chapter 14.5 for the main discussion of Memory), consistency looms larger as an issue than it used to. Achieving consistency is now more practical, but there are problems with using databases for this purpose.

Since a database typically contains material by several translators, unless they were themselves consistent with each other, or someone weeded out inconsistencies before the translations were loaded into the database, then you will find a variety of translations for a given source-language expression. Perhaps one translator used 'lifestyle' and another 'life-style'; perhaps one selected term X and another term Y in the target language for a given term in the source language. Under such circumstances, how will you use the information in the database to achieve consistency? All you can do is select the most popular target-language expression, if there are many instances of it in the database. But why is this expression the most popular one? Is it because several translators independently researched the matter and came up with that expression? Or is it because one translator originally chose that expression, and then one or two others copied it from the database, and then everyone else saw that it was a popular translation?

A further problem will manifest itself if you use the database to check correspondence between the translation wordings and the wordings in original target-language writing. Suppose you have a database that allows you to view both Spanish-English and English-Spanish translations for a single client or set of clients who commission work in both directions. Consider a Spanish expression S in the source text you are now working on, and its English translations E1, E2, E3 in the Spanish-to-English material contained in the database. Then look at that same Spanish expression S in the translations *from* English (in the English-to-Spanish material in the database). Did the writers of the English source texts use any of the expressions E1, E2, E3? When I have carried out this exercise, I have not infrequently found that the answer is no. Furthermore when I did a separate search for E1, E2, E3 in English source texts, I have often found that none of them were translated by Spanish S. (In other cases, I have found that E1 was used in original English, but not E2 or E3. This suggests that if I had selected E2, perhaps on the grounds that it was the most common rendering of S in the Spanish-to-English translations, then I would have made a poor choice.) The upshot of this is that relying on previous translations in a database to achieve consistency can result in consistently using expressions that are not in fact used in original writing in the target language.

7.4 Over-consistency

Usually when people think of the problem of consistency, they are thinking of its lack – too *little* consistency. But it is also possible to be *overly* consistent. In recent years, studies that compare a large corpus of translations with a corpus of texts in the same field that were originally written in the target language have suggested a number of interesting ways in which translations differ from original writing. For example, it appears that translators spell out connections between ideas that original writers leave implicit. They also tend to avoid specific words and prefer more general ones ('take' rather than 'grab'), even when the source text has a specific word. It would be interesting to find out whether translations are also more internally consistent (have fewer synonyms) than original writing. They certainly will be if extreme consistency is enforced by the reviser.

It's false that the use of synonyms by its nature creates confusion. Were you confused when I referred, at the beginning of this chapter, to the *American* essayist Emerson and then to the *U.S.* editor White? Did you find yourself wondering whether I was somehow referring to two different national origins? Probably you did not notice my use of synonyms at all. Such use of different words or phrasings to convey a single concept is a natural feature of human language production, and if you really want to write authentically in the target language, then you should not strive to eliminate it. On the other hand, if most of the readership will be people who are not well educated, or just learning the language, it might be best to remove synonyms.

Often when you are revising, you may find yourself wondering about phraseology. The translation in front of you has *evaluate the language capacity of employees*, and you think: should it be *assess the language skills of employees* or perhaps *evaluate the linguistic capabilities of employees*? Certainly it is possible that your client has a preference or even a set usage, but then again, it's possible that the client's original TL documentation sometimes uses *assess* and sometimes *evaluate*, with no intended difference in meaning; and likewise for *capacity/skills/capabilities* and for *language/linguistic*. I suspect this situation is extremely common, perhaps the norm, given the natural human proclivity to use whatever word comes to mind first.

Now, what about terminology? Should we not always strive for consistent cross-textual use of the 'correct term'? The fact of the matter is that if you read several documents originally written in the target language on the topic of your text, you will discover that different authors use different terms for the same concept, and that a single author will use synonyms within a single text. *This is even true, contrary to widespread belief, in technical and scientific writing.* Editors of scientific journals may remove certain inconsistencies but often they will ignore synonyms because they know that all the intended readers will recognize the different expressions as synonymous. Of course, you need to know what the recognized synonyms are, as well as the extent of the synonymy (in some contexts, terms x and y may be interchangeable, in others not).

If synonymy and paraphrase were not available to language users, people would often find themselves tongue-tied (i.e. if the single existing term for a concept failed to come to mind). Experts often make up their own terms or use a paraphrase if the 'correct' term does not come to mind. And when they are asked about a proposed translation containing a term invented by the translator, or a paraphrase that explains the concept, they will often say 'well I know what you mean', and that is the end of their interest in the matter, especially if the translation is being prepared for information only. Editors of specialist journals will naturally have a somewhat different attitude, combining linguistic and subject-matter concerns. As 'language people', editors and translators certainly need to keep an eye out for possible failures of communication; however it is simply false that successful communication requires the elimination of synonyms, explanatory paraphrases or terminological inventions.

One major hazard to keep in mind concerning terminological consistency is that the term which you have found in previous translations may be the wrong one. This danger is amplified when databases of previously completed translations are easy to consult. Perhaps one translator did poor research and made a mistake, then others copied that mistake, and now you consult the archive and see that most previous translations used that term. You then proceed to make your own contribution to this chain of errors, and you end up being consistent in the worst possible way...consistently wrong!

Synonyms may be very helpful to non-expert readers; those who did not fully understand a concept when it was first introduced in the text may understand it if another expression with the same meaning is used later on. Revisers who devote effort to eliminating synonyms in the name of consistency may then be doing the reader a disservice. On the other hand, it is true that non-expert readers may well find synonyms confusing. If a computer manual sometimes refers to the Trash and sometimes to the Wastebasket, non-expert readers may wrongly think two different things are involved. Or, conversely, they may wrongly take the instruction to 'enter' information to mean the same thing as the instruction to 'input' information, when different meanings were intended (perhaps 'enter' was intended to mean 'press the Enter button in order to incorporate the information you have just input'). A reviser might decide to eliminate such synonyms in texts for non-expert readerships, even though this means reducing the authenticity of the text (it will then not have the synonyms typical of original writing).

One point frequently mentioned in discussions of consistency is level of language. We are often warned to make sure that a text has a consistent degree of formality or technicality. Once again, it is possible to be overly consistent. For one thing, some types of writing typically do mix levels of vocabulary. In some English medical writing, for example doctor's notes, it is not uncommon to find medical terms of Greco-Latin origin mixed with lay language. So if you are revising the English translation of a medical text written in a Romance language, and authenticity is desirable, it may be important not to reproduce all the Greco-Latin terminology of the Romance text (perhaps write 'muscle pain' rather than 'myalgia').

It may even happen that a single concept is expressed at different levels of language within a single text. For example, a doctor's letter (consulted to help revise a translation into English) referred at one point to 'pneumectomy' and then later to 'resection of the lung' and later still to 'removal of a portion of the lung' – all of which have the same meaning. Perhaps the author was aware that he was addressing a mixed audience of doctors and insurance agents. In addition, doctors are often somewhat conflicted when addressing lay people: on the one hand, they want to seem scientific and authoritative (hence 'pneumectomy'); on the other hand, they want to be understood (hence 'removal').

More generally, editors need to recognize that over the course of the 20th century there was a shift in what was considered acceptable regarding mixing of levels. This was in line with a general cultural trend (mixing of 'high' and 'popular' culture). For example, if I had written this book in 1950, the editor would rightly have considered it to have both unacceptable informality and unacceptable mixing of the formal and the informal (for example, I have mixed the various forms of address discussed in section 7.2). Such mixing still causes some older people discomfort, but if they are editors, they must realize that eliminating the informality would constitute a markedly conservative editorial approach. Of course, as time passes, if the trend continues, then eventually a generation will appear that no longer experiences the combination of 'you should' and 'one should' as an inconsistent mixing of levels.

To sum up: consistency should not be treated as an end in itself. Inconsistency is only a problem if it creates a communication barrier. It is mainly a concern when a single text is divided among several translators, or when several texts of similar genre and topic for the same client are distributed among several translators.

Practice

1.   Discussion: Do you think you spend too much time on consistency? too little? just the right amount? If you are not sure, do you think it's important to look into this matter further?

2.   Exercise: Examine two or three completed translations which you have revised. Or examine a revised translation in a group. See if you can find any inconsistencies. Did you find any serious ones? Did you find many small ones? Decide whether, in view of the brief, it would have been better if you had focused on particular kinds of inconsistency (e.g. in terminology, in level of language).

3.   Scenario: You discover that your draft translation contains the expression 'an active lifestyle' in one passage and 'changing life styles' in another. Suppose the thought crossed your mind: "Is it lifestyle, life style or life-style"? Would you simply pick one spelling arbitrarily to create consistency or would you do research? If research, under what circumstances? What would your approach be: pick some dictionary as an authority? look at usage on the Internet? some other approach?

Further reading

(See the References list near the end of the book for details on this publication.)

Merkel (1998).

8.   Computer Aids to Checking

This chapter looks at the following questions: How can Internet search engines, multilingual sites and databases of previously done translations help me edit and revise? Shall I revise/edit on screen or on paper? How can word processors help with editing and revision?

8.1   Google to the rescue?

New technologies both solve and create problems. The advent of Internet search engines in the 1990s certainly brought us new ways of solving translation and revision problems, but it has also given rise to new issues for editors and revisers. In what follows, I refer exclusively to Google, the most popular search engine used by translators.

Throughout this chapter, 'wording', 'word combination' and 'expression' are to be taken as synonyms; they refer to any sequence of words, including the special terminology and phraseology of a field.

Authenticity of language

Imagine a situation in the pre-Google era, say around 1990, where a trainee translator has written a sentence containing the word combination 'at the service of'. The reviser has made a change, substituting 'in the service of', and when challenged on this, replies in an authoritative tone: "You can't say that in English". It being highly unlikely that the translator can supply a large number of instances of 'at the service of' from original English texts, the situation was simply one of conflicting intuitions, and the reviser would prevail if he or she was the one responsible for the linguistic quality of the translation.

Nowadays the situation is quite different. If a word combination is idiomatic, it will be easy for the translator to enter the expression in Google and supply a large number of instances within seconds. It may be that all or most of these are in texts not written by native speakers, or in texts which are themselves translations and thus suspect. But there may also be a great many instances of the expression in what are clearly original texts by native speakers. In that case, if the reviser still wants to make a change, it will no longer suffice to pronounce the expression in question 'wrong'. After all, an idiomatic expression is by definition a combination of words frequently used by native speakers, and the possible combinations in a language are not fixed forever; new ones arise regularly. So to justify a change, the Google-era reviser will need an argument: the samples you have found in Google are from a different genre; they are on a different topic; they have marks of orality whereas the translation is a piece of formal writing; there are no instances on Australian sites, and the text is for an Australian audience. With regard to this last point, it is often useful to restrict the scope of Google's search: if you want to see examples of (mostly) Australian English, add 'site:.au' at the end of your search string; if you want to see samples of the client's usage, add 'site:*myclient.com*'.

If you are working in a language pair that has many 'false friends' (e.g. Dutch/English or French/English), you may find yourself wondering whether a certain expression in the translation is really idiomatic. If your intuition does not supply an immediate answer, Google may help. Suppose that in working from French to English the translator has referred to the 'progressive introduction' of a procedure, but you think English 'progressive' may be a false friend of French 'progressif'. Google gives you 57,000 hits for 'progressive introduction' but 297,000 for 'gradual introduction'. Does this result justify revising 'progressive' to 'gradual'? The answer is no: 57,000 is a large number, and there is no reason why idiomatic English should not use both 'progressive' and 'gradual'. The fact that one synonym is less common is not a reason to reject it. Google tells us that 'wrong answer' occurs about seven times more frequently than 'incorrect answer', but that is not a reason to replace the latter with the former. However if the hitlist for 'progressive introduction' had been considerably shorter, and several of the hits near the top of the list had been from sites in non-English-speaking countries, that might justify revision to 'gradual'. (Bear in mind that asking for 'pages in English' does not limit the search to any particular countries, and of course it cannot distinguish native from non-native writers.)

When using Google, the engine's peculiar features must be kept in mind. Suppose you want to know whether 'the application he presented' is alright. Does one *present* an application? On the day I searched, there were indeed a vast number of hits for this expression, but almost all contained '...the application. He presented...'. Google does not 'notice' punctuation and capitalization.

A further difficulty is that while Google can tell you whether an expression exists, it cannot tell you how readers will understand it, that is, which meaning of the expression's constituent words they will select. For example, in some contexts, 'the application he presented' might be taken to mean the application which he 'showed' rather than 'submitted'.

A final word on word combinations: while care must be exercised when using Google, the ability it affords to check authenticity of language can be a great benefit to anyone self-revising a translation into their second language.

When it comes to syntactic structures, the situation is somewhat different than with idiomatic expressions. It's hard to check the occurrence of many structures, because you have to select a particular wording. Consider this sentence: 'It's not because you are in politics that you forsake the right to protect your reputation'. You can certainly ask Google for the sequence 'it's not because you are' and you will get 103 million hits, but a quick look at the first dozen hits reveals that none of them contain the above structure ('it's not because x that y'). If you ask for 'it's not because you are in politics that', you will get 0 hits, but that does not prove that the structure itself does not occur, only that it does not occur with the particular wording '...you are in politics...'. There do exist special databases of English texts that have been grammatically parsed, so that you can ask directly for all the sentences in the database that have a certain structure, but learning how to ask the corpus questions will take considerable effort (for more information, enter 'International Corpus of English' in your search engine). So if you are uncertain about a sentence structure, either rely on intuition (if you are a native or near-native speaker), or simply change the sentence structure to one you are sure exists.

Also to be borne in mind, if you do succeed in finding many instances of a sentence structure using Google, is that the mere occurrence of a structure does not by itself create 'correctness' in the sense of Chapter 3.6. The structure 'accept to + infinitive' ('he accepted to translate my text') can be found, but it should nevertheless be changed to 'he agreed to …'. Certainly frequency is a factor to consider: at a certain point, a structure becomes so common in published work that it will be deemed standard by all but linguistic conservatives. However 'he accepted to …' has not yet reached that stage.

Terminology and phraseology checking

Checking terminology and phraseology is rather different from checking idiomaticity. If the translator has used a term or phrasing which Google cannot find, that does not make it wrong. It may be a client-specific term. Also, bear in mind that engines do not search the Web directly; they search a database of selected pages. The Google database contains only a portion of all Web pages, though the actual percentage is no longer publicly available information. So the term you are checking may well exist but not be available through a Google search. On the other hand, if you find, again and again, that Google cannot locate the translator's choice of term or phrase, or worse, that it is found mainly on sites in countries where the target language is not the most common native language, then there is probably something wrong. Thus a Google query revealed that the word 'halieutic' does occur, but almost all the hits are bilingual dictionary sites rather than texts, or else they are English texts on sites in French-speaking countries, and the texts at these sites were thus probably written in English by French speakers or by careless translators (the French adjective 'halieutique' means 'having to do with fishing').

Sometimes you may suspect that the term the translator has chosen is not the most *frequent* one. Is a certain portion of the backbone called the 'dorso-lumbar spine', as the translator has written, or is it 'thoraco-lumbar spine', the term you found in a termbank? You can try a 'Google vote' to compare frequencies of occurrence, but care must be taken in interpreting the results. Consider three cases:

- You get approximately equal numbers of hits for both terms. Leaving aside the possibility that one of the terms mainly appears at non-native-writer sites, this result suggests leaving the translator's term unchanged, all other things being equal. (An example of other things not being equal: have you considered the possibility that the two expressions are not really synonyms? Since you are not a medical specialist, you cannot be sure. It may be that only one of the two items conveys the correct meaning.)
- There is a striking difference in frequency, say 300 hits for the translator's term and 12,000 for the term you found in a termbank. This certainly seems to suggest making a change, but there is another possibility: the

translator's term is not used much in most parts of the English-speaking world, but locally, it is in common use. If you were to use a 'site:xx' restriction when querying Google, you might get a very different answer about frequency.

- The translator's term has 9,000 hits as opposed to 18,000 hits for the alternative in your termbank. Here the point made earlier in the discussion about 'progressive introduction' applies: 9,000 is plenty to justify use of that variant, all other things being equal. If you were translating yourself rather than revising, you might decide to 'play it safe' by choosing the term with 18,000 hits, but when revising someone else's work, the situation is different (see Chapter 14).

A further consideration with 'Google votes' is that many hits are duplicates. There may be 5,000 hits, but if you go to the fourth page of hits, you may find a warning that 'we have omitted some entries very similar to the 34 already displayed'. In other words, there were really only 34 *different texts* found; one or more of those 34 texts appears at a great many sites. Also bear in mind that even if you place an expression within quotation marks, Google may try to be 'helpful' and find related expressions for you: it may include synonyms in the search, find results that match terms similar to those in your query, search for words with the same root and make spelling "corrections" (which, you may have noticed, result in searches for completely different words). To avoid this, when you arrive at the hits page, select 'Verbatim' (its location on your screen will vary) . This should restrict hits to sites containing the exact wording you entered.

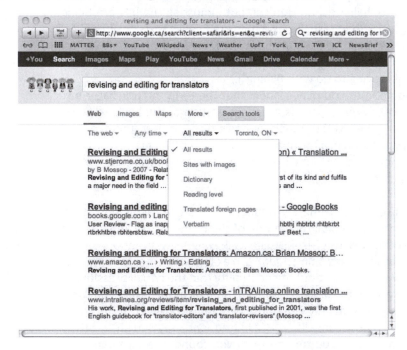

Location of Verbatim for a Google hitlist in the Safari browser, version 5.1.7

A general consideration regarding term research is that you are a reviser, not a terminologist. You do not have the time to do all the research a terminologist would do before establishing a terminological equivalency as correct. Indeed, you cannot spend as much time on research as you do when you yourself are the translator, for revisers are expected to move through the text far more rapidly than the original translator. This need to move along quickly does unfortunately create a problem because overly rapid Google research can easily lead to error. For example, if you inquire about the term 'shoreline development', the hitlist will suggest to you that it refers to the outcome of human development activities along a shoreline. You might then think that the translator has erred in using the term to mean the degree of irregularity of a lake's shoreline. However more thorough research would have revealed that this is in fact another meaning of the term.

When considering a hitlist, you also need to be sure that the items you have found do indeed correspond to the term you are searching. For example, suppose the translator has referred to a tree that has a 'true collar'. You wonder if such an expression exists. You get a lengthy hitlist, but on closer examination you discover that the hits mostly contain expressions like 'true collar rot', which may turn out to mean 'collar rot that is genuine' rather than 'rot in the true collar'. Another possibility is that the term the translator has used is very common, but in a completely different field from that of the text; perhaps the translator failed to look at the field designation in a term bank entry. So it's important to examine the first page of hits fairly carefully to make sure you are looking at relevant material.

Finally, Google can be used to find on-line bilingual or multilingual glossaries. Enter the words 'forestry' and 'glossary' to get forestry glossaries. Enter a particular forestry term plus 'glossary' or 'definition' to find a forestry glossary that contains your term. To find a bilingual glossary containing your term in both source and target languages, use Google's Advanced Search page. Enter the source-language term, along with 'glossary', then go to the languages menu and select the *target* language. You will thus be looking for all the target-language pages that contain your source-language term. The resulting hitlist will often include bilingual glossaries in your field.

Subject-matter research

Ideally, revisers only check work on subject matters with which they are familiar. Sadly, we do not live in an ideal world, and such a limitation may not be realistic. Internet search engines can then provide a means of rapid familiarization with the concepts of a field, allowing you to make up, to some extent, for the difference between your knowledge and the knowledge the translator has acquired through research while translating. You may find especially useful for this purpose the vast number of photographs and diagrams available by selecting the Images option above the keyword area on the Google search screen. If your text describes the three-toed sloth, you can quickly call up to the screen a photo of the beast.

As with term research, there is a danger in concluding concept research too soon or in reading the material you find too quickly. Suppose the translation you are revising says that the leaves of the butternut tree are composed of 11 to 17 opposite leaflets. You then look up information on the butternut tree and discover that its leaves are in fact not opposite each other; rather they alternate sides as you move along a branch. You decide there must be something wrong, but in fact the problem is your careless reading; the leaves are indeed alternating, but the individual leaf*lets* which *compose* each leaf are opposite each other *within* a leaf. The Internet seems to encourage overly hasty decisions.

The main problem with the Internet when it comes to concept research is that most material is unedited for content. Wikipedia articles can be improved by editing, but this can be done by anyone, and the result is a mixed bag, ranging in quality from excellent to awful. It's generally thought that the quality of any one Wikipedia article improves over time as it gets edited and re-edited by new contributors, but you have no way of knowing whether the article you are currently reading, about the latest advances in particle physics, was written by someone who knows what they are talking about. So if you are revising a natural science text, it might be better to restrict yourself to sites whose URL contains the name of a university or ends in .edu.

Searching within sites

Much information is available only through searches you do within a site. However this can be very time-consuming because the site's own search engine, unlike Google, may not display the hits in a useful order, and may not show a relevant passage from the various items it finds. As a result, you have to visit individual hits to see whether they contain anything useful. Revisers do not have the time to carry out such lengthy searches. Fortunately, many site owners are now employing Google technology for site-internal searching.

Multilingual sites

There are many sites on the Web where pressing a button on a page will give you a version in one or more other languages. There are lists of such sites by topic at www.multilingual.ch. Government Web sites in officially multilingual countries as well as the sites of multilingual organizations like the European Union or the United Nations typically have such a button on each Web page. Google can be used to retrieve from these sites material that may help you revise. For example, if you are checking the English translation of a French agriculture text, you can enter an expression from the source text in Google, then enter 'site:agr.gc.ca' and if that phrase occurs in any French text posted on the site of Canada's agriculture ministry, the relevant item will appear on the hitlist. Once you arrive at the site where the item is located, it is simply a matter of clicking a button, and the English version of the text will (usually) appear. Once you find the relevant phrase, you can compare it to the one in the translation you are checking. And of course other information or links on the English page may be helpful.

Online dictionaries

If you are looking for information on the meaning of a word, Google will take you to all sorts of online dictionaries if you enter "*word* define". Many of these dictionaries accept contributions from anyone. These contributions may prove useful for recent innovations in the source or target language, but in general it's best to rely on trained lexicographers, which means visiting, and perhaps subscribing to, the online site of a traditional dictionary-maker such as Oxford, Collins or Merriam-Webster in the case of English.

8.2   Bilingual databases

You may find it helpful while revising to consult databases that contain old (that is, previously completed) translations and their source texts, with each phrase of the latter aligned with the corresponding phrase in the former. For a few language pairs, such bitextual databases can be accessed free of charge. Try for example Linguee at www.linguee.com, or WeBiText at www.webitext.com. In addition, some Translation Memory programs allow direct access to the databases that underlie the memory. You can enter problematic expressions as search strings and then view extracts from texts in the database which contain that expression, alongside the corresponding expressions in the other language.

With the right computer skills, you can create your own database of texts on a given subject, possibly paired with texts in another language, but this is time-consuming, and only worthwhile if you are very frequently editing or revising (and translating) in that field. Unless this is the case, only pre-constituted corpora will be of use to you. So for example if you are revising a translation of a Canadian law text, you can check terminology and phraseology against the aligned French-and-English corpus of court decisions available (for a fee) at www.tsrali.com. The same site provides an aligned concordance of Hansard, the proceedings of Canada's House of Commons, for the past 25 years. Here you will find an edited version of everything Members of Parliament said in French or in English, with a translation into the other language. Such a database of everyday English and French can function like a bilingual dictionary, but with far more contextual information.

When you retrieve documents in this way, and compare them to the text you are currently revising, you always need to consider whether the contexts really match. The subject matter may be the same, but the writer of the present text may be saying something which is somewhat different from what the writer of the retrieved text was saying. The difference may be rather subtle, but it may nevertheless be significant. Perhaps it would be better not to revise the text you are working on by substituting the expression found in the retrieved text. When you find material of interest in a database, often a mouse-click will take you to the full source text or translation, if you need more context.

You can use a bitextual database to check authenticity of language, provided that it tells you which text is the source and which the translation (not all do, though often you can make a good guess). If the translator has rendered SL expression X by TL expression Y, can Y be found in the database in texts on the same topic that were originally written in the translator's target language?

Retrieval of wordings from databases gives rise to the following question for revisers: What shall I do when the translator has invented a new wording, but an old wording is available? Let's first consider the case where the text retrieved from a database is clearly a TL original rather than a translation. One might argue that, whatever the merit of the draft translation you are revising, the wording used in the original English document, presumably written by someone who works in the field of the document, is by its nature more 'authentic'. This argument has considerable merit, though objections can be raised. If a quick check in Google yields only a few examples of the wording in question, it could be a minority usage, or simply careless writing; if Google yields only a single example, it could be an idiosyncrasy of that particular writer.

Now let's look at cases where the old wording is in a translation into English, rather than a piece of original writing in English. (We'll assume for the sake of argument that you are able to decide whether a document you have found is a translation into TL or a TL original.) Two cases can be distinguished: (1) the expression of concern is field-specific and the question is whether the translation you are revising contains an expression that is indeed used by TL subject-matter experts in the required meaning; (2) the expression is not field-specific and it is simply a matter of deciding whether a new wording should be used in the current translation when a different wording has been used in previous translations.

Case (2) can be dispensed with fairly easily. If there are no issues of field-related authenticity, and if the translation being revised captures the meaning of the source text and is well written in the target language, and if the passage is not a quotation from a publication or legal decision, it is hard to see why an old translation should be privileged over the new one. You might wonder why the translator failed to draw on the material in the old documents. However, now that the translator has spent time preparing their own translation, rather than using an existing wording, why would you want to use up even more time replacing those new translations with old ones? If you make many such substitutions in a text, one can argue that you are engaging in pointless, time-wasting activity.

Turning now to case (1), amending draft translations on the basis of old translations brings with it the risk of *perpetuating errors*. *There is no particular reason to think that old translations are necessarily good translations*. In other words, the problem may be with the old translator, not the current one. Possibly the old translator was having a bad day and failed to do necessary research, or relied on faulty memory; possibly no one revised the old translation, or only checked passages other than the one currently of interest.

If you find several old translations of a relevant expression, and they all agree on the TL wording, this may be a good reason to substitute that wording for the one in the draft you are revising. Of course, it is also possible that all the old translations were done by the same person, or by a group of translators who work together and copy each others' 'finds' – including their erroneous finds!

More commonly, the old translations will not agree with each other. Some will have wording x and some will have wording y for a given SL expression. Archives of old translations, and institutional Web sites, are not overseen by super-editors who ensure overall consistency. Possibly some of the old translations are good ones, while others are not. Possibly some were done by neophytes in the field in question, and others by translators with considerable experience, but which is which?

If there are already, in old translations, three different TL wordings for some SL expression, and the translation you are revising has a fourth wording, it might be argued that one of the old wordings should be substituted simply to cut down on proliferating synonyms. But then which of the old wordings should be used? Perhaps they are all valid, but then again, perhaps one of them is not. The reviser will need to do more research to determine which of the old translations is valid. It might be faster to verify that the new translation is valid, and if it is, leave it.

The Linguee bilingual database site showing some results of a search for a German expression

8.3 Work on screen or on paper?

In *The Myth of the Paperless Office*, Abigail Sellen and Richard Harper write: "People tend to turn to the computer when they need flexible tools for a writing task and turn to paper when they need flexible support for a reading task. Very often, they use both together when doing combined reading and writing tasks" (2001:202).

If this is true, as I think it is, then it would follow that revisers and editors will work both on screen and on paper. And in fact this is just what happens. According to Dayton (2011), work on paper is still a common practice, and indeed best for certain jobs. He points out that flipping through pages is still an easier way to navigate through a document than scrolling on screen. Indeed it might be noted that the metaphor of a scroll is very apt in this regard: it was always much harder to consult a passage in a scroll than a passage in a book of pages.

There has, nonetheless, been a decline in paper editing. Dayton's surveys of Society for Technical Communication members asked about their primary editing method and found a decline in exclusive paper editing from 54% in 1999 to 27% in 2008, and a decline in those who do both paper and e-editing from 10% in 1999 to 3% in 2008. Use of Word's Track Changes or Compare (see section 8.4), or the similar features available in Adobe Framemaker, rose from 11% in 1999 to 33% in 2008.

Translators – to judge by self-descriptions given at professional development workshops – are divided on this issue. For self-revision, some work on screen, simply entering corrections as they go; others work on paper and then input any changes when finished. However, when it comes to revising someone else's translation, some on-screen self-revisers switch to paper so that they can provide the translator a document on which it is easy for the revisee to spot the changes.

Another possibility, if you are self-revising, is to work partly on screen and partly on paper: check a printout of the translation, but if you decide to make a change, enter the change directly on screen rather than first handwriting it on paper. One problem with handwritten changes is that there is an opportunity for introducing error when you are inputting these changes later. Your eye may skip over a change, or you may misread small or sloppy handwriting. Such errors can of course also occur if you are revising someone else's work on paper, and then that person (or a member of the office support staff) inputs your handwritten changes.

A survey of Belgian translation agencies found that two-thirds of respondents revised entirely on screen (they read the source and the translation on screen and they input all changes directly on screen), while fewer than 10% worked entirely on paper (see Robert 2008).

What are the factors to consider when deciding whether to revise on screen or on paper?

Speed

On-screen work may be faster because there is no handwriting followed by inputting of changes. However the quality of screen displays is such that reading speed on screen is significantly lower than on the printed page (this has been established through empirical experiments).

Error spotting

There is clear empirical evidence that errors in the text are more likely to be missed on screen, once again because the quality of screen displays is still not equal to the quality of print.

Eye strain

Print is easier on the eyes than the flickering screen image. In the case of translation, moving back and forth between two paper documents (source and translation) may be easier on the eyes than moving back and forth between one paper and one screen document.

Geometry

For comparative re-reading work, side-by-side viewing of source text and translation is impractical unless you have a very wide screen, because you will not be able to full lines of text without horizontal scrolling. Solving this problem by using two screens may clutter your workspace, or be unaffordable. One popular solution is to prop a print version of one text vertically on a paper holder next to the screen containing the text in the other language. However, you will not then be able to line the two texts up. Some people find that they cannot do comparative re-reading unless the texts are lined up side-by-side, and preferably on a horizontal surface in front of them.

A further 'geometry' consideration is that when revising, you will often be using more than just two documents. Aside from the source text and the translation, you may need to consult earlier versions of the source text (and possibly translations of those earlier versions), subject-matter documentation, dictionaries/term banks, databases of old translations, and so on. Theoretically, you could have all these on one screen, in different windows. In practice, however, flipping back and forth among six or seven windows is very likely to prove a nuisance. The option of splitting the screen among several documents will reduce the space devoted to each of them so much that you will be wasting a great deal of time scrolling. If you do need to consult multiple items at once, you will probably find it easier to work with a combination of screen and paper documents arrayed in front of you. Your eye can move back and forth faster than you can switch windows, and it can take in more of each paper document at once than you can display on a small section of screen.

If you are frequently consulting a reference document as you revise, it will often be easier to flip manually through a printout than to scroll through the on-screen version. The exception is when you are looking for a specific word, or a specific numbered section. Then it will be faster to use the Find option with an on-screen document.

Economics and environment

Both pennycounters and environmentalists will of course favour maximizing work on screen. This option will save money on purchases of paper and ink for the printer, and it will also save trees.

8.4   Editing functions of word processors

Most of the functions useful to editors and revisers can be found under the Review tab of the Word 2007 interface. To set preferences for functions, click on the Windows icon at the top left and choose Word Options at the bottom of the menu. In older versions of Word, the functions are scattered among the menus, though most can be seen on a Reviewing Toolbar which you can display when you start editing, and on which you can add or subtract functions.

Spellcheck

The Spellcheck function is valuable because it automatically catches typographical errors which the eye can easily miss (e.g. institututional). However, it is important to remember that Spellcheck software is only an *aid*. It does not automate the process of correcting misspellings and typos. As a matter of fat, there are many types of error which Spellcheck will not catch at all: 'fat' is a correctly spelled English word, and therefore Spellcheck will not signal the error in the fifth word of this sentence. Also, proper names (people, places, rivers and so on) will often not be in your Spellcheck dictionary, especially if they are source-language names. Certainly you can add to the Spellcheck dictionary the names of people and places that come up frequently in your work, but even then, you will need to check every single one of the proper names. For example, the draft may contain the proper name Macdonald, and Spellcheck will pass it by, but it may be that this particular individual spells her name Mcdonald.

You may also need to modify your Spellcheck dictionary to ensure that it signals spellings that fail to conform to the style sheet you are using, or else fail to conform to local spelling standards in your country (the country-specific spelling checkers provided with Word are not always accurate).

Find & Replace

This is probably the single most useful revision/editing function, but you have to be very careful when you enter the Find string. If you are not careful, the computer will make a search that is either too broad or too narrow. You will then have a revised/edited version in which either too many or too few words have been changed. Because it is so easy to make a mistake while specifying the Find string, it is probably best to avoid using the Replace All option (i.e. the computer automatically replaces all instances of the Find string with the Replace string you have specified). It is usually safer to examine each instance of the Find string, and decide whether you want to replace it.

Let's look at some examples of how problems can arise if you use Replace All:

- A word belongs to more than one part of speech, or has homonyms. If you are changing 'firm' to 'company', you don't want to change 'a firm commitment' to 'a company commitment'; if changing 'bank' to 'shore', you don't want to change 'data bank' to 'data shore'; if changing the plural noun 'acts' to 'facts', you don't want to change 'he acts funny' to 'he facts funny'. Sometimes you can get around this problem by entering long Find and Replace strings: replace 'bank of the lake' by 'shore of the lake'. The problem is that if the original text has 'on the south bank there are trees', this will then not be changed to 'on the south shore there are trees'.
- The Find string occurs as part of other words. If you change 'act' to 'fact', you will end up changing 'fracture' to 'frfacture' and 'action' to 'faction'. You need to specify the Find string as [space]act[space]. Of course, you will then have to do separate runs to change 'act' to 'fact' before a punctuation mark such as a comma or period; in the case of commas, the Find string will be '[space]act,'.
- One form of the Find word is not included in other forms of that word. For example, since the plural of 'activity' is not 'activitys', if you want to change 'activity' to 'action', you will need to do a separate run to change 'activities' to 'actions'. The same applies to many verbs: you can change 'think/thinks/thinking' to 'know/knows/knowing' in one run, but that won't change 'thought' to 'knew'.
- In translating the source-language phrase X, the translator has used the target-language word Y, but you decide that Z should be used instead. So you replace all Y by Z. Disaster! You failed to notice that not every instance of Y was being used to translate X. The translator had also used Y when rendering other source-language phrases.

Be sure to determine how your word processor handles capitals during Find & Replace. In most cases, you will want the Replace word to have the same capitalization as the Find word (e.g. capital letter at the start of a sentence; all caps in titles, etc). Experiment to make sure this happens. If on the other hand you want to change from upper to lower case or vice versa, then you will need to specify the appropriate case for the Find string, the Replace string or both. Again, experiment to make sure that you do not end up lower-casing the first word of a sentence.

Finally, Find & Replace provides a handy way of removing any instances of double spaces between words that may have crept into the text when the translator/writer Cut & Pasted or during your own revising/editing operations. Simply specify double space as the Find string and single space as the Replace string. (This assumes you also want to eliminate any double spaces between sentences.)

Grammar and style checking

The grammar checking utilities contained in word processors are by and large not very useful for finding errors in English syntax. For example, all too often they signal perfectly correct subject-verb number agreement as an error. And all too often they fail by omission, passing over a real error in number agreement. Grammar checkers are also quite useless at detecting mistakes that arise from accidental deletion of words. As a test, I randomly deleted words from this present paragraph:

> The grammar checking utilities contained word processors are and large not very useful for finding syntax errors. For example, all too often they signal as an error what is fact correct number agreement between subject and verb.

When I passed this through the grammar checker in Word 2007, it found no problems whatsoever!

Grammar checkers generally double as style checkers. Unfortunately, the concept of readable style they embody is an oversimplified one. They tend to stop at every instance of the passive or every sentence with more than a certain number of words – useful if you are editing work in a genre that calls for short sentences and no passives (for example, instructions), but otherwise a nuisance. Most genuine style problems will not be highlighted.

In Word 2007, you can turn off features you do not want signalled. Among the grammar features you can choose are capitalization, misused words, punctuation and subject-verb agreement; among the style features are cliches, wordiness, use of first person, sentence structure and 'sentence begins with And, But, Hopefully'! In older versions of Word, you can select one of four writing styles (casual, standard, formal, technical) or make up your own custom style. Each style corresponds to a selection of problems that will be signalled if present in the text.

Another possibility is to set the checker to provide what are called "readability statistics" once the spelling, grammar and style checks are complete. According to these statistics, the chapter you are now reading has an average of 3.3 sentences per paragraph, 23 words per sentence and 4.7 characters per word, and 13% of the sentences are passives. These figures are only useful if the texts you are editing are for children or for immigrants learning the language, or they need to be understood by people who may not have completed secondary school. For other readers, long words and passives are not difficult, and it is sentence structure rather than sentence length that will pose a readability problem. The statistics also provide something called the Flesch Reading Ease score (54.9 for this chapter) and the Flesch-Kincaid Grade Level (10.8). The latter means that the text will be hard to read for anyone who has not completed the eleventh grade in the U.S. school system (usually reached around age 16). The Reading Ease score of 55 supposedly means that the text will be somewhat difficult to read (the idea is to aim for a score between 60 and 70). However the formula for calculating the score is based on sentence length and word length (in terms of syllables), which are not helpful indicators for the readership of most texts which editors work on. A problem with this whole approach to readability is that you could score very high by editing a text into a monotonous succession of short sentences containing one- and two-syllable words, but such writing is unlikely to hold your readers' attention if they are much over ten years old. Also, note that an acronym like FRE (Flesch Reading Ease) is very short, and therefore highly desirable in Flesch terms, but a text full of acronyms will certainly be difficult to read!

One stand-alone style checker, called StyleWriter, is especially designed to deal with verbose bureaucratic prose. According to the maker's Web site (enter 'stylewriter' in Google for more information), this software will signal the italicized portions in the following passage and recommend changes which, if selected, lead to the corrected version underneath:

> *With reference to* the matter you raised *concerning* your tax free income, you must *make full declaration* of all sources of income within *the period of* the last tax year. This *situation* should be *reviewed on a regular basis* and information *forwarded* four times *per* year. I assume you *will be dealing* with this matter *in due course*, but should *any further action be required, please do not hesitate* to contact me.

> On the matter you raised about tax-free income, you must fully declare all sources of income within the last tax year. You should review this regularly and send this information four times a year. I assume you will deal with this matter soon, but if you need more advice, please contact me.

Displaying changes

As an editor (and sometimes as a reviser), you need to be able to show the author (or translator) the changes you are proposing. In Word 2007, turn on Track Changes under the Review tab. You can choose what the deletions and additions will look like in Change Tracking Options (in the Track Changes menu), and you can choose where on the page the changes will be displayed (in the Balloons menu). If you don't want any changes to be visible as you work, choose Final; if you want only certain changes to be visible, choose them in Show Markup. The author or translator can then turn these options on, or choose Final Showing Markup to see your changes. He or she can then Accept or Reject each change using the appropriate button.

One disadvantage of Track Changes is that, despite the colour used to highlight changes, the contrast between the original and the revised/edited text is never visually as striking as it is on paper. This is because the changes appear in the same typeface and on the same line as the original wording, whereas on paper, your handwriting appears above or below the original printed wording. Another problem is that if you are training someone, and you want to distinguish necessary changes from improvements, you will need to keep changing the highlighting colour – a very awkward procedure. It's much easier to put down your red pen and pick up a black one. On the other hand, if you are revising translations by someone who works in a location remote from you (e.g. a teleworker), and your procedure calls for returning the revised translation to the translator, you will probably not want to send handwritten changes by fax; colour will usually be lost, and your phone bill will rise. Instead, you will have to e-mail a version in which you have incorporated your revisions using Track Changes.

Inserting comments

You can write a comment to the translator using the Comment feature under the Review tab. You could decide to make suggestions using the Comment feature, reserving Track Changes for necessary corrections and improvements. The comment will be displayed in a bubble when the cursor moves over the word where the comment was inserted. You can also display comments at the side of the page, by choosing Comments in Show Markup.

Many editors and revisers find the Track Changes and Comment method of annotating texts highly unsatisfactory, and for that reason prefer to use paper. It is possible that e-editing will not replace paper editing until it becomes possible and affordable to handwrite changes and comments with a light pen on a large graphics tablet.

Before a text is delivered to the client, it's important that someone check to see that all tracked changes have been removed (unless the client wants to see edits), as well as all Comments (unless some of these are intended for the client). Simply Hiding them will not eliminate them; they will appear when the client opens the text. Each tracked change needs to have been either Accepted or Rejected and each Comment needs to have been deleted. To be double sure that this has been done, in Word 2007, click the Microsoft Office Button, point to Prepare, and then click Inspect Document; checkmark Comments, Revision, Versions and Annotations and click Inspect. If the Inspector finds comments and tracked changes, use Remove All. If you are training a translator, you can save your own private copy of the text with the tracked changes and comments for future reference.

Comparing documents

Word has a function that lets you compare any two files; to use it, choose Compare in the Review tab. This feature can be handy for training others or yourself. You can use it to see the differences between unrevised and revised versions of a text, or the differences between a text that has been partially self-revised (say for accuracy but not style) and a text that has been fully self-revised. To use this feature, you must save the revised and unrevised versions of the text under different filenames. When you choose Compare, you will be asked which two files you want to compare. You will then see a display in which the differences between the two documents are shown in colour (additions in one colour, deletions in another), though sometimes you will find that the display does not accurately reflect the changes.

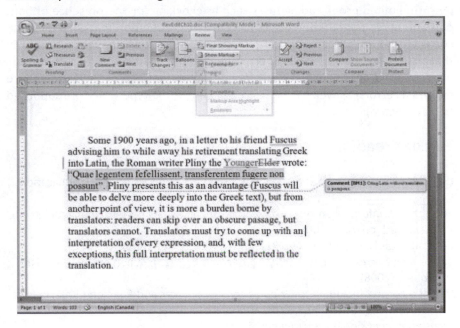

An early version of a passage from Chapter 10 of this book, showing an amended word, an inserted Comment, and the choices available under the Review tab

8.5   Tools specific to revision

Readers may have noticed that none of the computer tools discussed so far are specifically designed to help with revision; they just happen to be useful for that purpose. The central task of the reviser – identifying mistranslations – has not been (and perhaps cannot be) automated. No amount of automated searching in a database of paired SL/TL texts will tell you whether a source/target correspondence in the translation you are checking is acceptable; the fact that a source-language wording was previously translated in a certain way does not mean that the target-language wording was correct in those past cases, and even if it was, it may not be suitable in the case at hand. A machine will be useless at deciding whether a wording is stylistically suited to the genre or audience (e.g expert or non-expert) of the particular translation that is being prepared, or whether a sentence is properly connected to the previous sentence, or whether the right words are in the focus position in a sentence.

That said, automated translation checking tools, usually called Quality Assessment tools, are available either alone or more commonly as part of Translation Memory suites. However they are very limited in their scope. They can spot

failures to translate terms in accordance with a pre-approved list of terminological equivalences, as well as passages that appear not to have been completely
translated (because the translation is much shorter than the source). They also
perform limited proofreading tasks such as checking for the presence of both
parts of paired punctuation marks (parentheses, quotation marks) and for the
correct transcription of numerical expressions. These tools are perhaps useful in
that they may catch the kinds of error which a human eye may miss, but users
often find that there are too many false positives (perfectly good wordings are
flagged as errors) as well as undetected errors (of the type which are supposed
to be detected).

Further reading

(See the References list near the end of the book for details on these publications.)

For detailed information on doing Google searches, visit www.googleguide.com/
    advanced_operators.html
Computer tools: Austermühl (2001); Bowker (2002 and 2008).
Paper versus screen: Dayton (2003, 2004a and b, 2011); Sellen and Harper (2001);
    Robert (2008).
Use of a corpus, including the Web as corpus: Bowker and Pearson (2002: chapter
    11); Olohan (2004: chapter 10).
Translation checking tools: Drugan (2013).

9.   The Work of a Reviser

Revising is that function of professional translators in which they find features of the draft translation that fall short of what is acceptable, as determined by some concept of quality (see Chapter 1.4), and make any needed corrections and improvements. With some texts, the reviser's job is restricted to correcting: fixing omissions, major mistranslations, gross translationese, significant terminology errors, and departures from the rules of the standard language. With other texts, revisers must also make improvements: make the writing quality better (i.e. do stylistic editing; eliminate minor translationese) and make minor adjustments in meaning to better reflect the source text.

In this chapter we'll look at revision as an exercise in reading; revision terminology; the revision function in translation services; the relative roles of self-revision and other-revision; contract revisers; revision and specialization; revising translations into the reviser's second language; quality checking by clients; the role of the brief; the problem of balancing the interests of authors, clients and readers; measuring the quality of revision; the trade-off between time and quality, and the quantity of revision that can be expected of a reviser. We'll also look at how revision differs from certain related activities such as quality assurance and quality assessment.

In Chapters 9 to 12, the term 'revision' will be used to include both self-revision and revision of others, unless the context makes clear that only one of these is intended. Chapter 13 looks more specifically at self-revision, and Chapter 14 at revising others.

9.1   Revision: a reading task

In Chapter 1, I mentioned that there are various concepts of quality: it may be thought of as pleasing the client, creating a fit-for-purpose text, or protecting and promoting the target language. Under this last concept, revision will be seen as primarily a writing task – almost a literary exercise in improving language and style. Under the other two concepts, however, it is best to think of revision as primarily a reading task, that is, an exercise in spotting passages that may not please the client or may make the text unfit-for-purpose. The key skill of a reviser is an ability to read very carefully. It is a mistake to think that errors will simply jump out at you as you cast your eyes over the draft translation. It is in fact extremely easy to overlook gross problems (more on this in Chapter 12).

In order to have the right mental attitude as you revise (i.e. you are reading, not writing), don't have your correcting pen poised or your fingers on the keyboard ready to make a change. Your aim is not to make changes; it's to find problems, which is very different.

Unfortunately the English word 'revise', as used outside the world of translation, is not helpful when it comes to conceiving of revision as a reading exercise. The OED defines it as 'to look or read carefully over (written or printed matter), *with a view to improvement or correction*; to *improve or alter* (text) as a result of examination or re-examination'. Thus in everyday English, revising a text means making changes in it; it's a writing exercise rather than primarily a reading exercise.

9.2   Revision terminology

There is no generally recognized English terminology for revision activities. Terms such as *revise, re-read, check, cross-read, proofread, review* and *quality-control* are each used in a variety of meanings (see Appendix 5). Within a translation service, people will know what is meant by a given term, but when addressing outsiders, it will always be necessary to specify what is meant.

In this book, the terms 'revision', 'quality control', 'checking' and 're-reading' are virtually synonymous. To 'check' a translation is to revise or quality-control or re-read it, unless the context indicates that 'check' or 'quality-control' specifically refers just to the process of finding the errors and does not include making corrections. 'Re-read' is mostly used here in the phrases 'comparative re-reading' and 'unilingual re-reading', where the emphasis is on the distinction between revision that involves a comparison to the source text and revision which does not. Finally, while 'quality control' and 'revision' are synonyms, a distinction is made between 'quality controllers' and 'revisers'. The latter category consists entirely of qualified translators; the former category is broader, including anyone who performs a checking and correcting function. Thus non-translators (such as proofreaders or subject-matter experts) who do only those forms of checking and correcting that do not involve comparing the translation to its source, are quality controllers but they are not revisers. Many people use the term 'reviewer' to refer to a subject-matter expert.

Some translation services distinguish 'revision' from 'quality control', with the latter being used for the business-oriented (as opposed to text-oriented) activities which are discussed later in this chapter under the headings 'quality assessment' and 'quality assurance'. Alternatively, 'revision' may be used to refer to a full re-reading of the translation for accuracy and language quality, with each sentence being compared to the corresponding part of the source text; 'quality control' is then used to refer to less-than-full revision. A designated 'quality controller' may subject the draft translation to a partial check: only portions of the text are read, or there is no comparison to the source text unless a passage of the translation sounds odd, or the check is restricted to copyediting and layout matters. In this book, however, full revision (all aspects of the entire translation are checked, with comparison to the source) is simply the highest degree of quality control; lower degrees of quality control are still referred to as 'revision'. Degrees of revision are the subject of Chapter 11.

'Proofreading' is often used in translation services for any kind of linguistic checking, or in a more restricted way to checking for mechanical slips (typing errors, missing words, errors in page layout). Sometimes it is used specifically for the work done by professional proofreaders who work in a translation office but are not themselves translators. Finally, some people use 'proofreading' for the activity here called 'revision', i.e. checking and correcting translations.

The distinction I have made between 'revising' and 'editing' in this book does not always reflect the terminology used in the professional world. Thus many translators use 'editing' to refer to the process of reading a translation without referring to the source text, whereas I call it 'unilingual re-reading'. Meanwhile, others restrict the term 'editing' to the work done by professional editors after translations are submitted to publishers. Finally, many translators, especially in the United States, use 'editing' to mean the revision of translations.

Outside the world of translation, the term 'revision' is used in ways that may create confusion when revisers interact with non-translators. Writing teachers often use it to mean self-editing. Professional editors use it to refer to changes made in a text by its author. For example, when I wrote this book, I submitted my manuscript to the editor, who returned it to me with suggested changes. The work which I then did in response to those suggestions is commonly called revising. Similarly, the publisher has now decided to bring out what some would call a 'revised edition': a new version of the text in which I have made various changes, additions and subtractions in response to new developments in the field and in my own thinking about revision.

In large bureaucracies, documents go though many revisions (in the sense just described) before reaching their final form. If you translate for a multilingual bureaucracy, you may be asked to 'translate the revisions'; that is, to update an existing translation in order to make it conform to the latest version of a document in the source language.

In literary translation, situations arise when the term 'revision' (in the sense of correction and improvement of a translation) should be used but isn't. A publisher may bring out a 'new translation' of Proust, but it is not really freshly translated from the French; it is a revision of a previously published translation, which is treated as a draft.

The terms used in this book are listed and defined in Appendix 5.

9.3   The revision function in translation services

Sometimes, a few of the senior translators in a translation service or agency are designated as revisers. They occupy official 'reviser' positions and devote all or most of their time to revising the work of other staff translators. Such designated revisers may also have training, administrative and management responsibilities; they may be charged with training new translators, distributing texts to the other translators, and supervising junior translators (writing their annual appraisals, recommending them for leave or promotion and so on).

In other organizations, work is distributed by the manager of the service, a project manager or a member of the administrative staff rather than by a senior translator. Some of the senior translators may be assigned to training juniors or quality-controlling the work of other staff translators. Alternatively, senior translators may simply revise each other 'on request' (each translator decides whether to have a given text revised by a colleague).

Revisers may also check the quality of work done by contractors, and make any needed changes. Indeed, in some organizations today, all or almost all work is contracted, so that members of the translation staff spend their time checking the quality of contracted work and co-ordinating the members of teams of contract translators working on large projects.

In some organizations, the manager of the translation service is a qualified translator (rather than a professional administrator) and may act as a second reviser, taking a more or less detailed look at some or all translations. The manager may make changes and then take these back to the reviser or translator for action, or simply give them directly to a member of the clerical support staff for inputting.

9.4   Reliance on self-revision

A common issue today is the extent to which a translation service will rely on self-revision as opposed to revision by a second translator.

Freelances working directly for clients (not on contract for an agency) obviously need to pay special attention to self-revision since typically no other translator will see the text before delivery to the client. In recent years, however, especially with the advent of e-mail and translation discussion sites on the Web, freelances are developing contacts with each other, which may include revising each other's work.

For staff translators, things have been moving in the opposite direction. Some translating organizations have sought to save money by reducing the amount of time that highly paid senior translators spend revising the work of juniors. One way of doing this is to emphasize self-revision. Translators are given instruction in revision techniques and then asked to be more methodical about checking and correcting their own work. The result is then subjected to some degree of quality control (as described in Chapter 11), or it may simply go out to the client with no further examination.

One of the well known dangers of putting every text through a full revision by a senior translator is that, subconsciously (and sometimes consciously), juniors do not take responsibility for their own work. They think: "I'm not really sure about this passage, but it doesn't matter, because my reviser will be looking at it." There is nothing wrong with a junior marking specific passages as still uncertain despite research efforts; the problem arises when those efforts are not made in the first place.

A further problem arises when juniors do not know which of several revisers will look at their work, but know that each reviser has certain preferences. The result can be a certain despair about ever getting it right.

Replacing a revision system with self-revision plus quality control can make translators more self-reliant; they will then take greater pride in their work, and most will produce better translations and achieve greater job satisfaction. An interesting side effect is that, having gained more control over their work, staff translators become more like freelances.

A further advantage of reducing the amount of revision by a second translator is that there is less likelihood of unnecessary changes with self-revision. That is because there is a tendency, when revising others, to replace a perfectly good translation with the translation which the reviser would have produced. That is obviously not a problem with self-revision, though a parallel problem may arise with self-revisers who are perfectionists.

The disadvantage of relying on self-revision is that fewer errors will be detected: the translator has a certain blindness to the text. He or she may be especially proud of certain passages and not see an error which someone else will spot immediately. This second translator can act as the first 'reader' of the text – a role the original translator is not really in a position to play. Ideally, self-revisers allow time to pass between completion of the draft and self-revision, so that the wording of the translation seems somewhat unfamiliar, but surveys of translators suggest that deadlines often make this impossible; self-revision must begin immediately or at latest the next morning. Still, the translation can even then be made to seem unfamiliar if the font or page layout is changed on screen, or the draft translation is printed out and read on paper rather than on screen, or the draft is read aloud. If you want to focus on linguistic form, you can try reading the text backward, beginning at the last sentence; that way, you won't be distracted by meaning.

The need for other-revision is discussed in Chapter 11.1.

9.5   Contract revisers

Some organizations award contracts for revision, and the contract reviser's work must then be assessed before payment can be made. Sometimes a quantified assessment will be required, and you will need to count the number of errors missed and the number of errors introduced. (The number of unnecessary changes is not relevant to the final quality of the product. However, if you think the presence of many unnecessary changes may be the reason why the job was submitted late, and you had to levy a substantial financial penalty, you might give the contractor examples of unnecessary changes.)

If revision work is contracted out, it is vital that the external revisers have a very precise idea of what the translation agency or service expects. This can be achieved in two ways. First, you can hold a one-day session which contractors must attend. At the session, a text is revised in a group, and a representative of the translation agency or service explains what is expected and what is to be avoided. Alternatively, you can prepare a revision manual which you send to contractors. This contains examples in the appropriate language pair of do's and don'ts. In addition, for each individual job, you will need to specify the aspects of translation which are important and those which are not (for example, do not check field-specific terminology; do check accuracy of figures). Make sure you define all terms (if you use 'proofread', say exactly what you mean by it).

9.6   Revision and specialization

With specialized texts, that is, texts written by and for experts, and often concerned with the latest developments in some area of science or technology, revisers will need to decide whether they are qualified to revise the draft translation. If the translator is known to be, or seems to be, highly experienced in the field, the reviser probably does not need to check field-specific concepts and terms. However if that is not the case, then unless the reviser has some independent knowledge of the field, or considerable experience with specialized texts in that field, then it is best to find another translator who does have such experience or, failing that, discuss the translation with a subject-matter expert. With some assignments, you may be told that a subject-matter editor will check the field-specific content, so that you only need to check other aspects of accuracy. If you have occasion to discuss the text with a subject-matter expert who does not know the source language, be wary. Some of them insist on the interpretation which fits in with their own ideas on the topic; they may reject unorthodox concepts which are in fact present in the source text, or notions with which they are not familiar even though these may be commonplace among experts in the country where the source language is spoken.

   If you are a salaried translator, you may find yourself wishing that the manager had declined to accept the job. By the time it reaches you, it's too late; the job has been accepted and time has been spent preparing the draft. If you do not feel qualified, and you cannot find another reviser, or a subject-matter expert, you must signal to the client that the translation may well contain conceptual errors and needs to be seen by a subject-matter specialist for content and terminology before it is published. If you are a freelance, of course, you can accept or reject a revision contract.

9.7   Revising translations into the reviser's second language

It is often said that revisers should be native speakers of the target language, but this may in fact not be necessary. It depends on which features of the translation are important. If revision is mainly for accuracy and completeness, it does not matter which language is the reviser's native language. Indeed, it may be easier for a native speaker of the source language to spot a mistranslation! However, if writing quality is important, and the translation is to be published, then the reviser should be a native or near-native writer (not just speaker) of the target language.

9.8   Quality-checking by clients

Often clients treat translation as a professional service and therefore rely on the translator (and indirectly, a professional certifying body if any) to ensure quality. However many clients may also subject the translations they receive to some kind of quality check, using their own criteria. In addition, clients may put the completed translation through an editing process. For example, if the client will be publishing the translation of a scientific work, there will usually (but not always) be a scientific editor to check the content and terminology. It is a good idea to determine whether a subject-matter editor will be looking at the text you are revising.

One form of quality checking sometimes used by clients is backtranslation: the client has someone translate your revised translation back into the source language. Backtranslation may have its place in the process of testing question-naires that are to be answered in several languages, but otherwise it is a dubious method, even for checking accuracy, let alone other aspects of translation. For one thing, the backtranslator may well make a mistake, and then any discrepancy between the original source text and the backtranslation will be the backtrans-lator's fault. For another thing, the first translation may have been so literal that the backtranslator will arrive at a wording almost identical to the original source text; the client may then think the translation must be very good, when in fact it is almost unreadable because it is so literal.

If you hear from the client's subject-matter editor before you complete your revision work, and discover a conflict between the wording they want to see and the wording you believe reflects the source text, then you must keep to the wording you believe to be correct, especially if you are certifying a translation under your country's legislation. The Translator's Charter approved at the Du-brovnik Congress of the International Federation of Translators in 1963 makes the following statement that is relevant to these cases:

> The translator shall refuse to give to a text an interpretation of which he/she does not approve.

Since the final translation belongs to the client, they are of course free to change what you have written (unless you are being identified as the translator, or you have signed a certification of the wording you submitted). However you should never yourself make a change to reflect a view (about intended meaning, termin-ology, language usage or any other matter) with which you do not agree after careful consideration of other views. The function of a professional in society is to give his or her informed opinion, not repeat someone else's.

9.9   The brief

The work of both translator and reviser is ideally governed by a brief from the client. The brief is a set of specifications including such matters as who will be reading the translation, whether it is a publication, and preferred terminology. It may include instructions about revision (e.g. a full comparative revision is ex-pected) but even if it does not, you still need to be familiar with the instructions that were given to the translator.

The various parts of the brief may be obtained in three ways:

- They are explicit: the client states them orally or in writing when the request for translation is made.
- They are unstated but already known from previous similar jobs from the same client.
- They are elicited by the translation service, which takes the initiative of inquiring about this or that aspect of the brief.

The brief needs to be known in order to decide on the appropriate translation strategy. Many clients simply 'want a translation'. The idea that there may be several ways of carrying out this task does not occur to them. Or they may think that the nature of the source text implies the brief. As a result, they fail to specify who will be using the translation and why.

Suppose for example that an immigration official wants a translation of a prospective immigrant's medical records. To him, the purpose of the translation is obvious: it will be used by doctors to determine whether the person will be a burden on the country's health care system. However the translator and reviser may or may not find this obvious. It depends on how much information accompanies the text. It may not even be clear who is asking for the translation. If the request for translation comes with a form mentioning that the client is a 'hearings board', or if the form mentions an upcoming hearing date, it can probably be assumed that the translation will be used to make a decision. But questions still remain: Will someone with medical training read the translation and then summarize it for the board? Or will the translation go directly to the board members for their use before or even during the hearing, and if so, does the board include people with medical training?

It is hard to revise successfully or efficiently unless you have familiarized yourself with the brief. For example, as we'll see in Chapter 11, some briefs dictate much more thorough and time-consuming revision work than others. That said, cases will certainly arise where you simply cannot find anyone able to tell you who will be reading the translation and for what purpose. You will then have to make an educated guess, perhaps in consultation with other more experienced revisers.

As a reviser, you may or may not be the one whose job it is to actually determine the brief, in case it is not explicit. When you are distributing work to a trainee, or to a team of translators who are working together on a job, determination of the brief may be up to you. In other cases, it may be up to the translator, the project manager or the manager of the translation service. You may then find that you disagree with the translation strategy that has been adopted, but by the time the text reaches you, it may be too late to do anything about it, since the revision stage is not a good time to change strategy. Turning formal writing into informal writing, or a free translation into a close one, would be a very time consuming and wasteful exercise.

Some clients actually specify a translation strategy in the brief but this is really a matter for the translator to decide. Analogy from dentistry: it's up to the patient to decide whether she wants root canal work on a decaying tooth or a simple extraction, but once that decision is made, she does not tell the dentist how to perform the work. Given the users and use, the client's specified strategy may not be appropriate. For example, it may be better to use a less formal style than the source, rather than preserve the same style; or to summarize extremely verbose writing rather than write a verbose translation. Other specific instructions may also have to be politely ignored, or discussed with the client with a view to altering them. It may be best not to use the terminology requested by the client, if you believe it is liable to confuse the readers. And obeying the client's instruction to exactly follow the paragraphing of the source text may be disorienting if paragraphing habits in the target language differ. The client is not always right.

Consider this scenario. A written request is received for a 'verbatim translation' of a sworn statement related to an immigration matter. But how can a translation be verbatim, that is, 'in the same words'? Perhaps the intent was 'word-for-word'. But this would be in conflict with professional standards: translators render messages, not words. A call to the client is unhelpful; the only person available is a clerical go-between who cannot clarify matters (this is a common situation). The text is to be handled by a new translator or student trainee, so the supervising reviser provides advice on strategy. One solution might be to prepare a translation which is as close as possible to the lexical-grammatical structure of the source text while still being readable. The word 'verbatim' is then being interpreted as reflecting a view of translation very common among the general public – that a translation is a kind of transparent transcript of the source text, perhaps even slightly unidiomatic precisely to point to its status as a translation.

Postscript to the scenario: the originator of the translation request is finally reached. It turns out that 'verbatim' means a complete as opposed to a summary translation. The client has had bad experiences with court interpretation in immigration matters: the interpreter has summarized, and lawyers have argued that this invalidates the proceedings. Of course, in written translation, completeness is the norm; summaries are usually provided only on special request.

9.10 Balancing the interests of authors, clients, readers and translators

The final text a reviser produces may be seen by several people: the translator, the author of the source text, a proofreader, a subject-matter expert, an editor, the client, the employer, the project leader and of course the readers. Depending on their expectations and needs, their reactions may differ considerably. One task of the reviser is to reconcile interests if possible, or if it is not, then decide whose interests to favour.

Suppose you are revising a draft translation that is not close to the source (the translator has engaged in considerable stylistic and structural editing while translating, and perhaps even done some adapting). You realize that the translation will be communicatively successful, but you also know that the source author will see the translation and will probably not be pleased. As long as the source author is not also the paying client, then his or her pleasure is a minor consideration. But if the author is the client, then you have a real conflict. If you cannot persuade the author that a close translation is undesirable, then you may have to either decline to do any more work on the job (and risk non-payment) or revise the translation back to a close one. Ideally, such conflicts are cleared up before translation starts; for example, perhaps the job is not accepted unless the author/client agrees to editing and adaptation.

Here's a scenario where the draft translation seems to be successful from the reader's point of view but not a success from the client's. A request has been received from the head of a company's building maintenance department to translate a new edition of a repair manual. You observe that the translator has not used the new terminology which has just been decreed by a terminology-standardization body. The translator tells you that the technicians who will be the sole readers are not familiar with the new terms, so she has used the old, no longer approved terms with which they are familiar. However, the organization for which both you and the head of the maintenance department work has decided to introduce the new terminology, and the translators' association to which you belong supports the goal of having translators help disseminate new official terminologies. So in order to meet the standards of the client and your professional association, you must use terms which the readers will not understand. What will you do? The solution in this particular case might be to ask the translator to add the new standard terms, with the familiar ones following in brackets. Or prepare a temporary pull-out glossary, to be removed a year later once the new terms have been learned; the glossary would list the familiar terms in alphabetical order, with the new standard terms in a column opposite. That way the needs of all parties can be met.

Translators and revisers have an interest in creating respect for their profession, and this will place a limit on the degree to which they can comply with instructions from clients, even if it means some clients may go elsewhere for future jobs. Thus as a reviser you could not let pass a draft translation that reproduces inadvertent nonsense in the source text simply because the client has asked for a very close translation. It happens not infrequently that people end up unintentionally writing the opposite of what they clearly mean. The revised translation must then convey the clearly intended meaning, though a note might be sent to the client signalling the presence in the source text of such problems.

Apart from inadvertent nonsense, there is the question of how very poorly written source texts are to be handled. What should the reviser do if the translator has tried to reproduce the poor quality of writing in a job application, arguing that he wanted to help the reader by making clear the poor quality of the writing in the source text. But this is not a proper function of translation: if a multilingual organization is hiring, and one criterion for the position to be filled is writing ability in language x, all the members of the panel judging the application must be able to read language x. If any of them are reading a translation of the applicant's writing, they will be forming an opinion about the writing ability of the translator rather than that of the applicant. Also, it is next to impossible to create an equivalent that reflects the degree and nature of the poor writing. Translators who attempt this generally end up merely producing translationese, but a poor target-language writer would not produce translationese.

A distinction must be made between poor writing or careless mistakes in the source text on the one hand and factual or conceptual errors on the other. If the latter are discovered or suspected, neither the translator nor the reviser should simply correct them, with the idea that they are helping to smooth the passage of the source author's "true" message into the target language. If the source author is also the client, then there is no problem; one can simply ask the author about changing the wording of the problematic passage. But if the client is not the source author, then the reviser's duty is to the client, not the author: if the translator has made a "correction", then it must be undone, for the client (and the reader of the translation) has the right to see the factual and conceptual errors that were made; these are part of the message. In official multilingual contexts in particular, people who are reading a document in translation have as much right to see factual and conceptual errors as people who are reading the document in the original language.

You can be sure that situations will arise when you cannot satisfy everyone. You will have to decide whose requirements take priority; you may even have to decide whether your economic interests (as an employee or freelance) will always take precedence over other considerations. Will you always give preference to the interests and wishes of whoever is paying you? Or will you sometimes give preference to the interests of other parties? Or seek a balance where possible, with something for everyone as in the case of the repair manual discussed above?

9.11   The quality of revision

A translation agency or service may want to know how much value it is deriving from the time translators are spending on other-revision. For every hour of revision effort, how many necessary changes are being made? How many errors are being introduced? How many errors are being overlooked? How many inadequate corrections are being made? How many unnecessary changes are being made? Of particular importance is the question: how many of the *serious* errors are being corrected?

To answer these questions, a translation service may find it useful to conduct audits. To conduct a simple audit, collect a sample of revised translations delivered to clients over the past few months and count the number of errors (or better: the number of serious errors) that were not caught in a chunk of convenient size, perhaps 500 words. To find out more, you will need to arrange to have draft translations saved so that they can be compared to revised versions. You can focus either on 'good' revision work or 'bad' work. For the former, count the number of errors per 500 word chunk that were properly corrected during revision (or, if you want to examine entire texts, count the percentage of all errors that were properly corrected). If you feel more ambitious, you can distinguish types of error and assign weightings to the types. For example, you could count all the properly corrected mistranslations in a 500 word chunk and separately count the properly corrected linguistic errors in that chunk, and then calculate a score as $2M + L/2$: double the number of properly corrected mistranslations plus half the number of properly corrected linguistic errors.

Rather than consider the value that was added, you might want to look at the value that was not added, or was actually subtracted. A simple audit of this kind will count the number of errors introduced by the reviser in a chunk of given length (good translations made bad, or bad ones made worse) plus the number of errors not noticed. A more complex audit would consider not just errors introduced or not noticed, but also unnecessary changes and inadequately corrected errors. And once again, you could distinguish mistranslations from errors in language, style and terminology, and give these different weightings.

Of course you could also combine the good and the bad, using a formula such as $2MC + LC/2 - 3MI - U/3$: double the number of mistranslations properly corrected plus half the number of language errors properly corrected minus triple the number of mistranslations introduced minus one-third the number of unnecessary changes. And to repeat: you could count all errors, or only serious errors, though the latter will take more time since you will have to keep stopping to decide whether an error is serious. (See Appendix E on major, minor and critical errors.)

Individual revisers can also audit their own work for self-development purposes. If you are new to revising other people's translations, and there is no senior reviser who can look over your work, or no one with the time to do so, make a copy of a draft translation and then, a couple of months later, revise it again. Then compare the two revisions. The changes should be at more or less the same locations in both revisions, though of course the new wordings you selected on the two occasions may well differ. If the changes are at very different locations, then your work is clearly unsystematic.

9.12   Time and quality

A central issue for all translators, and in particular for revisers, is the trade-off between time and quality. From an economic point of view, time is money, and the faster a translation is completed, the better. The problem is most easily seen in situations where clients are billed (as opposed to situations where they receive translation as an apparently free service from the company's or ministry's translation department). Billing may be in textual units (the number of words or pages) or in time units (the number of hours spent on a given job). If a job takes 15 hours, someone will be worse off economically than if it takes only 12. If the client is being billed in hours, the bill will be 25% higher, and the client may look elsewhere next time. If the bill is so much per word or per page, the freelance translator (or the staff translator's employer) will have less total income over a given period of time. Suppose translator and reviser together take

15 hours to complete a 3000 word job. They are then working at 200 words an hour, whereas if they take 12 hours, they are working at 250 words an hour. If the client is paying 15 cents a word, the first pair are bringing in $30.00 an hour, the second $37.50.

But is the text completed in 12 hours as good as the text completed in 15 hours? Does it serve its purpose adequately? Are there more undiscovered errors in it, possibly serious ones? There is no getting around the fact that *quality takes time.* Achieving accuracy in particular is time-consuming for both the first translator and the revising translator. On the other hand, it does seem to be false that the longer you spend on a translation, the better it will become; there is a point beyond which no further significant improvement is being made, and time is simply being wasted. If you have been given a revision contract, your client does not want to be billed for pointless re-readings and unnecessary changes!

A full revision, covering all the features to be discussed in Chapter 10, is very time-consuming. Sometimes, as discussed in Chapter 11, less than full revision is perfectly acceptable. Also, time can be saved if revisers learn to avoid unnecessary changes. Finally, translators may be able to produce higher quality drafts more quickly, and leave more time for self-revision, if they have access to (and training in!) the latest technological aids, or if they can use the services of documentalists to track down quotations, titles and the like. However there are limits to these efficiencies. For example, when a new technology is introduced, the translation process may speed up: the research process was certainly speeded up by the advent of Internet search engines in the final years of the 20th century. However, after a while a limit is reached in what the new technology can achieve. Meanwhile, expectations about speed will now be higher. As a result, there will continue to be a conflict between ethical demands for quality and economic demands for speed.

There is a temptation under these circumstances to define quality in terms of client complaints. A translation is of adequate quality if the client does not complain about it. This is a very weak argument, indeed an unethical one that evades the professional responsibilities of revisers. Most obviously, few clients have independent bilingual checkers. As a result they may well not notice if, say, the forty-fifth paragraph of the text is missing (the transition from paragraph 44 to 46 of the source text may make sense). They may be in no position to recognize a major mistranslation (the translation as it stands may make sense, but not the sense the source-text writer intended). And if the text contains odd uses of target-language vocabulary, they may think that, well, all translations are like that.

In the struggle between time (that is, money) and quality, revisers face a dilemma: as employees or contractors, they must consider their employer's financial concerns, but as professionals (perhaps certified under legislation or by a professional association), they must give priority to quality. Freelance revisers are in the same position: they must earn a living, but they also have a professional duty. Clearly, there is no easy answer.

9.13   Quantity of revision

How much revision of someone else's translations should an experienced reviser be expected to complete per hour or day? This is a difficult question to answer: someone who spends much of the day revising translations in a single field, with well written source texts, and very good translators, will get a lot more done per hour than someone who spends much less time revising and often works with less than excellent translators, poorly written source texts, and materials in a variety of fields, some of them unfamiliar. Still, a reasonable answer can I think be given in terms of a multiple of translation time. With most European languages (those that do not have very long compounds that are written as single words), a translator with at least 5 years of full time experience, working with a mix of familiar and unfamiliar, poorly written and well written texts, should be able to complete (i.e. draft, research and self-revise) 1600-2000 words of source text in an 8-hour day, or between 200 and 250 words an hour (this is an average taken over a lengthy period such as a year). It should be possible for an experienced reviser to do comparative re-reading and correction of such a mix of texts at three times the translation speed (600-750 words an hour), and unilingual re-reading and correction at five times the translation speed (1000-1250 words an hour), assuming a reasonably competent translator. Comparative re-reading does not take twice as long as unilingual, even though there is about twice as much text to read. Using the above figures, a comparative re-reading of 1000 words would take somewhere between 1 hr 20 and 1 hr 40 minutes, or a third to two-thirds more time than unilingual re-reading at 1000 words an hour. One researcher (Robert 2012) timed her subjects and obtained a figure of just a third more time to do comparative re-reading than unilingual. It would be interesting to see further studies of this question.

9.14   Quality assessment versus revision

In addition to performing quality control work, your duties as a reviser may include the very different task of quality assessment. Unlike quality control, which always occurs *before* the translation is delivered to the client, quality assessment may take place *after* delivery. Assessment is not part of the translation production process. It consists in identifying (but not correcting) problems in one or more randomly selected passages of a text in order to determine the degree to which it meets professional standards and the standards of the translating organization.

Quality assessment may be done on single texts, to assist with hiring or promotion for example. It may also take the form of quality auditing: a sample of texts produced by a translation service is assessed in order to determine how well the service as a whole is doing. The purpose may be to identify areas that are weak so that training can be provided, or it may be to report to the senior body which funds the translation service.

Sometimes assessments must be quantified (for example to compare the results of candidates during a competition). On other occasions, assessments are qualitative; for example, as the supervisor of a translator, you may have to formulate their strengths and weaknesses (such diagnostic work is discussed in Chapter 14).

Note that contracted work needs to be both quality controlled (prepared for the client) and quality assessed (in order to determine, for payment purposes, whether the contract conditions have been met). These two tasks may be performed simultaneously by the same person, who assesses the text and also makes any needed amendments.

Whereas quality control is text-oriented and client/reader-oriented, quality assessment is business-oriented. It is a part of the work of managing the organization's current and future operations (payments to contractors and monitoring of their performance with a view to future contracts; hiring, firing and promotion of staff translators; determination of training needs; deciding on the balance of in-house versus contracted work, and so on).

Some of the problems of quality assessment are discussed in Appendix 2.

9.15   Quality assurance

Quality assurance is the full set of procedures applied not just after (as with quality assessment) but also before and during the translation production process, by all members of a translating organization, to ensure that quality objectives important to clients are met. Quality control and quality assessment are in part contributions to quality assurance. Quality assurance includes procedures to ensure:

- Quality of service: Are deadlines met? Is interaction between clients and translators or support staff pleasant? Are complaints dealt with in a satisfactory manner? Is each job tracked so that the client can be given a progress report? If the client has lost the electronic version of a translation done a few months ago, can the translation service provide a fresh copy?
- Quality of the physical product: Is the page layout satisfactory? Is it in side-by-side multilingual format if so requested? Has it been delivered in the manner specified – by fax, by e-mail, as a Word document, as an HTML document?
- Quality of the translation: Is the client satisfied with the terminology and with the writing (language and style)?

To improve quality, it may be useful (albeit time-consuming) to keep records that provide measurements of success: how many late texts? how many complaints from clients per month? how many unsatisfactory jobs from contractors as opposed to in-house translators?

In organizations which have cut back the quality control function (less time is allowed for quality control; fewer texts are given a full comparative re-reading), it is important to assure quality by *preventing errors from occurring in the first place*. This means paying extra attention to the earlier stages in the translation production process: Does the translator have the names of resource persons, access to the best possible documentation, a clear idea of the brief, and suitable computer technology? Errors can also be prevented if the right translator is chosen for the job. This may mean looking at a translator's record with previous texts (in general or for texts in the same field) or looking at their credentials: are they certified or otherwise recognized by some professional association or educational institution?

There is now a trend toward standardizing procedures for the contractual relationship between the client and the translation provider (freelance or translation company). The idea is that if certain procedures are followed before and during production of the translation, that will increase the likelihood of good quality. To this end, some translating organizations are applying a variety of standards and guidelines which have been issued in recent years. It should be noted that the documents in question tend to originate from committees which in the main represent owners/managers of translation services as well as major buyers of translations; input from organizations of professional translators and from translation schools may have been minimal.

These standards and guidelines typically cover such matters as: qualifications of translators and others working on a project; the process of negotiating a translation contract; interactions between the translation provider and the client during and after the project; and steps in the translation process, including of course the various types of checking work.

China's General Administration of Quality Supervision issued a document in 2003 entitled "Specification for Translation Service" (GB/T 19363, revised 2008). It is based in part on the 1996 German standard for the conduct of translation projects DIN 2345 (which has been superseded by EN-15038, described below). Concerning revision, the Chinese standard provides that "the intended use of the translation as specified by the client will determine how many times the translation is revised" (and, interestingly, that "the reviser should use a pen of different coloured ink from the translator"!).

The ASTM (formerly known as the American Society for Testing Materials) published a "Standard Guide for Quality Assurance in Translation" (ASTM F2575) in 2006. It "identifies factors relevant to the quality of language translation services for each phase of a translation project". Its definition of quality is contractual: "the degree to which the characteristics of a translation fulfill the requirements of the agreed-upon specifications". Regarding checking of translations, the document distinguishes editing, proofreading and quality control. The editor does a comparative reading for accuracy and completeness, as well as terminology, and also does a complete reading for readability. The quality controller reads randomly selected passages, or may read the entire text again. The proofreader checks for errors in formatting, typos and the like; proofreading can be combined with either editing or quality control.

The CEN (European Committee for Standardization) issued standard EN-15038 entitled "Translation Services – Service Requirements", also in 2006. It defines quality indirectly, in its statement about the task of the reviser: "the reviser shall examine the translation for its suitability for purpose". The wording is unclear as to whether the revision must include a comparative re-reading. The document does however specify that every translation must be revised by a second translator.

In 2009, the Canadian General Standards Board issued CAN/CGSB 131.10, entitled "Translation Services", which is an adaptation of EN-15038. It differs from the European standard in some interesting ways, most notably in not requiring revision of every text by a second translator. Instead the standard says "The Translation Service Provider shall identify the need for revision, taking into account the abilities of the translator, the requirements of the client and the nature of the assignment". However the wording is clear that if there is a decision to have a second translator revise the translation, then a comparative re-reading is required.

In 2012, the International Organization for Standardization issued ISO/TS 11669 entitled "Translation Projects – General Guidance". Like the ASTM guidance document, it defines quality by the degree to which the translation conforms to a project's pre-determined specifications. Specifications are to be agreed with the client for 21 suggested parameters. Thus the parameter "file format" might be specified as "HTML"; the parameter "in-process quality assurance" might be specified as "review" (the target content is evaluated by a subject-matter expert). Concerning revision, which is defined as comparative re-reading for content, this is one of the things that may or may not be identified as a requirement for a given project. It should be done by a second translator, but self-revision is acceptable if the first translator is the most qualified person available for that project. Concerning revisers, the guidance document suggests that they should ideally have subject-matter knowledge.

The ISO is currently preparing a standard ISO/DIS 17100 "Translation Services – Requirements for Translation Services".

Practice

1. Write out the sequence of quality assurance measures which you use (if you work alone) or which are used by the institution you work for (translation agency or department). Think carefully about each and every aspect of the work, from receipt of a request for translation to post-delivery (response to complaints from the client).

2. Scenario. You work for an organization which has moved from full revision of most texts to less complete forms of quality control together with more emphasis on self-revision. The result is that more text is being produced per employee-hour (income is up!), but when you look through a file of completed translations, you see several serious mistranslations. One day you tell the manager of the translation service that the text you

are quality-controlling requires a full comparative re-reading rather than a cursory scan. You suggest informing the client that the text will be two days late. The manager is not happy and lets it be understood that you might want to spend a couple of evenings doing (unpaid) overtime. You discover that other quality controllers have received similar hints. What do you do?

3. Describe a time-versus-quality conflict that has arisen in your work. What was the resolution? If the problem was one that arose frequently, did you decide (or did your agency or employer decide) to make some changes in policy or procedure? If you are attending a workshop or taking a course, present the problem as a case study to the other participants.

4. Scenario. A client has in the past complained about overly free transla-tions of the decisions of a semi-judicial administrative tribunal, and also about unwanted translator's notes suggesting alternative translations. In one passage of the decision now being translated, the tribunal states that a Spanish-speaking appellant had complained about not being able to understand the documentation used against him, because it was in French:

  il a déclaré ne comprendre que la moitié des textes français
  [he stated he understood only half the French documents]

The draft translation reads

  he stated that he could only half understand the French documents

The translator explains her reasoning as follows: "It's hard to see how he could have understood half the documents but not the other half, or half of each document and not the other half. Also, this text is a transcription from dictation. The transcriber may have made an error, and heard 'à moitié' as 'la moitié'; the former would mean 'half understand', i.e. not fully understand the meaning. This must therefore be the intent. If we write 'half the documents', the readers will be puzzled."

Bearing in mind the client's previous complaints, what will you do: leave the translator's draft or change it to 'half the documents'? Why?

5. If you work in a translation department, arrange a revision auditing session. Each participant examines a 500 word chunk of one already delivered translation before the session, and then presents it sentence-by-sentence to the group, first mentioning whether the translation was for information or for publication, and then pointing out problems that were not caught. Other participants then contribute.

Further reading

(See the References list near the end of the book for details on these publications.)

Quality of revision: Arthern (1983, 1987, 1991); Künzli 2009.

Quality assurance and assessment: Drugan (2013); Williams (2009); Colina (2008 and 2009); Picken (1994).

Briefs and approaching translations on the basis of their future function: Allman (2008); Nord (1997, especially chapters 3 and 4); International Organization for Standardization (2012).

Reviser's loyalty: Künzli (2006c and 2007b).

Revisers' domain knowledge: Allman (2008).

Office procedures: Risku (2004), Mossop (2006); Nordman (2003).

Balancing interests: Ko (2011).

Revision manual: European Commission (2010).

10. The Revision Parameters

The revision parameters are the things a reviser checks for – the types of error. An exhaustive listing of things that can go wrong when translating would be very long indeed. However in order to think about and discuss revision, it is convenient to have a reasonably short list of error types. In this book, we'll use twelve parameters, divided into four groups. Here they are, expressed as questions about the translation, followed by a single capitalized word for convenience of reference:

Group A – Problems of meaning transfer (Transfer)

1. Does the translation reflect the message of the source text? (Accuracy)
2. Have any elements of the message been left out? (Completeness)

Group B – Problems of content (Content)

3. Does the sequence of ideas make sense? Is there any nonsense or contradiction? (Logic)
4. Are there any factual, conceptual or mathematical errors? (Facts)

Group C – Problems of language and style (Language)

5. Does the wording flow? Are the connections between sentences clear? Are the relationships among the parts of each sentence clear? Are there any awkward, hard-to-read sentences? (Smoothness)
6. Is the language suited to the users of the translation and the use they will make of it? (Tailoring)
7. Is the style suited to the genre? Has correct terminology been used? Does the phraseology match that used in original target-language texts on the same subject? (Sub-language)
8. Are all the word combinations idiomatic? Does the translation observe the rhetorical preferences of the target language? (Idiom)
9. Have the rules of grammar, spelling, punctuation, house style and correct usage been observed? (Mechanics)

Group D – Problems related to the visual rather than verbal aspect of the text (Presentation)

10. Are there any problems in the way the text is arranged on the page: spacing, indentation, margins, etc? (Layout)
11. Are there any problems related to bolding, underlining, font type, font size, etc? (Typography)
12. Are there any problems in the way the document as a whole is or-

ganized: page numbering, headers, footnotes, table of contents, etc?
(Organization)

*Remember that this list is for discussion and reflection about revision practices. It
is not for use as a checklist while actually revising* in a professional setting (though
it might be used as such in a classroom setting). Obviously, you are not going to
go through each sentence twelve times! As we'll see in Chapter 11, however, you
may want to refer to the four groups of parameters before you begin, in order
to decide the degree to which you will revise.

Some translation departments and agencies do give their translators revision
checklists containing items such as "all translatable text has been translated" and
"client's terminology has been used". While such lists are useful as reminders,
it is hard to see how they could be used in any practical revision procedure. If
the checklist contains twenty items, there is no time to consider each of them
in turn after reading each sentence of the translation.

You may want to read some of the earlier chapters of this book for more
information on some of the parameters that are of concern not just to revisers
but also to editors (parameters 3 to 12). Chapter 3 looks in detail at the various
aspects of Mechanics as well as Idiom. Chapter 4 has sections on Tailoring and
Smoothness. Chapter 6 covers Logic and Facts.

If you work in a situation where a proofreader (who is not a translator) will
look at the translation prior to publication, you may not need to worry about the
Presentation parameters or about compliance with house style (parameter 9),
except for those aspects which affect meaning: you must always check commas,
which can have a serious impact on how a sentence is interpreted by the reader,
as well as words and phrases which are bolded, underlined or italicized, since
these features will affect focus. If there is no proofreader, then you the reviser
must deal with these parameters, and in particular ensure a certain minimum
'beauty' of presentation.

Aside from the parameters discussed in this chapter, revisers may also have
to check for consistency, which is considered separately in Chapter 7.

Let us now look at the twelve parameters in detail.

10.1 Accuracy

Unless you have specifically been asked to prepare an adaptation, or your client is paying a premium for extra high writing quality, accuracy will be the most
important feature of the translations you are revising. Generally speaking, the
first task of a professional translator is to guarantee that the translation means
(more or less) what the source means (or to be more careful – what you think
the source means). More particularly, you as a reviser must ensure that there are
no major mistranslations – passages which could seriously mislead the reader
about an important feature of the source text's message.

Accuracy is not limited to the level of words, phrases and sentences. Indeed,
perhaps the most important aspect of accuracy is the correct rendering of the

overall structure of the message: the sequencing of events or arguments must be the one in the source text. So when checking for accuracy, you need to pay special attention to words like 'however' and 'then'.

An accurate translation does not have to be a close translation. Accuracy has nothing to do with whether the translator has used vocabulary and sentence structures of the target language which are as close as possible to those of the source language. Accuracy has strictly to do with the message in a passage. More particularly, accuracy certainly does not mean reproducing poor writing; many translators consider it their duty to improve the quality of the writing.

Accurate does not mean source-oriented. A translation in which you have replaced or eliminated a metaphor, added a cultural explanation or used a functional equivalent of a cultural feature (sports, cuisine) can still be considered accurate, though there are limits (see the next section on Completeness).

Just how accurate does a translation have to be? Not as accurate as possible, but as accurate as necessary, given the type of text and the use to be made of the translation. Ephemeral texts, which will be read and discarded, and not used to make important decisions, do not need to be as accurate as publications, or documents which will be used for important decisions. There is no point spending five minutes searching for the *mot juste* which conveys the exact nuance if the translation is going to be read quickly and tossed away.

Suppose the source text is the minutes of a meeting. It mentions that an official gave an interview to a journalist at lunch-time. The draft translation says 'spent his lunch hour giving an interview'. This is not quite accurate – it implies that the entire lunch hour was spent giving the interview. But the key point has been made: an interview was given. What percentage of the official's lunch hour this occupied is utterly irrelevant. It would simply be a waste of time revising the draft.

In written translation, unlike oral, it is possible to go over and over a text, making it more and more accurate, so that not only the main message but even tiny details are reflected in the translation. But the fact that this is possible is not a reason to do it. Not only may it be a waste of time, but over-attention to accuracy can result in an unreadable text. Every scrap and nuance of meaning may have been crammed in, but the resulting sentence may be awkward, disjointed, in short hard to read. Readers of some texts (e.g. certain legal documents) may prefer such extreme accuracy, but others will simply stop reading or (if their jobs require them to read the document) they will be distracted from the message by the language.

More generally, there is a trade-off between Accuracy and the Language & Style parameters, especially Tailoring, Smoothness and Idiom. It is probably wishful thinking to imagine that a translation can be both extremely readable and extremely accurate. At the higher levels of accuracy, a degree of readability is inevitably sacrificed, while at the higher levels of reader-friendliness, accuracy must suffer. The trick is to identify the right balance for the job at hand.

The question whether a translation is accurate is actually two questions:

- Has the source text been correctly understood?
- Does the translation express that understanding?

The most common kind of inaccuracy arises from incorrect understanding of the source. But inaccuracy can also arise when the source has been correctly understood. The translator may believe that this understanding has been expressed in the translation, but in fact it has not. The readers are likely to interpret the wording the wrong way. This problem most often arises because the translator has written a syntactically ambiguous sentence.

Finding such potentially dangerous ambiguities is a good example of the superiority of revision by a second translator over self-revision. A second pair of eyes is more likely to see the incorrect reading, because there is no prior bias toward the correct reading.

Sometimes inaccuracies are actually necessary, for political or ideological reasons. Consider the institution in Quebec City whose official name until recently was 'Bibliothèque nationale du Québec' (national library of Quebec). It was sometimes just called the 'Bibliothèque nationale' (national library), but it could not be called the 'National Library' in English because that name would evoke, for English-Canadians, the institution in the federal capital Ottawa whose official name used to be 'National Library of Canada'. The problem for the reviser here is not simply that of ensuring the reader is not confused about which institution is being referred to. There's also an ideological problem, because the names reflect different understandings of the country: the French reflects the belief in a Quebec nation which happens to be part of a federation called Canada; the English reflects the belief in a Canadian nation consisting of three territories and ten provinces, one of which is called Quebec. With some clients and readerships, the reviser may need to ensure that the translation reflects the English-Canadian outlook: 'Quebec provincial library' or something of the sort. Some might call such deliberate inaccuracy a minor form of censorship.

A final point on accuracy: numbers are often an important part of the message. If the translator has turned an unemployment rate of 6.8% into a rate of 8.6%, that is a major Transfer error if unemployment is an important topic in the text. In any text where numbers are central to the message, it's a good idea to make a separate check for their accurate reproduction.

10.2 Completeness

Unless specifically asked to write a summary or gist, or provide an adaptation, translators are usually expected to render all the message, and only the message, that is in the source text – No Additions, No Subtractions (NANS).

Some 1900 years ago, in a letter to his friend Fuscus advising him to while away his retirement translating Greek into Latin, the Ancient Roman writer Pliny the Younger wrote: "What might have eluded your notice while reading cannot escape you when translating". Pliny presents this as an advantage (Fuscus will be able to delve more deeply into the Greek text), but from another point of view, it is more a burden borne by translators: readers can skip over an obscure passage, but translators cannot. Translators must try to come up with an interpretation of every expression, and, with few exceptions, this full interpretation must be reflected in the translation.

The most common completeness error is unintentional omissions, but the translator may also have unwittingly added ideas that are not present, even implicitly, in the source. The reviser must be on the lookout for such additions, for, as Andrew Marvell put it some 350 years ago:

> He is Translation's thief that addeth more
> As much as he that taketh from the store
> Of the first author. ...

Unwitting additions may occur when the text is on a topic about which the translator has strong feelings: an alleged child murderer's 'statement' becomes his 'confession'.

Apart from unintentional omissions and additions, the translator may also have deliberately eliminated a portion of the source text message or added material that is completely new (not even implicit in the source). For example, a tourist guide may have been used as a springboard for composing a guide in another language: much material has been left out because it was thought not to be of interest to target-language readers, and much else has been added to make the destination attractive to these readers. Another possibility is that the translator decided to make a dreary text more lively and interesting, perhaps by adding metaphorical comparisons or humour. Or the translator did some content editing because there are differences between what it is appropriate to say in an obituary in the source-language community and in the target-language community. If there are more than a few such additions and subtractions, the reviser turns into a bilingual editor, and might decide to turn the checking work over to someone else.

The NANS principle should not be taken too literally. First, small additions and subtractions are inevitable; there is usually no point going through a translation with a fine-toothed comb searching for tiny nuances of meaning that have been added or subtracted. For example, cultural or technical explanations may have to be added; as the reader's advocate, the reviser keeps an eye out for passages where the reader will need help.

Second, the NANS principle really only applies to *relevant* meaning. Some of the information in the translation will be very important to the readers, some less important. Thus if the text is a complaint containing a great many expressions of the complainant's emotional state, some of these can be omitted if the point of the translation is simply to allow an official to determine the substance of the complaint. Or take a text on the causes of avalanches which begins with a description of the researchers arriving in an alpine village and lists some of the flowers growing in the meadows. The whole passage could be summarized or omitted.

Third, always keep in mind that the NANS principle refers to the text's message, not to its wording. Completeness does not require the reproduction of the repetitiveness typical of poorly written source texts. Indeed, the reviser should generally ensure that such repetitiveness has been eliminated. However if this is likely to be a time-consuming task, and excellence of style is not a consideration in the job at hand, any repetitiveness can be left in the translation.

Completeness also does not require explicitness. Elements of meaning which are explicit in the source text can be left implicit in the translation. There is no problem of completeness as long as a reader can recover these elements by drawing either on general or expert knowledge or on knowledge conveyed *earlier* in the text (not later!). Now, it is not always obvious whether this condition of recoverability is met. You may err in either direction, thinking that the element is recoverable when it is not, or thinking that it is not recoverable when it is. The former error is more serious, since there will then be an omission in the final translation. The latter error merely leads to a needless (and therefore time-wasting) revision, as you make the element of meaning explicit. Obviously if you are in doubt, you will ensure that the element is explicit.

Leaving message elements implicit, together with elimination of redundancy, are especially important when only a small, predetermined amount of space is available for the translation. If these techniques do not work, then perhaps a different font or smaller font size, or reduction of interlineal spacing, might solve the problem. But in some cases, it may be necessary to simply omit material.

Completeness might be thought to be an aspect of Accuracy, but it is worth mentioning separately because the source of the problem, as well as the solution, is often mechanical in nature. The translator's eye may have skipped a point in a long list of bulleted points. Or a whole passage may have been skipped when a phrase was repeated in successive sentences or paragraphs: the eye, returning to the source text from the translation, went to the second occurrence of the phrase, even though the material after the first occurrence had not yet been translated. A key function of the reviser is to find such accidental omissions.

If the translation was produced by typing over the electronic source text, then it is unlikely that paragraphs, or items in a point-form list, will have been omitted. But if the translation was produced from a paper document (a printout of a .pdf document for example), it may be a good idea to make a count, in order to ensure that no list items or paragraphs have been left out. Note that if you do find a mismatch in the number of paragraphs, it may not be a case of omission, because the translator may have decided to combine or split paragraphs.

A final point on completeness: if the source text is provided electronically, bear in mind that there may be various forms of hidden writing which are not immediately displayed on the screen, and may not appear even on a printout. If the translator is not too familiar with the software, whole chunks of source text may have been missed. A very simple example: the translator is looking at the Normal view of the text in Word, and as a result does not see the headers and footers, which are visible only in Page Layout view. More complex forms of hidden text occur with presentation software (PowerPoint) and in HTML files.

You can find any hidden text by pressing the Microsoft Office button in Word 2007, pointing to Prepare, and then clicking Document Inspector; check Hidden Text, and press Inspect.

10.3   Logic

While a translation may well express ideas you find silly or outrageous, there should generally speaking not be any nonsense, contradictions between sentences, impossible temporal or causal sequences, or other logical errors. Each part of the translation must make sense to the reader in its context. Lack of logic can take two forms:

1. ***The source text itself is illogical, and the translator has not done anything about it.***

One can usually assume that the author intended something which makes sense, but poor expression has resulted in nonsense or contradiction as the reader's most likely interpretation. Sometimes the intention will be very clear from the context, as when an author accidentally self-contradicts by claiming that the unemployment rate has gone up from 9.8 to 8.9 percent. However care must be taken in such cases: *either* 'up' could be wrong *or* the figures may have become inverted. If the figures are confirmed by an accompanying graph, or by a reference to a smile on the face of the employment minister, then 'up' can confidently be changed to 'down'.

Here's an example of a passage that will likely be read as contradictory:

> Search the patent website to determine whether there are any inventions similar to yours. If your preliminary search is negative, you can either drop your invention or make an improvement to it.

Here the translator has not done anything about the source-text word rendered as 'negative'. It makes sense if 'negative' is taken to mean 'disappointing' (i.e. someone has beat you to this invention), but many readers will take it, on first reading, to mean a negative search outcome (i.e. no one has beat you to the invention). But then, if no one has beat you, why should you drop the invention or make an improvement to it?

Now consider this sentence:

> The short-term consequences are temporary and do not last very long.

In context, it was clear that 'short-term' meant 'short-lived'. So the first part of the sentence is a tautology; it tells the readers, regarding the short-term consequences, that they are short-term. Also, the word 'and' suggests that further information about the consequences is about to be imparted, but 'do not last very long' is nothing but a re-statement of 'temporary'; the second part of the sentence is redundant. Revise to 'The consequences are temporary'.

Let us note in passing that the logical connections between sentences in source texts may be very unclear because the author composed it by stringing together a collage of sentences from a variety of materials found in a database of corporate documentation, and then failed to do appropriate editing to create a logical sequence of thought, or worse, added connectors without careful thought (for example, added 'consequently' even though there is no cause-effect relationship between the sentences). In some cases, the lack of a logical link between sentences can be solved by starting a new paragraph at the beginning of the second sentence. However in other cases it may not be possible to create logical links unless the author is available and willing to clarify their intent.

2. *The source text makes sense but the translator has introduced nonsense or contradiction.*

Among student trainees, such nonsense often arises from lack of source-language knowledge; among experienced translators, it arises from attention waning when rushed or tired. Consider this bit of nonsense that crept into a translation from French about the medical consequences of excessive coffee drinking:

> There was fear of playing the game. Americans reduced their consumption of coffee.

A gloss of the source text for the first sentence would be 'fear played' (French 'la peur a joué'). The meaning is that fear (of negative health consequences) came into play and (therefore) Americans reduced their consumption of coffee.

Here is an example of contradiction being introduced by the translator:

> We are making use of innovative technologies because the latest advances are not affordable.

Now, if you cannot afford the latest technologies, how can you make use of them? Here the source text was actually discussing how to make innovative use of technologies, that is, how to use the older technology more cleverly. The translator was reading quickly or not being attentive, and read 'innovative' with 'technologies' instead of with 'use'. (The French was 'utilisation innovatrice des technologies', which means 'innovative use of technologies', but the word 'utilisation' appeared at the end of one line and 'innovatrice' at the beginning of the next line, bringing it visually closer to 'technologies'.)

Logic is also discussed in Chapter 6.3.

10.4 Facts

Although checking a text for factual, conceptual and mathematical errors is not a central task of translators, such errors are obviously of communicative importance; they will be spotted immediately by readers of the translation who are subject-matter experts. Clients will appreciate it if these errors are not simply skipped over in silence. They are most often present in the original, but they may sometimes be introduced inadvertently by the translator. If they are present in the original, you need to ensure compliance with the client's wishes, which may vary: make corrections in the translation; list and describe the errors in a separate document; call the author of the source text and get agreement to changes in its wording.

In some cases, the source text author's ignorance of the true facts may be significant; in this case, correction during translation would not be appropriate. However it may be necessary to indicate in some way that the error is due to the author, not the translator.

Here's an example of a translator introducing a factual error. While re-reading a translation of the findings of an administrative tribunal, you come across this sentence:

> The common law courts have already dealt with the charges of robbery
> and extortion in the matter before us.

The intended readers will all be knowledgeable about the law, and will immediately see that there is something very wrong here: robbery and extortion are matters of criminal law, not common law. Furthermore, the reference is to a trial in Quebec, which does not use English common law but French civil law derived from the Napoleonic Code. A glance back at the French source text reveals that there was no error in the original, which referred to 'les cours de droit commun'. This means 'the ordinary law courts'. (The French term for courts outside Quebec that deal with common law matters is 'cour de common law').

Note that this is not merely a mistranslation. There is an important difference between the Content parameters (errors in Facts and Logic) and the Transfer parameters (Accuracy and Completeness). For someone comparing the translation to its source, there may not seem to be much difference between Content and Transfer errors, but the effect on the readers of the translation is not the same. Transfer errors will often pass unnoticed, if they make sense, but the same is not true of Content errors. Logical errors and in particular factual errors are immediately obvious to subject-matter experts and they call into question the competence of either the source-text author (if the reader does not know the text is a translation) or the translator.

For more on factual and conceptual errors, see Chapter 6.2. For mathematical errors, Chapter 6.4.

10.5 Smoothness

This parameter and the next two (Tailoring and Sub-language) cover the area commonly called 'style'. Smoothness is discussed in more detail in Chapter 4.2.

Generally speaking, the meaning should come across to the reader on first reading at normal reading speed. If it does not, the problem will often be one of poorly organized sentence structures or poor connections between sentences, perhaps due to careless imitation of the word order or the connector words ('this', 'therefore') of the source text. An example of a common problem is poor sequencing of verb tenses from sentence to sentence, as well as improper selection of tense. In translation from French, for example, a common form of the verb can be rendered in English either by the simple past or the perfect (a translator was hired / a translator has been hired); both may be perfectly grammatical, but often only one will fit the flow of the argument.

Unsmooth writing in the source cannot justify unsmooth writing in the translation. Varying degrees of smoothness are acceptable, but the appropriate degree is determined by the user and use of the translation, not the smoothness of the source text.

One thing that can definitely interfere with a smooth reading experience for the typical reader (i.e. one who does not know the source language) is the presence in the translation of many source-language phrases, for example, names of institutions and titles of publications. In some genres, notably legal documents, source-language names may be required. In others, action should be taken to reduce them. Since the first duty of a translator is to translate, it is important for the reviser to check that the translator has minimized source-language words.

Smoothness has become a more pressing concern in recent years because many translations now include passages pasted in (manually or using Translation Memory) from previous translations or from client documentation that was originally written in the target language. The joins between the pasted parts and the translator's own work may not be smooth. More on this in Chapter 14.5.

> *Terminology note*: The literature on translation sometimes uses the term *cohesion* to refer to Smoothness and the term *coherence* to refer to Logic. Simply put, cohesion is the flow of words, coherence the flow of ideas. The problem with these two terms, which have been borrowed from linguistics, is that they are so similar. The result is that if you read a reference to 'cohesion', for example, you have to stop and try to remember whether it refers to Smoothness or Logic.

10.6 Tailoring

The translation has to be suited to its readers and to the use they will make of it. For example, if the document gives instructions for installing a video card in a computer, you must imagine a typical computer user following the sequence of actions set out in the translation.

The translation must have the right 'level of language', that is, the right degree of formality and technicality and the right emotive tone, and the vocabulary must be suited to the education level of the readers and to their knowledge of the subject matter of the text. The degree of formality of the source text is largely irrelevant; the reviser must instead ask whether the text in the target language has the right degree of formality or technicality for its future readers. Consider:

> While no cure has yet been found for AIDS, there are a number of treat-
> ments which can prevent the opportunistic diseases from appearing.

An opportunistic disease is one of the diseases which people are prone to if their immune systems have been impaired by HIV. The expression is well known to doctors and AIDS activists, but is not really suited to a general readership. If this translation will appear in a pamphlet to be distributed to the general public, it needs to be tailored to its audience, perhaps with a paraphrase: 'prevent the diseases which HIV-positive people often get'.

The readership may be very narrow or very broad. With narrow readerships (that is, all intended readers are subject-matter experts), you may need to check that the translator has used what would normally be undesirable language, for example, the latest fads of bureaucratic jargon. Otherwise, the text may not appear to be addressed to its intended audience.

Even if the readership of the translation will be similar to the readership of the source text, the use to which the translation will be put may well differ from the use of the source text. For example, the source text may be a transcript of oral proceedings – the words were used to make an argument in court – but the translation will be read silently as a reference by attorneys working on another case. You need to check that most of the features of oral language (false starts, repetitions) have been removed, since they are liable to cause confusion or slow the process of reading. Just the occasional repetition or interjection should be left to remind the reader of the oral nature of the source text ('he...he said that, well, ...').

Tailoring is discussed in more detail in Chapter 4.1.

10.7 Sub-language

Each genre (text type) and each field of writing in the target language draws on a different selection of the lexical, syntactic and rhetorical resources of that language. A syntactic example: minutes of meetings are normally presented in the past tense in English; French, on the other hand, uses the present. Thus minutes would be grammatical but inauthentic if they contained a sentence like 'Mary reports on client complaints'. Genres may also differ in the degree to which they prefer noun-based structures ('the exigencies of penury') or the less formal, more speech-like verb-based structures ('the things that you have to do if you're poor'). Finally, every genre in the target language will have its own structure: there is a typical way of structuring recipes or academic papers that may differ from what is found in the source language.

The most obvious aspect of sub-language that requires checking is field-specific terminology. In most translation jobs, the terminology has to be that used by specialists who are native speakers of the target language, or else the in-house terminology specified by the client. However, with texts being translated for information only, clients may accept wordings that convey the meaning even if they are not terminologically correct. Many revisers believe that subject-matter experts will be annoyed if they find anything other than the correct term in the translation. I think that in general this is not true. The subject-matter experts who read our translations are not 'language people' like us; the typical forest scientist is interested in trees, not the language used to talk about trees. Experts tend to 'read through' language to the non-linguistic world in which they are interested. We should not project onto them our own interest in linguistic matters.

One common problem is that it may not have occurred to the translator that a sequence of ordinary words of the source language is in fact a term. In meteorology, French 'vents en altitude' should not be translated 'winds at high altitudes' or 'high above the ground'. Instead one speaks of the 'upper winds' or the 'winds aloft' – an expression which sounds faintly poetic/archaic in everyday English but is quite neutral and very common in meteorology journals.

In some translation jobs, revising to create authentic phrasings would be a waste of time. For example, if the authorities who decide on eligibility for disability benefits have asked for translations of an immigrant's old medical reports, the important thing is to get the medical content correct. The readers know perfectly well that they are reading a translation, so there is no need for it to sound authentic, i.e. just like original writing by doctors in the target language.

Authentic phrasing and terminology should actually be avoided in some cases. For example, if revising the translation of an inquiry from a citizen about a legal matter, make sure it does not contain legal phrasings that would only be used by a lawyer, so as to avoid creating the impression that the source-text writer is a lawyer. If revising a translation of a letter from an unemployment insurance recipient, use the expression 'apply for benefits' even though the civil servants who deal with this matter use 'apply for benefit' (with 'benefit' in the singular) in their own writings. If revising the translation of a Belgian court proceeding for reading by British attorneys, it may be a good idea to make sure the translator has *not* used British legal terminology, so as to avoid creating the impression that the Belgian justice system is just like Britain's; if French 'procureur du roi' or Dutch 'procureur des Konings' has been translated 'Crown prosecutor', revise to something like 'king's prosecutor'.

10.8   Idiom

In every language, only some of the grammatically possible combinations of words are actually used. These are the idiomatic combinations. If a text contains unidiomatic wordings ('Immigrants are needed to match gaps in the workforce', instead of the idiomatic 'fill gaps'), that will distract native speakers of the language from the informational content of the text. In some cases, an unidiomatic turn of phrase may also make them wonder whether something different is intended (perhaps 'matching gaps' means something other than 'filling gaps'). Of course, if most of the readers will not be native speakers (as is quite often the case with texts in English these days), this problem of distraction will not be so important.

In editing work, lack of idiomaticity is usually not a problem unless the writer is not a native speaker. However in translation, the situation is very different. Notoriously, translators – even good ones – are prone to producing, under the influence of the source text, unidiomatic combinations such as 'washed his teeth'. This combination of words is perfectly grammatical in English, and understandable, but it is not used. In English, you clean or brush your teeth. There is no rhyme or reason to idiomaticity; you simply have to know which combinations are the idiomatic ones. This is perhaps the main reason why those revising the work of others should ideally be native speakers of the target language.

Some instances of unidiomatic language may be considered creative or witty by native speakers (innovative language is by definition unidiomatic). However, outside literary and marketing texts, or humorous passages that call for unusual language, this is not a consideration.

After years of translating, you may sometimes find that you are not sure whether a certain expression really is idiomatic English, rather than a calque of the source language. A good dictionary will then reassure you that, for example, 'set a process in train' is definitely English, not a calque of French 'mettre en train'. Or simply look up the uncertain expression in Google (see Chapter 8.1).

In an extended sense, checking for idiomaticity also includes checking for anything that 'we just don't say' in the target language. Consider this passage from a translation on peregrine falcons:

> Despite the various protective measures that had been taken, there was a slight unexplained decrease in the peregrine population in the area. This clouded the previously hopeful outlook and was feared to be the sign of a new and this time disastrous decline of our peregrine, possibly leading to extinction.

In French, 'notre pèlerin' (literally 'our peregrine'), meaning the peregrine populations living in 'our' area of the world (in this case, French Switzerland), is perfectly acceptable. But in English, we don't use the first person plural possessive adjective this way, at least not in an article in an ornithology journal (perhaps it might work in a birding column in a local newspaper). 'Our' needs to be replaced with 'the'.

In this extended sense, checking for idiomaticity also includes keeping an eye out for differential frequencies of linguistic features. For example, a sentence structure may be perfectly grammatical in the target language but not as frequent as in the source language. Generally speaking, the less frequent a feature, the more punch it has, so the effect in the target language will in such cases be too strong. In translations from French, one often finds sentences like the following, already discussed in another connection in Chapter 8. It comes from an English-Canadian newspaper reporting, in translation, what a Quebec judge had written in French:

> It's not because you are in politics that you forsake the right to protect your reputation.

This structure is grammatical in English, but it simply isn't used much. It appears in draft translations as an imitation of the common French structure 'ce n'est pas parce que x que y' (it is not because x that y). French sentences with this structure should usually be inverted: 'You do not forsake the right to protect your reputation simply because you are in politics'. Or, if the word 'reputation' needs to be stressed: 'The fact that you are in politics does not mean that you forsake the right to protect your reputation.'

The question of frequency also extends to checking matters that may be ranged under the broad heading of comparative stylistics. For example, French often uses rhetorical questions where English would not; it frequently repeats a sequence of nouns where English would use a shortened version of the noun sequence or a pronoun ('your request for legal opinions...your request....it'); and French has a tendency to express a point in the negative where English would use the positive ('The fact that he controls less than 40% of the shares doesn't mean that he doesn't control the company any more' instead of 'He may still control the company even though he controls less than 40% of the shares').

Idiom is also discussed in Chapter 3.4.

10.9 Mechanics

Aside from finding any errors in grammar, spelling, punctuation and usage, you may need to ensure that the text conforms to any style manual or house style sheet that has been specified for the particular job you are revising. See Chapter 3.2 for more on style sheets.

It is especially important to find mechanical errors when revising text that will appear on homepages, on public signage and in prestigious publications.

If the translation has been prepared by typing over an electronic version of the source text, be sure the punctuation and number-writing conventions of the source language have been replaced with target-language conventions. For example, in French-to-English translation in Canada, the shape of quotation marks must be changed from «....» to "..." , the space before a colon must be eliminated, and 4 000,21 $ must be replaced with $4,000.21. There are, unfortunately, dozens of such small mechanical details that may need to be checked, depending on your language pair.

Capitalization may require special thought when it comes to the translation of proper names, titles of articles and so on, in order to avoid misleading the reader. For example, if the title of a source-language document is referred to in the source text, and this title is then capitalized in the English translation, that will lead the reader to think, possibly wrongly, that the book is available in English.

The two languages may differ in the way they use devices like parentheses. Consider:

> Glass walls must offer a good view from the guard post in order to ensure security (riots, suspect parcels, etc).

where the material in the parenthesis has no syntactic link to the rest of the sentence. This is acceptable in French but not in English. The wording needs to be changed to something like: '...from the guard post so that staff can handle security problems (riots, suspect parcels, etc)'. With this change, 'riots' and 'suspect parcels' are in apposition to 'problems'.

10.10   Layout

A page crammed with type is hard to read, so check for adequate margins and adequate spacing between sections.

Check too that layout remains consistent. Are all paragraphs either indented or not indented (or as in this book, all indented except for the first paragraph in a section)? Are all point-form listings similarly positioned? Are parallel headings similarly placed on the page (e.g. are all chapter titles centred)?

Checking the layout is particularly important if some readers are likely to compare the source and the translation (for example, the text in both languages is to be published as a single document). If the texts are both simultaneously visible, and one is noticeably shorter than the other, some readers may think elements of meaning are missing. You may want to avoid this by using layout devices that give the illusion of equal space being devoted to each language (for example, if the texts are side-by-side, use a narrower column for the shorter text).

Clients may specify as part of the brief that the layout should follow that of the source text. Revisers should check that this has been done, unless the genre rules of the target language dictate a different layout (as in letter-writing).

If the translation will be published, there may be a proofreader who will check layout, which can then be ignored by the reviser.

10.11   Typography

The main things to check for here are moderation and consistency. It will be hard to read a text in which too many words are bolded, italicized, capitalized, underlined or coloured. Also, be sure each device is consistently used for the same purpose (e.g. bolding to pick out special terminology; italicization for any source-language words retained in the translation).

Where the source text uses bolding, italicization or underlining for emphasis, make sure this has not been mechanically repeated in the translation. The emphasis must make sense in the target language. Even if there is a proofreader, this aspect of typography needs to be considered by the reviser because it affects meaning.

Check that all headings of the same depth (e.g. subsections) have the same typographic treatment. Are they all bolded? Are they all the same font size? If font size changes for indented material, does it change back to the original size after the indent ends?

10.12 Organization

The organization of the translation as a whole is important in enabling readers to navigate through the text and perceive its structure.

Check, for example, that page references in the body of the text are correct; the passage referred to may well be on page 26 of the source-language document, but it may be on page 24 of your translation. (If the translation will be published, the precise page numbers will not be known until after delivery of the translation, so this potential problem needs to be signalled to the editor of the publication.)

Also make sure that the numbering or lettering of headings, subheadings, chapter/section titles, figures and tables, as well as their wording, exactly match that found in the Table of Contents. Sometimes translators (or revisers!) change a section heading in the body of the text but forget to make the same change in the Table of Contents. Word processors do contain a feature for automatically creating and revising a Table of Contents, but many source-text writers find it hard to use.

If there is an error in numbering in the source text (e.g. section '6' is followed by another section '6'), make sure this is reproduced in the translation unless the client approves a correction. Signal the error in a note.

If material is presented under each of a series of alphabetized headings in the source text, make sure to alphabetize the headings in the target language after you finish comparing the two versions.

Finally, don't forget to check isolated bits of prose such as headers and footers, and captions.

Further reading

(See the References list near the end of the book for details on these publications.)

Error types and terminology: Delisle *et al.* (1999); Hansen (2009b); Bertaccini and Di Nisio (2011).

11.   Degrees of Revision

To revise or not to revise. That is the question to be considered in this chapter. Will a translation be looked at by a second translator, and if so, will the entire text be revised or just parts of it? Will it be compared to the source or will it simply be re-read? Will all parameters be checked or just some?

If you look hard enough, you will always be able to find more things to change. Imagine that you are taking a final glance through a lengthy English translation. To your horror, you notice that some subheadings have all words capitalized while some have only the first word capitalized. Does this mean that quality control has failed, and that you should immediately set about making the capitalization consistent? No. The question is: just how important was it to catch this problem? With one text, it may be very important; with another, not important at all. Many readers may not notice, and even if some do, it may not create a bad impression in the case of a relatively ephemeral text, one which will be read by only a few people within the organization for information purposes, and then discarded. Tolerance for errors of various kinds, even minor mistranslation, varies with the type of text. It may also vary with urgency: the client will prefer to have an awkwardly worded document *before* the meeting at which it will be used than a beautifully worded document *after* the meeting.

As we saw in Chapter 1, there are a great many things that can go wrong when writing or translating, and consequently there is a very long list of things you might check – or not. In this chapter, we'll look at how to determine the degree to which you will revise a text, and the consequences of less-than-full revision.

11.1   The need for revision by a second translator

Having a second translator look over a translation is costly, especially if a comparison is made with every sentence of the source text and all parameters are taken into consideration. Such revision work is usually done by a senior, more highly paid translator, and every minute devoted to revising someone else's translation is a minute not devoted to preparing a new translation. A 'second look' becomes time-wasting and therefore even more costly if the reviser has not been properly trained and makes large numbers of unnecessary changes. The whole exercise becomes largely pointless if the reviser misses many significant errors, and it becomes positively harmful if the reviser introduces errors – and there is reason to believe that these things happen with alarming frequency.

The predominant view, as expressed in the policies of translation services and agencies, and surveys of translators (see for example Morin-Hernández 2009), is that not every text requires a second look, and that even when it is required, the revision can sometimes be partial (less than the entire text is examined), need not be comparative (a simple reading of the translation is sufficient), and need not cover all parameters.

It should be noted that actual practices may vary considerably from policy (see for example Rasmussen and Schjoldager 2011). Interviews with revisers show that it is not always practical to do what policies require, usually for lack of time or non-availability of personnel. Or the opposite: the policy calls for less checking work than the revisers think is necessary; they may then ignore the policy. Some translation services and agencies emphasize checking certain micro-aspects of a translation where errors will be immediately visible to clients: spelling, grammar, punctuation, client-specific terminology. However the revisers may not actually follow this preference strictly, and instead devote quite a lot of time to style: smoothness, tailoring, a consistent level of language and phrasing suited to the genre. That is because professional translators tend to think such things are important, regardless of any policy.

How is the decision made about whether to have a text revised? The policy at the translation service of the Organization for Economic Cooperation and Development has been summed up by two of its revisers as follows (Prioux and Rochard 2007):

Translator has→ Text has↓	High reliability	Good reliability	Fair reliability	Poor reliability
High importance	1 /2 Revision recommended (re-reading)	2/3 Revision important	3/4 Revision essential	5 Retranslate
Medium importance	0/1 No revision	1 Decide case by case	2/3 Revision recommended	3 Revision important
Low importance	0 No revision	0 No revision	1 Decide case by case	1/2 Revision recommended (re-reading)

At the OECD, the need for revision by a second translator (as opposed to reliance on self-revision) is based on risk, with risk being a function of the importance of the text and the reliability of the translator: 0 represents very low risk, 5 very high risk. As can be seen, the main factor is the importance of the text: the top line on the chart, representing texts of high importance, is the only one where the risk ever rises above 3. Even with a translator of poor reliability, revision is not seen as essential (only 'recommended') with texts of low importance. And even with high importance texts, if the translator is highly reliable, revision is also only recommended (not 'important' or 'essential') and it takes the form of re-reading the translation rather than comparing it with the source. The OECD's approach assumes, of course, that one knows who has translated a text, which is not always the case with outsourced material.

Translation services and agencies often have lists of text types which are deemed to be of high importance. Typically this will include laws and regulations, documents in which errors could have negative health and safety implications, and documents in which errors could harm the image or reputation of the corporation or government which has commissioned the translation (e.g. the front page of a Web site, or a pronouncement by a Very Important Person). Translations that are for information only (not publications) will have medium or low importance, though they may still require revision by a second translator if the drafting translator was inexperienced (as a translator, or in the field of the text). In addition, translations supplied by freelance contractors will need to be checked to at least some degree in order to determine whether the work is satisfactory before payment is made. Finally, clients may specifically request a full comparative revision by a second translator, though they may have to pay a higher price for this service.

For self-employed translators, the key factor in deciding whether to have a second translator take a look is self-confidence. Are you confident in your own translation, or do you feel uncertain about it? Of course, one can be over-confident, especially if one has years of experience. It is therefore probably a good idea to have your work looked at occasionally, but you will need to find someone with an equal or preferably higher level of subject-matter knowledge.

11.2   Determining the degree of revision

In professional work, one does not have all the time in the world. The client is expecting the revised text by a date which is often not far off. You (or the translation service you work for) must therefore consider whether you are going to do a time-consuming full comparative revision of the text, checking for problems in all four groups of parameters discussed in Chapter 10 (Transfer, Content, Language and Presentation).

If you have several jobs going at once, you must also consider whether they all merit equal attention. Better to devote the available hours to texts which merit more work. There is not much point in spending vast amounts of time on the stylistic editing of a text which is relatively ephemeral. If you do a less than full revision of these texts, you will have more time for a full revision of texts that merit it (those which will be read by many people over a long period of time, or by people outside the organization, or possibly by a few highly placed people who may get an unfavourable impression of the translation service if they find errors).

Here are the choices available to you, expressed in the form of questions:

1. Shall I check for one, two, three or all four groups of parameters?
2. Within each group, shall I examine all parameters or just some of them? Thus within Transfer, you might decide to focus on Completeness; within Language, you might decide to focus on Smoothness.
3. What overall degree of accuracy and writing quality should I aim at?
4. Shall I check the entire text, or just part of it?
5. Shall I compare the translation to the source text?

6. What degree of consistency shall I enforce, and for which aspects of the text?

(On consistency, see Chapter 7.)

Which parameters will be checked?

How will you decide which parameters to check (Questions 1 and 2)? Here are some of the factors, again expressed as questions:

A.   Who will be reading the translation?
With some types of reader, it may be important to pay special attention to Tailoring (see Chapters 4.1 and 10.6): readers who are not experts in the field of the text, those with less than secondary education, immigrants still learning the target language, and readers in other countries who are not native speakers of the target language. If people outside the commissioning organization will be reading the translation (i.e. it's a publication), then all parameters become more important. If the author of the source is likely to read the translation, it may sometimes be necessary to cater to this person by checking that the translation is not only Accurate but also as close as possible to the source in terms of syntactic structure and correspondence of vocabulary items, though obviously there are limits to this.

B.   Why will the translation be read?
If some of the readers are going to make decisions based partly or entirely on the content of the text, then Transfer and Content are more important than Language and Presentation. If the translation will have a readership consisting of a single person, who will use it as a source of information for writing a further document in that field, then it may not be necessary to check Sub-language (terminology); readers who are subject experts will know the right terms, as long as the ideas have been correctly conveyed.

C.   For how long will the translation be read?
If the text will probably still have readers many years hence, then it is worth looking at all four groups of parameters, and being fussy about Consistency. If the text is ephemeral, there is no point in worrying about Presentation.

D.   How will the translation be read?
Will the readers skim through it quickly, or will some of them read very carefully, and possibly re-read? Skimming will be easier if the text is highly readable in the sense of having good inter-sentence connections, and plenty of structural signposts. Careful readers will be disturbed by logical problems that may not be obvious on a quick first reading (a contradiction between two successive sentences; a use of 'therefore' where there is no cause-and-effect). If the text is a manual for consultation (i.e. it will not be read from start to finish), then you

must ensure that each section is understandable on its own, and does not require a knowledge of the preceding sections. If the translation will be read aloud (it's a speech, for example, or repair instructions read aloud by one person to another person who is performing the repair), then Smoothing (including euphony) will be especially important.

E.   Where will the translation be read?
Will it appear in a book? a manual for consultation while doing something else? on a webpage? on signage? The issue here is whether the readers will be sitting in a quiet environment as they read. Or will they be consulting the text in a busy environment with many distractions, perhaps performing some other task as they read, or walking past a translated sign, or reading their smartphone screen as they amble down the street? In these cases, brevity and simplicity of language will be extra important.

F.   Am I familiar with the work of this translator?
If you have looked at the translator's work before, you know the kinds of error they are prone to. If you are self-revising, then you already have considerable knowledge about the kinds of errors that are likely to be present in the draft.

G.   Was the text translated in a hurry?
Generally speaking, the faster one works, the more mistakes one is likely to make. Consequently, if the deadline is very tight, and the translator had to work very quickly, then *more* rather than less quality control is needed.

H.   Will anyone else be quality controlling this translation?
If a proofreader will be looking at your revised translation, then you can ignore house style sheet matters and the Presentation parameters, except for those aspects directly related to meaning (commas to signal sentence structure, bolding for emphasis).

Determining which parameters to check for is a matter of experience and common sense. Theoretically, one could attempt to set up a complicated system based on the above eight questions (A to H) about user and use. Such a system would tell you that if the answer to the first question is such-and-such, and the answer to the second question is such-and-such, and so on through the questions, then quality control should consist of spot-checking for Language and Presentation parameters. However, in the absence of any empirical evidence that a given degree of revision is best suited to a particular answer to the eight questions, such a complicated approach seems pointless.

Knowing the answers to questions A to E amounts to knowing the brief. Before you revise someone else's translation, it is vital that you know at least the answers to questions A and B: who are the readers and why will they be reading?

Here's a chart showing the OECD's policy on which parameters to check.

Parameter→ Text has↓	Accuracy	No additions or subtractions	Grammar	Style	Terminology
High importance	H	H	H	H	H
Medium importance	H	L	H	L	L
Low importance	H	L	L	--	L

As can be seen, the decision about which parameters to check depends primarily on the importance of the text. The letter H means that there is a high requirement to eliminate problems; the letter L means a low requirement; in other words, undiscovered problems related to that parameter can be tolerated. Thus errors in terminology can be tolerated in medium and low importance texts. As for writing style, it receives no attention at all in low importance texts! Problems with accuracy, on the other hand, require careful attention at all levels of importance.

Bear in mind that this policy is being applied to the particular type of text that is translated at the OECD. For example, it seems that the audience of the translation always consists of the same type of individuals as the audience of the source, so tailoring to a different audience is not an issue.

What degree of accuracy and what writing quality is required?

Aside from picking out the parameters of interest (Questions 1 and 2), you need to consider how accurate the translation needs to be and what writing quality is called for (Question 3). Here are four possible levels, though you may want to define your own:

Commissioner's Purpose	Accuracy	Writing quality (readability and clarity)	One-word descriptor
For speedy, basic understanding	Roughly accurate	Minimally readable and clear	Intelligible
For information	Fully accurate	Fairly readable and clear	Informative
For publication	Fully accurate	Very readable and clear	Publishable
For image	Fully accurate	Finely crafted wording and very clear	Polished

The third column covers two aspects of writing quality: readability (the smooth-ness of the reading experience and the degree of tailoring to readers) and clarity (the logic of the sequence of ideas). The table does not apply to adaptations such as marketing materials, where a high degree of writing quality may be required, but correspondence to the source text is not a consideration. The table also does not distinguish degrees of accuracy beyond 'roughly' versus 'fully' accu-rate. Legal texts typically require accuracy down to very small details, whereas other texts often require accuracy only with respect to primary and secondary elements of meaning. In addition, decisions of high courts may deserve finely crafted wording.

So to be really complete, one might add two rows to the table:

For court use	Accurate down to very small details	Very readable and clear *or* Finely crafted word-ing and very clear	
For marketing	Accuracy not an issue	Finely crafted wording and very clear	

Let's look in more detail at the first four degrees of writing quality.

Intelligible

Depending on the user and the use of the translation, you may be aiming for a revised translation which is merely intelligible, that is, it has a bare minimum of readability and clarity, and is roughly accurate (it will not seriously mislead the reader about central aspects of the message of the source text). There may be question marks in the final product indicating passages where meaning remains uncertain because you decided that additional research was not worthwhile. At this level, there is no point applying house style rules, worrying about Pre-sentation, correcting unidiomatic expressions, or creating even text-internal consistency, never mind consistency with other texts.

Post-editing of machine translation output may aim at this level (see Chapter 14.4). In some situations, it may also be the level expected of translators working into their second language. For example, if a salaried translator has been hired to translate mostly from language X into his or her mother tongue, but must occasionally translate in-house texts into language X, the key criterion may be intelligibility. With these texts, no one will be comparing the translation with the source; unidiomatic expressions and even certain kinds of ungrammatical expression may be acceptable, and accuracy may only be needed with respect to primary aspects of meaning (the central message).

Informative

At this level, the final product avoids misleading the reader about primary or secondary aspects of the message of the source text, but it need not be more than fairly readable and fairly clear. This might be acceptable, for example, when the first draft of a document is being translated; there is no point in creating a nice smoothed version of a sentence which may later be deleted or completely altered. Again, do not apply house style rules or spend much time on Consistency or Presentation.

Publishable
The final translation is fully accurate, clear, well tailored and smoothed. House style rules are applied, Presentation is checked and corrected, and a reasonable level of text-internal Consistency (and perhaps some degree of consistency with other texts) is sought.

A clarification about 'publication' is in order. A 'publication' is to be understood as a document which will be available to an audience outside the organization which commissioned it. As the term suggests, it's a document for the 'public', or some segment of it. To put it another way, there is no such thing as an 'internal publication'. An organization may well publish full-colour documents on expensive paper that are distributed only in-house, but this glossiness does not turn such documents into 'publications' as understood here.

Polished
At this level, the reading experience is in itself interesting and enjoyable, quite apart from the content. Creating such a finely crafted text can be *extremely* time consuming even if you are not aiming at that ultimate level of craftsmanship where you become the new Flaubert, re-writing a dozen times until each sentence is *just perfect*.

You will also be aiming for this level if you are self-employed and your pricing strategy is to charge a high price and become known for exceptional writing quality, for example in commercial translation.

To clarify the concept of levels, here's an example from a translation of an in-house newsletter that discusses a company's response to public complaints about a possible removal of trees from their property:

> The firm does not intend to remove the lime trees but it is necessary to carry out pruning of the trees to keep them healthy

Does this need to be revised? Perhaps you could change it to:

> The firm does not intend to remove the lime trees, but to keep them healthy, they will need to be pruned.

This is certainly a better quality of writing, in particular because it places the key word 'pruned' in focus position at the end. But there is no need for the change, because the translation will not be published; a 'fairly readable' translation will do. There is a tendency for revisers to enter an abstract mental space in which they are always aiming at the 'publishable', or worse, the 'polished' level, when this is not at all necessary.

Most revisers will mainly find themselves working at the 'informative' and 'publishable' levels, but it can be useful to have the other two levels in mind to help you keep your bearings. If you are aiming at 'publishable', you need to have in mind that you are not aiming at 'polished'. If you are aiming at 'informative', you need to have in mind that you are not aiming at 'publishable'. 'Informative' is perhaps the hardest level to revise for, because you need to refrain from making a great many improvements that occur to you. To help you refrain, it may be useful to have the 'intelligible' level in mind: while you are indeed not making sentences smoother or more concise, you are certainly not sinking to the merely 'intelligible' level!

As 'language people', translators may find it hard to refrain from improving writing quality. You see that that a sentence is wordier than it needs to be; the idea could be expressed in 13 words instead of 20. But will you stop to ask whether any useful purpose is being served by making the sentence more concise? It's important to bear in mind that the people who read our translations, especially those who are subject-matter experts, are interested in the world, not in words. If an agronomist is reviewing the literature to see what work has previously been done on wheat yields, and finds something in a language she cannot read, she may ask you for a translation. You must keep in mind that she is interested in crops, not in language. It probably does not matter to her whether the sentence you are revising has 20 words or 13.

There may be a problem justifying less-than-publishable quality if clients are paying a set rate per textual unit, whether it be the word, the character, the line or the page. Why would someone pay a certain amount for 'informative' quality when 'publishable' quality costs the same? Ideally, a client who submits large numbers of texts for translation could be persuaded, at a given price level, to accept 'informative' quality for certain pre-determined text types. However a 'levels' approach is most easily justified with in-house translation departments where clients do not pay, or when billing is by the hour, since generally it will take less time to achieve 'informative' than 'publishable'.

Full or partial check?

Will you read the entire text or just parts of it? Rasmussen and Schjoldager (2011) found in interviews with revisers that although a company's policy may be to always compare source and target, the revisers do not necessarily perform a comparison for the entire text. Similarly, the revision manual of the Spanish department at the European Commission's translation service (EC 2010) says that "In principle, the whole text must be revised, but in certain circumstances (e.g. if the translator is an expert in the subject) partial revision may do". The Canadian Government's translation service used to have a policy of checking one, two or three 400-word segments of outsourced work (depending on the length of the text); if these were satisfactory, no further checking was done. Now it is up to the reviser to decide how much of the text to check, unless the client is paying extra for full revision. Here are some of the possibilities:

A.   Full reading
Read the translation in full. If you are checking for Accuracy and Complete-

ness, compare each sentence to the original text. Otherwise do a unilingual re-reading, that is, refer to the source text only when a passage is questionable (you suspect a Transfer problem, or you have found a Logic error and you need to see what the source says). When self-revising, you should always do at least a full unilingual reading

B. Spot-check
Read the title or the cover page and the first paragraph, then read either at regular intervals (e.g. the first paragraph on every other page) or randomly selected paragraphs or pages spread over the entire text. Compare the selected passages to the original, or just refer to the original when a passage is questionable.

C. Scan
Read the title or the cover page and the first paragraph, then read by 'following your finger' across each page, focusing on just one or two parameters. Refer to the original when a passage is questionable.

D. Glance
Read the title or the cover page, and the first paragraph.

Reading the title and first paragraph is a bare minimum. Why? Because if there are any typographical errors or missing words at the very start of the text, that will immediately create a bad impression on the reader or client.

When a text was translated in a hurry, and the translator did not have much time for self-revision, there may well be more errors toward the end of the text. So spot-checking might be focused on the last quarter of the text.

The choice of scanning or spot-checking is only a starting point. If you are using one of these methods and discover several language errors, or several cases where a check with the original reveals mistranslation, then you will want to revert to method A, or even return the job to the translator for further self-revision.

If time permits, it is a good idea to scan the text for accurate reproduction of numbers in any text where numbers are important to the message. Scanning can also be used to look for those errors that you know are common in translations from language X into language Y. For example, when I am scanning an English translation from French, I keep a lookout for the expression 'by (verb)ing', because very often the formally similar French expression 'en (verb)ant' does *not* indicate 'how' something was done (the manner or the means used). 'He gave a speech during the opening conference at the university, by presenting the historical context' is nonsensical: presenting historical context was not the manner or means of giving the speech. Either the 'by' should be deleted or it should be replaced by 'in which (he presented)'.

Compare or re-read?

Unilingual re-reading (i.e. not looking at the source text unless a passage seems suspicious) can be very effective. At workshops, participants who have never tried it are often surprised at how many errors can be detected in this way. In particular, one can get quite good not only at spotting probable mistranslations in the draft but also at avoiding the introduction of mistranslations while correcting. You may at first worry, while making a change, that you have departed from the meaning of the source. However if you regularly check the source to avoid this, and keep track of your findings, in all likelihood you will discover after a while that almost all your changes are consistent with the source. You will develop a sixth sense about when you really do need to check the source.

That said, it is true that with unilingual re-reading, you may miss omissions and mistranslations. The text may read smoothly even though a sentence or paragraph has been omitted, and it may make perfect sense – but not be at all what the source-text author intended.

If you keep discovering mistranslations when you check the source during unilingual re-reading, then you will of course switch to comparative re-reading. However while comparative re-reading does no doubt increase the number of mistranslations and omissions that will be caught, it has its own disadvantages. The back-and-forth between source text and translation creates an unnatural reading process which may make it difficult to properly monitor readability and clarity. Comparative reading tends to focus attention at the sentence and sub-sentence level, so that errors in 'macro' features of meaning or grammar (e.g. pronouns referring to a previous sentence, the logic of an argument) may not be noticed. Consider the following translation about the problems which ship crew members may have when they are under stress because they are trying to get passengers into lifeboats in an emergency:

Negative effects of stress

– Lack of concentration
– Recourse to improvisation at the expense of established procedure
– Focused attention
– Alternative solutions ignored
– Inability to solve complex problems
– Inflexibility

If you are doing a unilingual re-reading, and paying attention to meaning, it will be fairly easy to notice that 'focused attention' does not fit because it is not 'negative'. However during comparative re-reading, you will probably compare each item in the list with its source-text counterpart. If the source text contains the same error, you will likely accept it as a good translation of the source, and not notice its lack of fit with the other items in the list. (Perhaps the intention was 'overly focused attention', that is, not seeing the forest for the trees.)

Appendix 4 contains a sample unilingual re-reading with commentary.

11.3   Some consequences of less-than-full revision

Levels of risk

Obviously, any quality control system which allows for less than full revision contains a risk of letting errors pass uncorrected. Your system may assume that if there are no errors on pages 1, 5, 10, 15 and 20, then there are no errors elsewhere. Of course, this is just a probability; in reality, there could be a serious error. The translator's attention may have lapsed on page 13, with the result that a whole paragraph was omitted. Furthermore, this can happen to anyone; even an experienced translator working on an easy text of a familiar type can make such mistakes. To err is human.

It is true that if the translator is experienced and working under the best possible conditions, the likelihood of error is reduced. But ultimately, the only way to be sure that the whole of a translation is good is to give it a full re-reading.

Both forms of full re-reading (comparative and unilingual) have their attendant risks, as discussed in the previous section. So if you are doing anything less than a full comparative plus a full unilingual re-reading, you will need to define an *acceptable level of risk*. This may be done on economic grounds: are clients coming back or going elsewhere? Or it may be done on professional grounds: what will the impact of an error be on the translation's user? The worse the potential impact, the higher the degree of quality control you should apply. An error in a document that will be used as evidence in court is more likely to have negative consequences than an error in the minutes of a routine meeting. An error in a document that will be used by many people over a long period of time is more likely to have negative consequences than a document used only once by a single person.

Generally speaking, unilingual re-reading can be justified as a time-saver unless the longer comparative procedure is dictated by a combination of serious consequences and a greater likelihood of mistranslation or omission being present (the text was a difficult one, the translator's ability is unknown, the text was translated very quickly).

Types of error sought during partial revision and unilingual re-reading

In addition to the problem of errors in passages that are not checked, there is the problem of the type of errors found in passages that *are* checked. There is a great temptation, when doing partial revision, to devote one's time to looking for relatively superficial, easy-to-spot errors. How satisfying to have found another case where the translator left a space between the last letter of a sentence and the period! But just how important a find was this? Perhaps it would have been better to notice the mistranslation in that sentence.

The same danger arises with unilingual re-reading. It can easily degenerate into proofreading, in the sense of a hunt for errors in Mechanics and Presentation: typos, wrong indentations, grammar mistakes and the like. *Re-reading means reading for meaning* first and foremost, and secondly for writing quality. Does the argument, description or narrative make sense and is it easy to follow and suited to its intended readers?

What is the psychology behind the tendency to look for proofreading errors?

Perhaps unconsciously one is thinking: "I've been assigned to find mistakes, so I must find some. I'm not earning my pay if I just leave the text the way it is. But there's not a lot of time available, so I'll look for things that are easy to spot."

If you do spend most of your time searching for errors in Presentation and Mechanics, then you are definitely *not* earning your pay. This is work that can be done by a copyeditor or proofreader, whose time is probably much less expensive than yours. Your services are required only if the quality control includes at least one of: Accuracy, Completeness, Logic, Smoothness, Tailoring, Sub-language or Idiom. In some circumstances (if you are a freelance working alone), you will have to check Mechanics and Presentation because there is no one else to do so, but if you are combining this with unilingual revision, make sure you are still reading for meaning. Ideally (if you have time), you will proofread in a separate step.

Research during revision

How much term and concept research will you do while revising the work of others? If you are training a newly hired translator, or checking the first text submitted by a contractor, then unless you are fully familiar with the field, you may need to repeat much of the translator's research in order to check that it is being properly done. In other cases, you should strive to minimize research. For example, junior translators could be asked to indicate their sources; experienced translators could be asked to put a checkmark beside any passage where they believe you might have doubts, to indicate that the translation, despite appearances, is correct.

11.4 The relative importance of transfer and language parameters

This chapter has been concerned with how the features of a particular translation job determine the appropriate degree of revision. However there is a factor that goes beyond the particular text at hand. Revision is traditionally thought of as being concerned with two things: accurate transfer and good writing in the target language. Or to put it negatively, the elimination of mistranslation and of unidiomatic or incorrect language. Now, the relative importance of these may vary not just with the particular text but with the general social-historical situation in which translation is being done. For example, there have been times in history when accuracy was not deemed especially important; what was important was to create a beautifully written text in the target language.

The situation in Canada is interesting in that while accuracy is important whether one is translating from English to French or in the opposite direction, things are different when it comes to the importance of the language parameters. This is partly a matter of different attitudes toward language in the French- and English-speaking worlds. In English, we have long accepted a more relaxed (some would say sloppy) approach in non-literary writing, where language is seen as a means to an end, not something important in itself. In the French-speaking world, language has been valued more for itself (some would say it has been excessively and obsessively fussed over), though this is now changing as U.S. cultural norms become ever more influential.

In Quebec, however, there is an additional factor at work. To simplify somewhat, revision in Quebec has traditionally been first and foremost concerned with the quality of French. This is partly because such a large percentage of what Quebeckers read has been translation rather than original French, so that the quality of language in translations has a significant effect on the quality of language in Quebec society generally. In addition, the writing of Francophones (including junior translators) has often been laden with anglicisms to an extent unknown in Europe – and this has met with strong disapproval by French-speaking members of the translation profession. Defence of the quality of French has therefore been the central concern of revisers with all texts, not just the more important ones.

The situation in English-speaking Canada is completely different. Only a very small percentage of what people read is translation, and (with the exception of the small English minority in Quebec) people's speech and writing are hardly influenced at all by French. So revisers of French-to-English translations need only be concerned with eliminating those linguistic features that arise from the influence of the source text. They can focus on Accuracy, on Language, or on both, as the brief dictates.

You would do well to consider the relative importance of the language parameters in the social/historical context within which your readers will be receiving the product of your revision efforts.

11.5 A "good enough" approach to revision

During workshops on revision, a few people always express shock at the idea of 'degrees' of revision and varying quality targets. Their goal, they proclaim, is excellence or even perfection. The first thing to say about such proclamations is that if most of the translations produced in the world were 'good enough' for their purpose, that would represent an enormous improvement on the current situation. Making 'fit-for-purpose' a reality is a difficult enough goal without aiming for the best possible translation every time. Second, a distinction needs to be made between self-revision and other-revision. If some translators want to make excellence their personal goal with their own translations, that's fine, but when they are revising others, they should take the goals of the first translator (or the first translator's employer or the commissioner) as given. If the first translator was aiming to create a translation that is fit-for-purpose, then the reviser must accept this.

Practice

1. If you currently use varying degrees of revision, try to formulate the factors you consider.

2. Scenario. You find that the translation you are revising (the introduction to a manual used by workers in a repair shop) contains this wording:

> follow the manufacturer's recommendations (General Motors) closely

In the source language, the structure was '...recommendations of the manufacturer...' so that 'manufacturer' was right next to 'General Motors', but the translator chose the above structure. Now, will you stop or not stop to make this read more smoothly:

> follow the recommendations of the manufacturer (General Motors) closely

or more smoothly still:

> closely follow the recommendations of the manufacturer (General Motors)

What factors will determine your decision? Suppose the text is a very long one, and you keep coming across such awkward wordings in your draft. If you decided to make a change the first time, will you continue to do so?

3. Suppose that Google informs you that the expression 'black, dense smoke' occurs 60,700 times, while 'dense, black smoke' occurs 2,060,000 times on the portion of the Web which Google searches. If you encounter the former in the translation you are revising, will you change it to the latter? Why? Will you be more likely to make a change if English is not your first language?

4. Exercise on revising to different levels. Take the draft translation given you by your instructor and make it 'informative'. Thus you will consciously ignore awkward wordings for example, or wordings that are not very concise. Stop for discussion. Then continue revising to make the text 'publishable' (but not 'polished').

Further reading

(See the References list near the end of the book for details on these publications.)

Quality in relation to purpose: Samuelsson-Brown (1996 and 2010 ch. 8.2); Wagner (2005).
Revision policies: Bertaccini and Di Nisio (2011); Prioux and Rochard (2007); Rasmussen and Schjoldager (2011); United Nations (2003), Annex 6.
Types of revision: Matis (2011).

12.   Revision Procedure

Almost all discussion of revision tends to focus on the types of error the reviser should look for – the parameters of Chapter 10. But that is not enough. You need to know not only *what* to look for, but *how* to look for it. To state the obvious, *you cannot correct a mistake until you have found it*. It is all very well to know that the translation should have a level of language suited to the readers. The question is: will you *notice* that a particular phrase has an unsuitable level of language? You need to have a procedure that increases the likelihood that you will find the errors in a translation. And when you arrive at a passage that you think perhaps requires correction or improvement, you also need some *principles* to help you decide whether in fact to make a change.

Noticing problems in a translation is the most difficult aspect of revision. Revisers frequently overlook clear-cut problems. Why is that? Two possible reasons are that they are working too fast and that they are not paying the right kind of *attention* to the text. The reviser's mind may be focused (perhaps to some degree unconsciously) on language and style problems, and the result is that transfer problems are not noticed, or vice versa. In addition, the reviser may be attending to micro-problems such as an error in number agreement and not notice macro-problems. So in this sentence:

> Customers are reminded that the sale of tobacco products are limited to those 18 years of age and younger.

you might notice the error in number agreement (*sale...are*) but not notice that the sentence says the opposite of what is intended. Or, depending on your focus of attention, you might notice the meaning problem but not the grammatical one (the plural verb *are* is right next to the plural noun *products,* so the error might escape your notice, especially if you are reading quickly).

12.1   Procedure for finding errors

We'll assume that if you are revising someone else's work rather than self-revising, you have already determined who the users of the translation will be and what use they will be putting it to, and you have made yourself aware of any special instructions the client may have given (about terminology, about layout etc). We'll also assume that you have selected a degree of revision; that is, you've answered the following two questions:

- Am I going to check the entire text, or just parts of it?
- Am I going to check only Content, Language and Presentation (henceforth CLP) parameters, or am I going to check Transfer parameters as well?

Suppose you have decided to check Transfer parameters (Accuracy and Completeness) as well as CLP parameters. In other words, you are going to make a comparative check, not just a unilingual check of the translation itself. The question then arises: in what order are you going to check the parameters? More specifically, you need to ask the following questions:

- Shall I check the CLP parameters at the same time as I make the comparative check, or shall I make two separate checks?
- If I make separate checks, shall I make the comparative check first, or the CLP check first?
- If I make separate checks, shall I do the entire text at once (for example, read the entire text for CLP, then for Transfer) or shall I work a paragraph or two at a time, or a section at a time (for example, read a couple of paragraphs for Transfer, then read them for CLP, then move on to the next few paragraphs)?
- Shall I read the source text first or the translation first during comparative checking?
- How many words should I read at one go during comparative checking?

These five questions will be considered in the sections that follow.

One check or two?

If you have enough time, you may find it best to perform separate checks for Transfer and for CLP. The reason is that detecting one type of error can get in the way of detecting the other type. For example, you are less likely to spot a lack of Smoothness in the transition from one sentence to the next if you are comparing sentences one at a time against the source text. You are also less likely to notice that a sentence in your translation is unidiomatic if you have just read the source text: the wording of the source text may get in the way of your target-language judgments. If you do have time for only a single check, this latter problem can be avoided by reading each sentence of the translation *before* you read the corresponding source sentence.

Unfortunately, even if you do two separate checks, you may still encounter a difficulty we'll call the micro/macro dilemma. Some errors manifest themselves in a single word or phrase. Is this term right? Is this word combination idiomatic? Other errors manifest themselves over larger stretches of text. Is the sequence of tenses right? Are the inter-paragraph connections clear? Are the headings consistently formatted? You may find it hard to focus on problems of the former kind (micro-problems) at the same time as you check for problems of the latter kind (macro-problems).

The micro/macro dilemma mainly affects the unilingual check, where you are reading the translation without comparing it to the source. (Comparative re-reading by its nature tends to have a micro-level focus.) Take the example of Logic. A contradiction may not come to your attention unless you are reading the text through with a specific focus on the flow of the argument or narrative. If you are also looking for micro-problems of Language and Presentation as you read along (e.g. Mechanics), your attention may be distracted from a contradiction in the thoughts being expressed.

If you have time, you could do two unilingual checks, first looking for macro-problems, and then for micro-problems. Even then, you may not be able to attend to all macro-problems at once. Consider consistency of Layout. If you are focused on Logic, will you spot the fact that, starting at the top of page 20, paragraphs are no longer indented? (Perhaps the translator started page 20 one morning and forgot that the previous day they had been indenting.) This argument suggests yet a further separate check, but of course that will most often be impractical. With practice (and depending on your own psychology) you may be able to attend to several types of macro-problem at once, or, hopefully, both macro- and micro-problems at once. One possible way of helping yourself focus on microlinguistic problems, without getting distracted by the overall message of the text, is to read the text backward, beginning at the last sentence.

It is perhaps worth bearing in mind that there is as yet no empirical confirmation that doing two or more checks yields a better result than a single check. Many translators are sure that it does, and it would certainly seem that it should, but the whole point of empirical testing (see Appendix 6) is precisely to determine whether what seems obvious is in fact true. Robert (2012) found that the final quality resulting from comparative re-reading was higher than with unilingual re-reading, but she also found that doing two re-readings, one of each type, failed to make a further significant improvement. Presumably many of the errors that would have been corrected during a single, unilingual re-reading were corrected during comparative re-reading. (This by the way suggests that anyone who wishes to focus separately on accuracy and on language and style, and to that end decides to do two re-readings, should do the unilingual re-reading first. If the comparative re-reading is done first, there will be a tendency to make language and style changes as soon as they are noticed.)

Comparative check first or last?

To answer this question, there are three considerations, which unfortunately may not all lead to the same conclusion.

First, all other things being equal, you should read the translation alone first, without comparing it to the source text. This is especially so when you are revising someone else's work, because you have a golden opportunity to see the translation from the user's point of view. You are not burdened by prior knowledge of what the text is supposed to be saying – knowledge which the translator possessed from reading the source text. Your knowledge of the message is coming from the translation alone.

A second consideration is the problem (discussed in greater detail later in this chapter) of introducing errors while revising. Suppose you do the CLP check first, and then the Transfer check, but during the Transfer check you introduce

Language errors. There is no further check that would enable you to find these new errors. So it may be worth determining which type of error you are more prone to introducing – language errors or mistranslations. If you are more prone to introducing language errors during the Transfer check, then check for language errors last. If you are more prone to introducing mistranslations during the Language check, check Transfer last. Determining which type of error you tend to introduce is unfortunately not easy. In the course of revising a half dozen texts, you will have to save a copy of the text after you complete the first check, then save a copy after the other check, then compare the two using the Compare function of your word processor (see Chapter 8.4). Ideally, you will discover that you don't introduce errors, but it is a good idea to be sure that this is indeed the case.

The third consideration is related to the second. Quite apart from your own error-introducing tendencies, there is the question of whether the job is one in which language and style are especially important. If they are, you may want to do the CLP check second, to ensure you catch any Language errors that you introduced during the Transfer check. Of course this runs counter to the first consideration mentioned above: you will not be reading the translation the way the user will, without benefit of prior knowledge of the source text.

Read the whole text or work a few paragraphs at a time?

Once again, if you want to try to duplicate the final user's experience, you will start by reading through the entire translation from start to finish. If you come to an odd passage, where you wonder what the source text says, make some kind of mark and come back to it later during the comparative check. If you keep interrupting your reading to make a comparative check, you may lose track of macro-features such as the flow of the argument. Your attention to flow is going to be interrupted enough as it is whenever you stop to make a correction.

Read source text first or last during comparative checking?

Let's take special note of an issue that was mentioned briefly earlier in this chapter, namely the order of reading during comparative checking: translation first or source text first? Here, happily, all the considerations point in one direction. Read a sentence of the translation first, then the corresponding sentence in the source text. Reading the source text first has several disadvantages:

- If you are checking Language at the same time as you check Transfer, your reading of the source text may influence your judgment about the language quality of the translation. In particular you may fail to notice that the translation is unidiomatic.
- Reading the source first may make you think of your own translation – the last thing you want to have in your head when revising someone else. You should never compare the translation in front of you with your

own mental translation.

- Your reading of the source text will put in your mind the meaning which the translation is supposed to have. When you come to read the translation, you may project this meaning onto the translation. You may not see that the translation does not in fact have this meaning. This is particularly a problem if the target-language sentence happens to be ambiguous: it has two possible interpretations. Reading the source sentence first may have the effect of cueing in your mind the interpretation which corresponds to the source, whereas the reader of the translation may take the other interpretation.
- You will not see the text from the user's point of view (the user will not be reading the source text first!)

If you are self-revising, and you want to avoid the last two of these disadvantages, it is a good idea to leave the longest possible time between completing your draft and starting your revision. Unfortunately this is very often not practical: because of the deadline, you may have to start your self-revision as soon as you have completed the draft translation.

It should be pointed out that there is only a single empirical study (Künzli 2009) which looks at this question of reading order, among other matters, and the result was inconclusive: reading the translation first made a difference with one of the texts under study but not with the other two. In the absence of empirical grounding, we must rely on logic, deducing a recommended procedure from a hypothesis (in this case, the hypothesis that reading the source first will make it more difficult to make an independent judgment of the translation).

Size of unit to read during comparative checking

The answer to this question partly depends on individual psychology. How big a unit of text in one language can you keep in mind while you read the text in the other language? One general principle does seem valid: avoid reading a *very* small unit in one language and then turning to the text in the other language. Such a practice will not give you enough context, and it will increase the likelihood of your overlooking bad literal translations. Consider this sentence:

> Given the concentration required by translation, and the numerous details a translator must deal with, often within more or less reasonable deadlines, one cannot expect a perfect translation.

If you read the whole sentence paying attention to meaning, you can immediately see that something is wrong: 'more or less reasonable' means 'fairly reasonable' and this doesn't fit. Given our knowledge of the topic, we expect to read 'often within unreasonable deadlines'. Now if you were reading this sentence phrase by phrase, and you compared 'often within more or less reasonable deadlines' to the French source text ('souvent dans des délais plus ou moins raisonnables'), you might not detect any problem. The match seems perfect: at the word level, 'plus ou moins' equals 'more or less'. However, French 'plus ou moins raisonnable' means 'not so reasonable', emphasizing the negative, whereas English 'more or less reasonable' emphasizes the positive. If you are lucky, a warning bell goes off in your mind every time you come across 'more or less' in a translation from French, but a surer way to avoid disaster in such a case is to avoid reading small chunks of sentences.

12.2   Principles for correcting and improving

Having looked at procedures for finding errors, let us now look at some principles for making changes as you check. It is important to keep checking and correcting (or improving) distinct in your mind. Revising is checking a translation and *possibly* making changes. You may identify a passage as a candidate for a possible change, but then decide not to actually make any change. For example, you see that a sentence is somewhat awkwardly structured, or not as concise as it could be, but you decide not to do anything about this.

It is best to use a three-step process: 1) spot a potential problem; 2) decide whether a change is merited; 3) make a change if you deem it necessary. Step 2 is the crucial step.

The first two correcting/improving principles we'll look at concern cases where you absolutely must make a change. The remaining four tend in the opposite direction; they are variants on a single principle: Minimize corrections.

1. If you cannot understand the translation without consulting the source text, a correction is definitely necessary.

2. If you have to read a sentence twice to understand it correctly, a correction is needed. For example, if you need to read a sentence twice to see how it relates to what precedes, that means there is a problem of Smoothness. Or again, if a passage sounds nonsensical on first reading, but then you realize that the translator's wording could make sense after all, there is nevertheless a problem of Logic, for the future reader may at first make the same 'mistake' you did.

   This principle does not apply to certain texts which are by nature difficult to read: the extremely long sentences of English legal texts are very often hard to read; some passages in a scientific text may have a very complex argument which you may find hard to follow.

   Try as much as possible to read at normal reading speed in order to capture the future reader's experience. If the future reader will be reading aloud, then read the text aloud yourself.

3. Avoid perfectionism.
   As you go through the text, avoid asking yourself: *Can* I improve this? Of course you can, but that's not the question. The question is: Do I *need*

to improve it? Your aim is not to achieve a flawless text. Your client or employer cannot afford to have you revise, re-revise and re-re-revise. And there are diminishing returns on revision effort: your fifth re-reading will take almost as long as your first, but will probably reveal few if any errors. What you can do is guarantee that you will correct, free of charge, any mistakes the client finds. Your goal as a professional is to achieve acceptability – a text that meets needs. Perfection is a personal goal, not a business goal.

Achieving adequacy is no mean feat. Because there are so many things that can go wrong, and it is so hard to attend to all aspects of a text, it is in fact quite difficult to get everything adequate, and to do so from first page to last. This last point is very important. What is the use of a brilliant translation of the first three pages of a text if the last three are riddled with errors because you ran out of time?

So do not even *think* about an alternative wording until *after* you have decided that improvement is needed. And once you do so decide, use the first adequate alternative wording that comes to mind. Do not try to generate several useable alternatives and choose among them.

If in doubt about whether to make a change, don't agonize. Make no change and move on. Unless new research, or newly discovered evidence from elsewhere in the text, has revealed a definite error, any change you make while you are in an uncertain state of mind about its necessity is just as likely to make your translation worse as it is to make it better.

Remember: there are not just two degrees of quality – excellent and dreadful. There are many degrees of acceptable quality; it depends on the brief.

4. Don't retranslate! Don't retranslate! Don't retranslate!
   Whenever possible, make small changes in the existing translation. Work with the wording that is already there. Don't restart the drafting process by working from the source text and inventing a whole new translation of a sentence. If a whole new translation does pop unbidden into your mind, ignore it, no matter how absolutely fabulous it may be. There is no reason to consider this new translation at all if the existing translation is acceptable as is, or with a small change.

   Write 'do not retranslate' on a piece of paper and post it in front of you; recite it 100 times before going to bed; play a quiet recording of it while you sleep so that the idea enters your subconscious. A reviser who constantly retranslates is an economic burden on the organization and a cause of low morale among the translators whose work is being wasted.

   There are of course occasions when, unfortunately, there is no choice but to retranslate some or even many passages of the text. First, the translator may simply be unqualified; the job should never have been assigned to them. Second, the translator was wrongly informed about the level of quality required (as discussed in Chapter 11.2): they were working to the "informative" level but should have been working to the "publishable" level. (The opposite case is far more common though: the translator was rightly working to the "informative" level, but you – perhaps not entirely consciously – are thinking of "publishable" as you revise.)

If you are working from your first language into your second, you may find it much easier to re-translate a sentence than to work with the existing wording. If you are self-revising into your second language, and come across a sentence you have doubts about, the quickest procedure may be to mentally paraphrase the corresponding sentence in the source text (which should be easy for you as a native speaker of the source language) and then prepare a whole new translation based on that re-wording.

5. Beware of introducing errors.
    In the course of making changes to achieve Accuracy or Completeness, you may introduce Language errors. Conversely, as you make corrections pertaining to the Language parameters, you may introduce Transfer errors. In addition, one Language change may call for other Language changes elsewhere in the sentence, or in a preceding or following sentence, and it is easy to forget to make these additional changes.

    Introducing Accuracy errors: As you re-arrange a sentence to achieve Smoothness, you may unwittingly remove an important bit of content, or unwittingly change the meaning (see example in Chapter 4.5). If at that point you have not yet done the comparative check for Accuracy and Completeness, there is no problem. But if you have already finished the comparative check, then you have done the worst thing a reviser can do: you have made the translation worse. If you discover that you do tend to introduce mistranslations, you may want to recheck Accuracy right after you re-arrange a sentence, or always do your Accuracy check last.

    Introducing Language errors: Language errors tend to be introduced when you are focusing on one small segment of a sentence and you are not attending to the surrounding text. A very common error in English is to change a singular noun to a plural (or vice versa) and then forget to make corresponding number changes in words like 'this' and 'it' (which may be in the next sentence, referring back to the noun you have changed). Another type of error that results from parcelizing your attention is lack of euphony: you change 'took place' to 'occurred' in 'the exodus of Iraqi Kurds took place last week', and you fail to notice the uneuphonious and unintentionally humorous result 'Kurds occurred'.

    You may also introduce a Language problem while correcting for Accuracy. For example you change 'implemented environmental management systems' to 'instituted environmental management systems'. Unfortunately, the sentence as a whole then reads '...instituted environmental management systems within penal institutions', with two occurrences of the root 'institut-' that have very different meanings. If you find you are making such mistakes, the solution is simple. After making a change, re-read the whole sentence, and possibly the next and previous sentences.

Deleting too many or too few words while correcting: With the advent of electronic writing in the 1980s, missing words became more common because it is so easy to press the key combination that deletes words once too often when you are removing a part of a sentence. Conversely, you may not press the delete keys often enough. Again, the solution is to re-read sentences after you delete portions of them.

6. Minimize corrections of features you are not currently checking.
   Suppose you are doing several checks, and currently you are check-ing Accuracy. You spot a Language problem and decide to correct it, thinking perhaps that you may not notice it later, during your unilingual check. Making such a change is harmless provided that you do not then get diverted by other Language problems, to the point where you find yourself tailoring and smoothing the sentence in question. This defeats the point of separate checks. Some people have no problem shifting mentally back and forth from accuracy-checking to language-checking, but others will find that they miss errors if they keep shifting the focus of their attention.

12.3   Order of operations

Below is an ideal but lengthy order of operations, for use when making correc-tions directly on screen rather than on paper (see Chapter 8.3). Such a procedure would be suitable with texts that will be used for many years, or for making important decisions. If you are self-revising rather than revising someone else's work, you may already have made some of these checks while drafting (see Chapter 13.1). If so, then you need to decide whether to recheck. It is also a good idea when self-revising to do an initial Spellcheck to remove annoying ty-pographical errors. You don't want to be distracted by the temptation to correct these manually as you move through the text. (But don't forget to do another Spellcheck when you have completed all your revision work, in order to catch errors you introduced while revising!)

1. Read the entire translation for Logic, Smoothness, Tailoring, Sub-language and Idiomaticity, as well as those aspects of typography and punctuation which are important for meaning.
2. Do a comparative check for Accuracy and Completeness. If the client wants the translation to follow the Layout of the source text, check this at the same time.
3. Read the entire translation from start to finish for Mechanics (other than

spelling), Layout, consistency, and any Language errors introduced during steps 1 and 2.

4. Do a separate check for numbers if they are important to the message.
5. Check the document's Organization.
6. Run Spellcheck after all changes have been made in case you have introduced any errors.
7. Press Control-S to make sure you have saved all your changes.

Never forget step 7, which is important in *any* revision procedure, however brief. Before you print out a copy of the text, or send it off by e-mail to your client or to the translator, you must be sure that you are indeed printing or e-mailing the *final* version of your revision, *with all corrections included*. If you print from screen, you will be fine, but if you print or e-mail from the list of files on your hard drive, you will be printing or e-mailing the last version that you saved. The best practice is to save frequently. You may have set your computer to make a timed backup every so often, but if you don't actually press Control-S, then your final version, with all corrections included, will be in the backup file, not the main file.

Now very often (indeed, perhaps almost always, depending on your own situation), it will not be practical to carry out the lengthy procedure described above. Here is a selection of shorter procedures, beginning with the briefest:

A. Check the Presentation parameters. Also count paragraphs and lists of points to ensure there are no gross omissions. You may also want to pay special attention to correct reproduction of proper names, dates and other figures. With this procedure, you are essentially functioning as a proofreader.

B. Do a single reading of the translation for the CLP parameters. Look at the source text only if this is necessary to clear up a Logic problem.

C. Do a single comparative check. Don't stop for style changes (problems in Smoothing, Tailoring and Sub-language); correct only gross language errors if found, and run Spellcheck. Don't use this procedure if working into your second language; you have more need than native speakers to do a reading for Language only, so use (B) or (D).

D. Do two read-throughs – one unilingual and one comparative – in whichever order you think best.

12.4   Handling unsolved problems

Let's now consider the question: what do I do if the deadline is approaching, there is no time for further research, the author cannot be reached (or is simply unknown), and I have been unable to solve a problem? If creating the final version for delivery to the client is your job (not the original translator's), then it is your duty as a professional to admit that you have failed to find a solution. A professional is not someone who knows all the answers; a professional is some-one who knows how to go about finding answers, but if they fail, they admit it.

Ask the client how the problems should be signalled: translator's notes in-corporated into the body of the text? translator's footnotes? a separate page of notes? translator's notes in Comment boxes? question-marks or highlighting incorporated into the text? If the client will do more work on the text before it goes to a printer or to readers, then highlighting or Comments or a separate page of notes will often be acceptable. Similarly, if the text is being translated for information only (it will not be published), the client may be quite happy to have question-marks indicating uncertain passages. Otherwise you will need to prepare a finished version with translator's notes.

One difficulty with incorporating question-marks is that they may be mis-interpreted by the reader. If a doctor reading my translation of a medical text comes across '?no foraminal encroachment?', he may think I am not certain whether there is such an expression as 'foraminal encroachment'. But that was not the problem. The problem was that I was not certain whether the source-text author was in fact saying that there was no foraminal encroachment. In such a case, you might use the Comment function to distinguish 'term uncertain' from 'meaning uncertain'.

Finally, remember that many clients do not want to spend a lot of time dis-cussing problems in the translation. Clients who happen to be the author of the source text may be very happy – indeed anxious – to do so, but many others will want *you* to handle the problems.

Here are four common situations:

1. You understand the concept but can't find the right way to express it in the target language.

Write something which conveys the concept. Or take advantage of context: if the translator has referred to something called a 'blanky knife' and you cannot find any evidence for the existence of this term, perhaps you can write 'use an appropriate knife'. If the text is one where correct terminology is important, signal your problem to the client.

2. You can't decide which of two interpretations is right.

Fudge, that is, write something which has both meanings. This can often be ac-complished through an ambiguous syntactic structure: a certain word order or punctuation device will allow the sentence to bear both meanings. If fudging is not possible, or the text is one where fudging is unacceptable, provide both pos-sible translations. Here's an example using an incorporated translator's note:

> It is possible that helicopters will be used [*or perhaps*: use of helicopters is permitted] when ferrying heart-attack victims to the hospital.

3. You can't resolve a contradiction between different passages of the text.

If you are sure the contradiction is a genuine one (that is, it is not simply that you have failed to see the true meaning of one of the two passages), you must somehow indicate the problem. Otherwise, readers who know the text is a translation may wonder if the contradiction is due to the translator rather than to the source-text author.

4. *You don't understand the passage at all.*
One solution is to make an intelligent guess. Here's an example using question-marks:

> He said that ?boldness? was the secret to moving ahead.

When using question marks, it is best to use two marks: one at the outset of the uncertain passage and one at the end of it, to signal the extent of the problem to the reader. It may also be a good idea to italicize the question marks, or place them in square brackets, or highlight them in colour, in order to distinguish them from indicators of interrogative sentences.

Another possibility is to signal such problems with literal or unidiomatic translation:

> He said that the audacity of our abilities was the secret to moving ahead.

When you really do not understand a passage, literal or unidiomatic translation is actually better than smooth-reading, idiomatic translation, because you want to be sure that the reader recognizes the passage as a translation. Conceptual errors expressed in idiomatic language are more likely to be (wrongly) attributed to the source-text author than to the translator. However I hasten to add here that normally, revisers must wage unrelenting war on literal translation, by which I mean the substitution of bilingual dictionary equivalents. Translators, perhaps tired at the end of the day, sometimes stop attempting to figure out what the author of the source text meant, and start to engage in bilingual word substitution. This frequently happens when the source is very poorly written, or it is a transcript of spoken language. Word substitution cannot create a target-language equivalent, for speech or poor writing produced by native speakers of the target language does not sound anything like literal translation from another language.

Returning now to cases where all attempts to understand the source have failed, question marks and literal translation can be combined:

> He said that ?boldness? [*literally*: the audacity of our abilities] was the secret to moving ahead.

If question marks are unacceptable, use a suitably vague word suggested by context. Suppose you had to revise a translation of this passage:

> The strike sent a very strong message to the government that its workforce was becoming radicalized, with poignant implications for future relationships in the workplace.

Neither the translator nor you have been unable to determine what 'poignant' means here. So substitute an uncontroversial word (say 'significant') and translate.

Occasionally, if you are in doubt about the meaning of a passage, you can simply delete it from the draft translation. Sometimes it is obvious that a word or phrase is of no importance and could have been omitted from the source text. For example, if there is a parenthesis containing four examples of the author's point, and you can't understand the third one, omission will cause no harm. Another example: connector words can often be omitted if you cannot see how one sentence is related in meaning to the next; it may be better to leave it to the reader to fill in the connection rather than write something misleading.

If the obscure passage is a complicated description of a natural process or technological object, the solution may be to simply delete the description and refer the reader to an accompanying diagram or photograph.

If entire passages are obscure in their detail, but clear in overall intent, you can sometimes substitute a summary for the full translation which appears in the draft. This approach, along with omission and fudging, will be necessary if the brief is to produce a text whose status as a translation is to be concealed; in that case, obviously, no alternative translations or translator's notes will be possible.

12.5   Inputting changes

When corrections and improvements are made on paper, they have to be input on the computer. Two questions arise: who does this work and who is responsible for ensuring that it is done accurately? There is no point in painstaking revision work followed by sloppy inputting of changes.

With student trainees and new employees, the matter is clear. They input the changes, and then the supervising reviser checks that this has been done properly. One of the points to cover in evaluating trainees and new employees is how good they are at this task. Skipping over some of the handwritten changes is a not uncommon problem.

In other cases, changes may be input by the translator, the reviser (with con-tracted work), a proofreader or a member of the clerical support staff. In a large organization, a particular approach to this task may be laid down by senior or local managers; alternatively, it may be left up to teams of translators to decide on a system. The important thing is to have a definite system with clear-cut responsibilities.

The best system, if workable, is to have the translator input the changes (or Accept/Reject changes in a Track Changes display). That is because there is al-ways a danger that the reviser, who is less familiar with the text, has unwittingly introduced errors.

12.6   Checking Presentation

Checking certain features of Presentation is especially important if your revision falls at the end of the production process; that is, after you input corrections, the text will not go to a proofreader, or a secretarial support unit or page layout designer within the translation department. Indeed, the client may use your output as such, printing it out for distribution, or placing a link to it on a Web page. Here are some common problems, expressed as questions:

- Are there any section headings isolated at the bottom of a page?
- Are there any widows (first line of a paragraph isolated at the bottom of a page) or orphans (last line isolated at the top of a page)? You may find that the widow/orphan protection option in your word processor does not in fact prevent widows and orphans.
- Are there any unintentionally blank or almost blank pages? (The translator may have unintentionally introduced a hard-page code that causes the next word to appear on a fresh page.)
- Are tables or columns skewed?
- Are some lines of point-form lists indented more than others or less than others?
- Are there pages where all words are bolded?
- Are the last few words of a footnote on the next page?
- Is the footnote indicator on the same page as the footnote?

You might also want to check the legibility of the text. Of course, clients and readers can manipulate e-text themselves to make it legible, but they may find the need to do so annoying, or worse, they may receive printouts of hard-to-read text rather than adjustable e-text. To make it easy for the reader's eye to follow the text, you should ensure that:

- It uses a serif font (serifs are fine lines finishing off the main strokes of letters).
- The font size is no smaller than 10 points.
- The lines are not too long.
  Long lines make it hard for the eye to keep its place and return to the next line. When producing landscape text (text parallel to the long side of the paper), use two or three columns in order to achieve shorter lines.
- The text is not full-justified (lined up with both left and right margins). Without added manipulation, full-justified text may have irregular spacing between words, and this is hard on the eyes. Check how your word processor handles justification; there may be no problem. If you do use full justification, make sure it is turned off for the last line of the paragraph; o t h e r w i s e   t h i s   w i l l   h a p p e n .

12.7   Preventing strategic errors

A considerable amount of correcting work can be eliminated if the translator avoids making strategic errors. A strategic error is a wrong decision about how to handle a certain category of translation problem. This decision then leads to multiple errors that cannot be quickly corrected with Find & Replace. For example, suppose a new translator is working on a lengthy text that contains large numbers of names of organizations, companies or committees in the source language. There are many ways such proper names can be handled, but it may be that some of them are not appropriate in the text at hand. It is therefore important to find out, at an early stage, how the translator is handling this issue. In the case of a contractor, you can send instructions about strategy along with the text, for example: "leave all organization names in the source language, italicize them, and where appropriate add a translation in brackets". Another scenario: suppose you are heading a team of translators working on a very lengthy text. You do not want a situation to arise where one translator regularly uses the personal pronouns 'I' and 'you' but another translator favours impersonal forms ('Earlier I suggested that you avoid rewriting' versus 'A suggestion was made earlier that rewriting should be avoided'). Once again, you need to decide early in the translation process how formal you want the writing to be and advise the translators accordingly.

12.8   Helping the reviser

If another translator will be checking your work, signal passages which you found especially difficult so that the reviser can concentrate on these if time is limited. If you have translated an expression in a way the reviser might find odd, write a note or use an agreed-upon mark to signal that in your view this is a good translation, despite its oddness. If you have obtained confirmation of a technical term, check-mark it so that the reviser does not need to recheck it.

It's also a good idea to check-mark confirmed terminology in long texts, so that when you come to self-revise, possibly a week later, you will know what you have already checked and what remains to be checked.

12.9   Procedures, time-saving and quality

In this book, there has frequently been occasion to distinguish things that are matters of rule-following from things that require judgment. Spelling is rule-governed, but tailoring a text to readers requires judgment. Now, when a reviser (or a translation service) creates a procedure, in the sense of a predetermined sequence of steps for checking translations, what happens is that rules replace judgment. If the procedure calls for just scanning a particular kind of text, or a job done by a senior translator, rather than giving it a fuller check, then one does not stop to consider what would be best in that particular case. If the text is of type x, or it has been done by translator y, then it is scanned because the approved procedure says so.

Generally speaking, it takes less time to follow a rule than to make a judgment and act on it. So every time you leave room for judgment, you increase production time. On the other hand, you probably also increase the number of errors caught. Thus in deciding what procedures to adopt, and how rigidly they will be applied, the time/quality trade-off discussed in Chapter 9.12 comes into play once more.

Summary of techniques for spotting errors

1. In self-revision, leave as much time as possible before starting the post-drafting phase.
2. In self-revision, change the appearance of the text on screen, or print it out, or read it aloud.
3. In comparative re-reading, read the translation before reading the corresponding bit of source text.
4. Have someone diagnose the kinds of things you miss. Read separately for these.
5. Do one reading with a macro-focus, one with a micro-focus.
6. To help focus on microlinguistic problems, read the text backward, starting at the last sentence.
7. Read draft translations on paper, not on screen. (See Chapter 8.3.)
8. After a stylistic change, check that you haven't changed the meaning.
9. After any linguistic change, check whether this calls for change elsewhere in the sentence or in the next (or previous) sentence.

Practice

1. Try to formulate the revision procedure you use. Does it vary with the type of text?
2. The term 'satisfice' (a combination of 'satisfy' and 'suffice') was coined by computer scientist Herbert Simon to refer to the act of doing what is good enough, what suffices while satisfying needs minimally; choosing the first solution that works rather than continuing to search for the best possible solution. Look the term up in Google, exploring its uses in various fields (economics, artificial intelligence, moral philosophy). In light of your reading, do you think that satisficing is a justifiable approach to revision?
3. In a workshop or course, divide up into groups and have each group take a different approach to revising the same draft translation. For example, one group might do a single check for Transfer and the CLP parameters, another group two or even three separate checks. Members of each group then exchange their revised versions with members of another group. Examine the translation you receive and compare it with your own revision. Discuss the results with other members of your group. Can you correlate procedure with types of error found or not found? Each group then makes a presentation on its conclusions to all course participants.

Further reading

(See the References list near the end of the book for details on these publications.)

Horguelin and Pharand (2009); Samuelsson-Brown (1996 and 2010, chapter 8.10).

13. Self-Revision

According to the European standard EN 15038, "On completion of the initial translation, the translator shall check his/her own work". Skipping self-revision is simply unprofessional. The minimum acceptable is a full unilingual re-reading of the translation – no scanning or spot-checking. If time permits, a comparative re-reading may be done as well, depending on how confident the translator is about the accuracy of the translation. When the translator is a freelance producing directly for a client (not for a translation agency), this may be the only check the translation receives, unless the translator has another freelance look at it. When the translator is an employee, self-revision is still very important because in many translating organizations today, designated quality controllers most often do not carry out a full revision of the draft translation. In some organizations, senior staff translators operate like freelances in the sense that their self-revised translations may go straight out to the client.

Many of the matters discussed in Chapter 11 (degrees of revision) and Chapter 12 (procedures) are applicable to self-revision.

In Chapter 1, I pointed out that it is easy to make mistakes when writing or translating, and easy not to notice these mistakes. Now I should add that it's probably easier not to notice your own mistakes than the mistakes others have made. That is because the wording is yours, so you have a familiarity with it and a certain personal attachment to it. There may be passages of which you are particularly proud and as a result you fail to notice problems that may be obvious to others.

13.1   Integration of self-revision into translation production

In this chapter, we'll be concentrating on an issue that is peculiar to self-revision – the different ways you can integrate checking and amending work into the overall process of producing a translation. How do professional translators integrate self-revision into their work? Self descriptions by translators during workshops on revision, as well as empirical studies of self-revision (see Appendix 6), suggest that there is no one recognized approach; different people do the job quite differently.

The production of a translation can be described in terms of three phases and five tasks:

Three phases of translation production
    (1)   pre-drafting (before sentence-by-sentence drafting begins)
    (2)   drafting
    (3)   post-drafting (after sentence-by-sentence drafting is complete)

Five tasks to be performed
(1)   Interpret the source text.
(2)   Compose the translation.
(3)   Conduct the research needed for tasks 1 and 2.
(4)   *Check* the draft translation for errors and amend if necessary.
(5)   Decide the implications of the brief. How do the intended users and use of the finished product affect tasks 1 to 4?

Different translators distribute the tasks over the phases differently. Perhaps they will develop a default strategy for texts with which they are familiar (say, texts in the field of finance that are reasonably well written, under 3000 words, and have a deadline that allows 4 hours per 1000 words). They will vary the strategy when confronted with unfamiliar texts: those that belong to other fields, are not well written, are much lengthier or have a shorter deadline.

I should make it clear before proceeding that, in speaking of strategies, I am referring only to what translators do more or less consciously. By 'more or less', I mean that some things have become so much a matter of routine that a translator may not be immediately aware of them. But apart from that, much that goes on in the mind when we use language is completely inaccessible to our awareness, and is therefore not part of 'strategy'.

There are two types of strategy: for comprehension of the source and for composing the translation. For comprehension, the default strategy may be to do considerable preparation before beginning sentence-by-sentence composing of the translation. Translators who adopt this strategy may read the source text through entirely or at any rate in some detail, mark difficult passages, do a considerable amount of conceptual research (i.e. research needed to understand a passage), and perhaps even jot down some possible target-language wordings. Other translators work quite differently: they take a quick glance at the text (perhaps to see if they need to ask for reference documentation) and then start composing the translation. They may do a certain amount of research as they go, or simply leave a blank, write down alternative translations, or take a guess at the meaning preceded by a question mark; they then do further research after drafting is complete. Thus the post-drafting phase may not consist simply in checking-and-correcting; it may include research and composing work as well.

As regards the composing work, there are several default approaches. Some translators we may call 'Architects', borrowing a term from the study by Chandler discussed in Chapter 1, but using it somewhat differently, to refer not to a strategy for creating an entire text from the pre-drafting to the post-drafting phase, but rather to a strategy for composing individual sentences during the drafting phase. Architects are so called because they do a lot of planning: they consider several possible target-language wordings in their minds before finally picking one and typing it out; they then move along immediately to the next sentence of the source text. Others, whom we may call 'Steamrollers', type out something as soon as they have read the source sentence, and then proceed immediately to the next sentence of the source text. They do not ponder possible wordings in their minds before their fingers begin moving on the keyboard. A third group – the 'Oil Painters' – also type out something (often a rather literal translation) as soon as they have read the source sentence, but they immediately revise it, perhaps several times, before proceeding to the next sentence. They translate-by-revising so to speak. They are called Oil Painters because they lay down one wording, then another on top of it, and then another. Oil Painters and Architects both try to get down a fairly finished translation during the drafting phase, the former through revision, the latter through mental planning.

Thus the term 'self-revision' does not refer only to checking-and-correcting that takes place during the post-drafting phase (though many people do use the term that way); the drafting phase includes some degree of checking-and-correcting work as well, this being especially true of Oil Painters.

Some translators need to Oil Paint (revise during the drafting phase) because they do not read whole sentences before beginning to compose, just enough to get started. It is then sometimes necessary to backtrack because the unread portion of the sentence forces changes in the already translated part. Consider this sequence:

> Source text:
> Le nombre d'évasions a diminué dans la majorité des pénitenciers à sécu-rité minimale durant la première moitié de l'année fiscale 1999-2000.

> Gloss:
> The number of escapes has diminished in the majority of the peniten-tiaries with minimum security during the first half of the financial year 1999-2000.

After reading as far as the French for 'minimum security', the translator wrote:

> The number of escapes has dropped at most minimum-security penitentiaries

Then after reading the remainder of the French, it became necessary to back-track and change the tense ('has dropped' to 'dropped') because the text was written during the 2000-2001 financial year, and the perfective was therefore not permissible. Presumably some people use this approach because they have found that only a few such changes are necessary after the remaining portion of the sentence is read. As a result, time is saved, and the translator can compose more continuously, with relatively short gaps for reading. Those revisions which do prove necessary are not terribly time-consuming; even a bigger change (e.g. moving 'at most minimum-security penitentiaries' to the front of the sentence to improve the link with the preceding sentence) is simple using the word processor's click-and-drag option.

Translation Memory (see Chapter 14.5) disrupts the Architect and Steamroller strategies, to a greater or lesser extent depending on how much target-language material has been found in the Memory's database. The translator unavoidably becomes an Oil Painter, constantly stopping to revise bits of target-language material inserted from the Memory.

People who speak their translations using a dictation machine appear to be either Architects or Steamrollers; Oil Painting is impractical because it calls for frequent backtracking, which is awkward with such a machine. For those who dictate using speech recognition software that turns speech into text, there is a need to speak very clearly or risk having the machine fail to recognize words. But it is hard to concentrate on speaking clearly if you do not know exactly what you are going to say, so you must plan a good stretch of translation before opening your mouth; otherwise there will be a great deal of on-screen correcting required. Thus users of such software will probably be Architects.

After drafting is complete, Steamrollers will often find that they need to do a considerable amount of revision. Architects and Oil Painters will probably have less to do at the post-drafting phase, the former because of their careful consideration of several possible wordings before writing, the latter because of all the revision they have already done during the drafting phase. Of course, during the post-drafting re-reading of the translation, translators get a more synoptic view of the text, and certain macro-level problems that were not evident when focusing on individual sentences may be identified as needing revision. Those who dictate may discover during this phase that unwanted features of the spoken language have crept into their drafts.

In one empirical study, Englund Dimitrova (2005) found that highly experienced translators tend to make most of their changes during the drafting phase; students, and translators with only 2-3 years' experience, more often wait until the post-drafting phase. In another such study, Jakobsen (2002) found that professionals spend more time on the post-drafting phase than students but make far fewer changes during that phase than students.

Another aspect of the drafting phase where translators may differ is focus of attention. Some focus on the Language parameters (especially Idiom) when working on familiar texts. That is, their aim during the drafting phase is to set down readable, flowing prose. They do not want to pause to work in every single secondary idea in the source text, as this interrupts the composition process. Then they use the post-drafting phase to bring an idiomatic but not entirely accurate or complete translation into closer conformance with the source text.

Some people do the opposite: in the drafting phase they try to get down a very accurate and complete translation. Then they use the post-drafting phase to fix up the Language parameters. You may not be aware of such a focus, but it is useful to *become* aware of it in order to spend your post-drafting time wisely. If you have been focusing on Transfer during the drafting phase, then perhaps you need to pay critical attention to Language during the post-drafting phase. You may find that this is not easy, because you tend to accept wordings you have already composed unless they are truly awful.

Another function of the post-drafting phase may be to correct the effects of 'automated' drafting. It is well known that as translators gain experience, they increase their speed by automatically translating source-language expression

X by target-language expression Y. Ideally, a bell goes off in the mind if Y is in fact not appropriate in a particular passage, but sometimes this bell may not be functioning properly. The post-drafting phase affords an opportunity to correct the resulting errors.

You might also consider whether some of the revision work you are doing during the post-drafting phase could be avoided. For example, if the source text is poorly written, are you improving the writing as you compose your initial draft, or are you leaving such improvements until the post-drafting phase? The latter approach is probably more time-consuming overall. Another example: the post-drafting phase is not a good time to make decisions about things like the level of formality of language. Changing the level will be very time-consuming; it is not something you can do by search-and-replace. Better to come to a final decision about such matters early in the drafting phase.

With longer texts, you may be wasting time during the post-drafting phase by checking points you already checked (perhaps days earlier) during the drafting phase, but have forgotten about in the intervening period. If you often find yourself checking a point and then realizing that you have already checked it, place a mark on that passage of the translation the first time you check it.

To sum up, people differ in how they integrate the checking task into the translation production process, and as a result there are differences in how much checking remains to be done in the post-drafting phase, and which parameters need to be checked during that phase. We do not know how many people use one approach, how many another, though informal shows-of-hands during workshops reveal that Steamrolling is very common when translating familiar texts.

Is there a best way to work? No one knows, because empirical studies have not yet advanced to the point where we can say that one particular way of integrating the checking task into the translation production process is superior (that is, it results in a translation which is better, or is produced more quickly, or both). In all likelihood, the best way to work will vary from one person to another. So the question is whether you have found the way that is optimal for you. Perhaps if your default strategy is to be an Architect, you should give Steamrolling or Oil Painting a try.

13.2 Self-diagnosis

If you think there may be a problem with your current approach to self-revision, you could attempt a formal diagnosis of your work methods (if you cannot find someone else to do it). Here are some of the questions you will need to answer:

(a) What are the weaknesses in my draft translations? That is, what types of problem are typically present at the end of my drafting phase? Your self-revision procedures should focus on these. There is no point wasting time on your strengths. In other words, you don't want to be *over-checking.* Why check consistency of heading treatment if your drafts are already consistent?

To diagnose the weaknesses in your drafts, save a copy of your translations at the end of the drafting phase. After a while, you will have accumulated a body of drafts which you can use for diagnostic purposes. (See Chapter 14.2 for more on diagnosis.)

(b) What are the weaknesses in my final output? That is, what types of problem are typically still present at the end of my post-drafting phase? These are the weaknesses which your checking procedure is not currently catching. So you need to change your procedure to deal with them. If you discover that your inter-sentence connections are still not very clear at the end of the post-drafting phase, then you need to be spending more time on unilingual re-reading, and perhaps that should be your final check.

(c) To what extent am I *over-correcting*? How much time do I spend making unnecessary changes in my draft? Can I justify each change to myself, in terms of the revision parameters ("I've left something out", "that's the wrong level of language"), and more particularly in terms of the readership and future purpose of the translation ("that won't be understood by the non-expert readers", "this is a prestigious publication"). To some extent, over-correcting is a matter of confidence, or rather the lack thereof. Inexperienced translators find it hard to quickly decide that a wording is alright. Being uncertain, they make changes, which may in fact not be necessary.

(d) To what extent am I *introducing errors* while self-revising?

To answer questions (c) and (d), you will need to save several versions of your translation as it comes into being during the drafting and post-drafting phases. You can then compare the versions using the Compare function of your word processor (see Chapter 8.4); as you examine the changes you have made, you can see whether you are over-correcting or introducing errors.

If you are very ambitious, you can install a screen recorder like Camtasia in your computer. You will then be able to record everything that happens on your screen while you work, after which you can play it back and observe your self-revision habits. There is also software that will record all your keystrokes and play them back (for more information, enter the two words "Translog" and "translation" in Google).

13.3 The term 'self-revision'

Some people may prefer to reserve the term 'revision' for the process of checking someone else's translations (discussed in Chapter 14). There is a significant difference between checking the work of others and checking your own work. While the former obviously takes place after the translation is complete, the latter, as we have seen, is distributed over two phases: the drafting phase and the post-drafting phase. The European standard EN 15038 uses the term 'checking' for the self-revision work which occurs in the post-drafting phase and makes no reference at all to self-revision during the drafting phase. Many people may regard the self-revision work done during the drafting phase, especially by Oil Painters, as simply a normal part of the writing process rather than a distinct process: as you compose sentences, you monitor what you've written, and occasionally you recompose.

Practice

1. Write down how you think you distribute the tasks over the phases. Do you do a lot of comprehension work before you start or do you try to understand-as-you-go? When it comes to drafting the translation, are you an Architect, a Steamroller or an Oil Painter? Do you focus on Transfer or on Language during the drafting phase?

2. If you are one of those who make quite extensive changes during the post-drafting phase, do you think this means there is something wrong with the way you work during the drafting phase?

3. Do you think your self-revision procedure varies with any of the following factors:

   - length of text?
   - urgency of translation request?
   - topic (familiar or not)?
   - quality of the writing in the source text?

   If so, how?

4. Exercise in self-revision.
   This exercise will inevitably be quite time-consuming, because each individual workshop or course participant must first translate a text (300-400 words is a suitable length). It is not a good idea to have people bring a pre-drafted translation with them, for two reasons. First, they may pre-revise the text to avoid embarrassment. Second, an important part of the exercise is to notice checking and amending work done during the drafting phase. People who bring a pre-drafted translation may have forgotten what they did during the drafting phase.

   Ideally the exercise would be done in a room where everyone can work on a computer and share his or her self-revised texts with other participants, by email or by posting on a commonly accessible website or by projection on a screen at the front. However this will very often be impractical. The exercise can also be done using pen and paper or printouts. The instructions below assume no electronic sharing.

There are four steps. With a one-day workshop, allow a lengthy mid-day break during which participants can both eat lunch and do Step One. With a two-day workshop, you might do Step One the afternoon of the first day, and Steps Two to Four the morning of the second day.

If participants will not have access to the Internet and electronic term banks, the instructor will need to distribute photocopied documentation. The simpler alternative is to use a text that does not call for any research except in printed dictionaries (which should be available). The disadvantage of using such a text is that participants will not then experience the interaction that often occurs between conducting research and making changes in the draft.

Step One - Pre-drafting and Drafting

(a)   Proceed through the pre-drafting and drafting phases using your normal method and working at your normal speed. (This will not be possible if the circumstances of the workshop mean that you have to use paper and pencil instead of a computer, or a computer instead of a dictating machine.)

(b)   If working on paper, do not erase anything when you make changes. Simply cross words out, leaving them legible. Write on every other line or every third line so as to leave room for changes. If working on a computer, you can keep track of any revisions you make during drafting by turning on Track Changes (see Chapter 8.4) under the Review tab. This tab also allows you to display only the changed version on screen as you proceed, so that you will not be distracted by coloured markups of your insertions and deletions. Select Final, or deselect Insertions and Deletions in Show Markup.

(c)   Do not go over your draft once you come to the end of the text. In other words, do not proceed to the post-drafting phase.

(d)   If you were working on paper, give the workshop leader your handwritten draft showing the changes you made during the drafting phase. If you were working on screen, give the leader a triple-spaced printout of your draft, showing the changes. To do this, select Final Showing Markup under the Review tab, and make sure Insertions and Deletions are selected in Show Markup. Then go to the Print dialogue box and choose Document Showing Markup.

(e)   Write down a brief description of how you carried out the pre-drafting and drafting phases:
  •   Did you read the entire source text, or just glance at it and then start drafting?

- Did you do any preliminary research? Any research while drafting?
- Did you use the Architect, Steamroller or Oil Painting approach?
- Did you focus on Transfer or on Language while drafting?

Step Two - Post-drafting

(a) Take up to five minutes to decide how you are going to revise:
- Which parameters will you check?
- Will you do separate readings for Language and Transfer, and if so, in what order?

(b) The workshop leader will announce how much time you should take to do your self-revision. You will have more time if you Steamrolled through the drafting phase, or if you are doing a full comparative revision, or if you are doing two separate readings.

(c) Write corrections in by hand; don't use a computer. If you prepared the draft on paper, print the changes in block capitals. (Using a different colour of pen will not work unless a colour photocopier is available. Printing in block capitals will distinguish changes in the post-drafting phase from those made during the drafting phase when a black-and-white photocopy of your work is made for other participants.)

(d) If you identify a problem but do not find a solution fairly quickly, just underline the passage and move on. The focus of the exercise is finding problems rather than finding solutions.

(e) Do not repeat any procedure (e.g. do not do two read-throughs for Accuracy).

(f) Hand in your revised draft.

Step Three - Presentations

(a) Prepare to give a five-minute presentation on your work either to the entire group (if small) or to a subgroup (if the entire group is large). The presentation should explain:
- how you prepared the draft (using the description you wrote down at Step One (e));
- how you worked during the post-drafting phase: which parameters were you especially concerned with and why did you chose them? Did you do separate readings for Language and Transfer? If you did a single reading, did you focus on Language, on Transfer, or both equally?
- subjective aspects of the self-revision process (e.g. Did you find yourself agonizing over a point? Did you suddenly realize that you were pondering a change when no change was really needed?)

(b) Receive from the workshop leader, for each participant, a copy of the drafting phase output showing changes as well as a copy of the post-drafting phase output showing changes made during that phase, so that you can follow the presentations of other participants.

(c)   Give your presentation when your turn comes.

Step Four - Small Group Discussion

Take 45 minutes for discussion with a small group of 3-5 other participants. For example, each of you might say, for selected points, why you made a change or decided not to make a change. This is an opportunity to see things you may have missed.

Further reading

(See the References list near the end of the book for details on this publication.)

Dragsted and Carl (2013).

14.   Revising the Work of Others

No passion in the world is equal to the passion to alter someone else's text. (H.G. Wells)

When revising others, you may have two different functions. You will always have a business function: preparing the text for delivery to the client, and perhaps writing performance appraisals for the personnel department. In addition, you may have a training function: showing people where their strengths and weaknesses lie, and advising them on how to improve. In both functions, interpersonal relationships are very important.

The great danger when revising others is to treat the task as similar to self-revision. In self-revision, you naturally feel free to change your own wordings. But when revising others, you have to be more careful, even if the person you are revising will never see your changes. That is because you are wasting time (and money) if you keep substituting what *you* would have written for what the other person has written.

These days, revising translations which you did not produce yourself may mean several different things. It may, as in the past, mean revising work done by contractors or by colleagues, but it may also mean revising the output of Machine Translation, or revising passages in your own translations which consist of wordings inserted from a Translation Memory database that contains translations done by others. In the first part of this chapter, the focus will be on the interpersonal aspect of revising translations prepared by colleagues or contractors. We'll then look briefly at Memory and MT.

14.1   Relations with revisees

When you are assigned to revise the work of others, you may be in one of a number of different situations:

(1)   The person you are revising (the revisee) is a colleague at your own rank, or another freelance. You are revising each other's work.
(2)   The revisee is an employee at a lower rank. If he or she is a new employee, you may be responsible for on-job training.
(3)   The revisee is a student on a practicum whom you are training.
(4)   The revisees are members of a team translation project which you are heading. They are each contributing to a single text, and you are ensuring the unity of the final product.
(5)   The revisee is a contractor.

In situation (1), you will give the revisee your suggested changes and perhaps have a discussion about them. The revisee may or may not accept your revisions. The translator, not the reviser, bears the ultimate responsible for the quality of the translation.

In situations (2) and (3), the revisee has no choice but to accept your changes, though your employer may require you to always discuss the revisions (as part of your training function) and perhaps try to come to an agreement. However you have the final say, because you – not the translator – are the one with responsibility for the quality of the translation.

In situation (4), some members of the team may be colleagues at your level, but if there are disagreements, someone has to make final decisions, and that someone is you.

In situation (5), you may simply revise the translation and then send it out, not informing the contractor of changes you have made unless they complain about a financial penalty. Some organizations, however, strongly encourage their revisers to provide feedback to contractors. Such feedback will help eliminate future errors arising from the fact that contractors inevitably have less familiarity with the client (they are in the same position in that respect as new staff translators).

The interpersonal aspect of revising others makes it quite different from self-revision. During self-revision, making unnecessary changes merely wastes time. When revising others, such changes will in addition create difficult interpersonal relationships. Assuming that the revisees take pride in their work, they will probably not be pleased if their drafts come back to them with vast numbers of changes. To ensure no unnecessary displeasure on their part, you must be more careful about unwarranted changes than you are when self-revising.

To avoid unwarranted changes, one thing you must do is recognize the validity of approaches to translation other than your own. For example, different translators tend to work at different points on the literal-free scale. There is a certain acceptable range, recognized by professional organizations and by translating organizations. It is important not to unconsciously define acceptability in terms of your own habits with respect to this range.

Many translators tend to favour superordinate words: they will write 'take' when the source text has a more specific verb. That may be perfectly acceptable; don't rush to change it to 'grab', 'snatch' or 'seize'. A few translators tend to do the opposite: write 'grab', 'snatch' or 'seize' even though the source text has a general word. That too will often be perfectly acceptable, since English tends to like specificity in verbs of motion. This illustrates an important difference between revising others and self-revision: in self-revision, you might want to stop and change a general term to a specific one if it occurs to you; it's your work after all. But when revising others, the situation is quite different: it's someone else's work, and you must respect their approach unless the word they have used could mislead the reader about the intent of the source text.

Another way to avoid unwarranted changes is to bear in mind, when you start a job, that the translator knows more about this particular text than you do. If you come across a wording that strikes you as odd, especially near the beginning of the text, you should consider that the translator may have had a good reason for that wording, a reason which is not yet apparent to you because you have not yet advanced very far into the text. The translator may also have consulted the client, the author or a subject-matter expert about the passage, or the translation may be based on some documentary source with which you are unfamiliar. It's a good idea to have new translators write marginal notes indicating their reference sources, so that you do not end up repeating their research. And when experienced translators are quality-controlling each other's work, they can anticipate which passages may cause the quality controller puzzlement, and either indicate the source or simply use an agreed symbol such as a check-mark next to such passages.

You may find revision more difficult if the translator tends to translate quite freely compared to you. Generally, it is easier to do a comparative re-reading of a close translation, because it is easier to coordinate the two texts with your eye. However, that is not a reason to encourage a free translator to adopt a closer approach. The translator is working for the client and reader, not for you. Each person must be left to find the approach that suits them, within the range generally recognized as acceptable.

Don't rush to impose your own interpretation of a passage. Bear in mind the inherent vagueness of language. For example, the source text may contain one of those words which is more general in meaning than any word in the target language. A more specific target-language word must be used, and the translator has selected one possibility. You would have selected another, but really when you think about it (and it is important to think about it when revising others), the context allows for both interpretations.

Another point to bear in mind is that the translator is a qualified writer just like you. It is important not to impose any personal linguistic preferences: perhaps you tend to write 'keep in mind' rather than 'bear in mind', but that is not a reason to change the translator's 'bear in mind'; there's no difference in meaning or style between these two expressions. Also, avoid getting the reputation of being a linguistic fussbudget: perhaps you don't like so-called 'split infinitives' but they are in fact perfectly grammatical and acceptable. More generally, it is important to make language and style changes only when these are warranted by the communicative goal. Revisers have often been seen in a bad light because they have attempted to impose a single absolute notion of language quality based on literary tradition. In professional translation today (at least as far as work into English is concerned), there can be no place for the notion of a single, universally applicable language standard. You must operate with a multiplicity of standards corresponding to differing communicative purposes.

If one of your functions is to train the revisee, then a good way to avoid ruffling feathers is to make a visual distinction between necessary changes and suggestions. For suggestions, use a pencil or a different colour of ink, and instead of crossing out the draft translation, simply write the suggestion above it. If revising on screen, place suggestions in a Comment box. The suggestions will show revisees how a problem might have been better handled, or just differently handled, without labelling their work as 'wrong'.

Something else you can try if you have a training function, and the text is reasonably short, is to sit with the translator and have him/her read the translation aloud while you follow along in the source text, making comments and suggesting changes as you go.

A final way to avoid unwarranted change is to ask yourself the question: can I justify this change? A good rule of thumb is that you should be able to justify nine out of ten changes by reference to some authority (e.g. a dictionary), or by invoking some specific category of error (e.g. wrong level of language) or principle of translation (e.g. "it's not sufficient to include the same points as the source text; you have to have the same focus") or instruction from the client ("use these terms"). "It sounds better my way" is not a satisfactory explanation for a change you have made (unless the problem really is a matter of euphony!). Notice that by justification is meant not a reason for the proposed new wording but *a reason for making a change in the first place.*

Why nine out of ten instead of ten? The answer is time constraints. For example, the translator has written 'cropland' and you would need to do research to determine whether this is right. You are certain, however, that 'farmland' would be correct. If the deadline is looming, you may not have time to do the research or ask the translator why 'cropland' was chosen. You will then have to make the change to 'farmland', even though 'cropland' may well be perfectly acceptable.

Justification of changes is important not only to avoid unnecessary changes but also to win the respect of those you revise. If you can explain why you made your changes, you will be seen as someone the revisees can learn from; if you cannot, you will be seen in a negative light, as arbitrary, authoritarian or worse.

In order to justify your changes, you will need a set of categories and a vocabulary for talking about translation. You could start with the parameters of Chapter 10 ('not smooth', 'not the right sub-language for this field'), and then make up more specific categories if you need them. You may find it difficult to explain changes if you do not have a knowledge of basic translation theory. Also, if grammatical instruction was not part of the curriculum when you studied your mother tongue at school, you may be at loss to explain certain language-related changes you have made.

All these cautions should be especially kept in mind by anyone new to revising others. The main mistake new revisers make is over-revising, not under-revising. And of course, the more revisions you make, the greater the risk that you will introduce errors, and make the translation worse. Revisers would do well to adopt as their motto "First, do no harm"! Your default revision action should always be to do nothing. (This is not to say that under-revising is never a problem. A desire to get to the end of a long and dreary text may lead you to overlook wordings which you really should change.)

Even if you take precautions to minimize changes, and even if you give reasons for your changes, there will inevitably still be cases where the translator just does not agree with you. Sometimes this is just an inability to accept correction – a stubbornness which new translators must get over if they are to succeed. However if the translator has a good counter-argument, and time is available, you might try submitting the dispute to a third party. If the dispute is over the meaning of the source text, the third party could be a native speaker of the source language, such as a colleague who works in the opposite direction (from your target language into your source language). If time is not available, just point out the practical realities: time is pressing and someone has to decide; it may be that you are wrong and the translator is right, but given your greater experience, the opposite is more likely. If it does turn out that you were wrong, don't conceal this fact. The same applies if you are discussing a change you want to make and you suddenly realize that the translator is right after all. Admit this immediately. Most people will think more highly of someone who admits mistakes, and they will then be more open to accepting criticism of their work.

One way to reconcile junior translators to revision is by occasionally asking them to revise the work of senior translators. This creates an appreciation for the difficulties of revising, and it shows that everyone makes mistakes. It's also an excellent way to learn about the fields with which the translation unit deals, the translation strategies appropriate to the unit's clients, and the tricks senior translators have acquired.

While newly hired translators must learn to accept revision, it is important not to create a dependency. You do not want translators to think "I don't need to bother checking this point because the reviser will figure it out" or "There's no point making stylistic changes because the reviser will just make a different set of changes." To avoid such a situation, it's important to identify, as soon as possible, one or more types of text which the translator does well, and announce that these texts will no longer be revised (unless there has been a specific request from the client to do so). If you go on revising every text, long past the time where this is really necessary, that will be seriously demotivating for the translator.

In larger organizations, junior translators are often annoyed when they are assigned to a new reviser, and the new reviser makes very different kinds of changes. The United Nations (2004) translation service conducted a study which found much greater than expected differences among revisers. Ideally, revisers will attend workshops where participants revise a translation together, and differences in approach are ironed out.

If you have a training function, you need to keep in mind two distinct tasks as you revise the translator's work: preparing the translation for the client and training the translator. The two functions call for a different attitude toward error. In preparing a translation for delivery, an error is just something that needs to be corrected. For training purposes, however, you will also want to consider matters that are completely irrelevant when preparing a text for delivery:

- The type of error. Which types of error is the translator most prone to?
- The cause of error. What can the translator do to avoid such errors in the future?

The remainder of this chapter will be concerned with these two issues: diagnosis of a translator's strengths and weaknesses, and advising juniors and trainees on steps they might take to improve.

14.2 Diagnosis

For purposes of delivery to the client, there is no reason to assign an error to a particular category. For training purposes, however, some sort of categorization is needed in order to formulate the translator's strengths and weaknesses.

Organizations that have a need to evaluate (translation schools, professional associations that test translators and so on) have developed classifications of errors and corresponding terminologies. However, no standard terms are in use by revisers themselves, in the English-speaking world at any rate. Individual revisers simply devise their own ways of talking about draft translations.

To prepare yourself to give oral or written assessments of someone's work, it is perhaps best not to start with a long list of error types. The main purpose of such an assessment is to identify the main areas of strength and weakness. Decide whether the translator's problems are mainly with Transfer or mainly with Language, and then go into more detail, using the parameters of Chapter 10. Here are two sample diagnoses, as they might appear in a formal appraisal addressed to personnel managers. Each identifies a main strength and a main weakness, and then adds a couple of other points.

> Her drafts read well but tend to be full of minor departures from the meaning of the source text. The formatting is sometimes inconsistent, and she keeps forgetting to use the client's special terminology.

> His drafts are accurate but there are too many un-English turns of phrase. Also, the connection between sentences isn't always clear, and he sometimes skips over parts of sentences.

The first translator is strong on Smoothness, but weak on Accuracy, and there are some problems with Layout and Sub-language. The second translator is strong on Accuracy, but weak on Idiom, and there are problems with Smoothness and Completeness.

In formulating a diagnosis of a particular translation for discussion with the translator, avoid quantitative statements. It is not very helpful to tell someone that their draft translation had 3 omissions, 6 unidiomatic word combinations, 2 mistakes in number agreement and 11 minor mistranslations. Some of these mistakes may be accidental – the product of momentary inattention rather than a symptom of an underlying problem in the translator's methodology. The question is not how many mistakes the translator made, but what general areas they need to work on. Perhaps the minor mistranslations are not so important but the lack of idiomaticity is egregious and needs immediate attention.

Diagnosing a translator's problem areas is not easy. Not all revisers are good at it. Perhaps it ought to be a qualification for anyone applying for a reviser position that will have a training function.

14.3 Advice

It is all very well to point out someone's mistakes in a particular text, or to provide a general diagnosis of their weaknesses; it is certainly useful for junior translators to be aware that they are making certain kinds of mistakes. But there is not much point in them merely resolving to 'do something about it'. The main problem for juniors is not *that* they made mistakes, but *why*. What was it that led to the mistakes being made in the first place? A good training reviser should try to point out possible causes, and then give suggestions about how to avoid that type of mistake in future.

In keeping with the topic of this book, we'll look briefly at advice that touches on the translator's self-revision process, leaving aside advice about research and other matters.

Some of the common problems of junior translators are easily remedied. If there are frequent omissions of a paragraph, a sentence or a point in a list, the translator should get into the habit of counting paragraphs, sentences and listed points. The methodological sources of many problems, however, may not be so clear; what goes on in a translator's mind remains more or less a mystery.

One possible way you may be able to help is by ascertaining the translator's work procedures. Junior translators have often not yet developed an order of operations that will help them avoid error (see Chapter 12). For example, suppose the problem is lack of Idiomaticity. This problem can be tackled in two ways: avoid writing unidiomatic wordings in the first place; or notice unidiomatic wordings once they are present. Now many new translators claim that they do indeed read their translations over without looking at the source text; in theory, this should reveal unidiomatic passages, especially if the translator is a native speaker of the target language. If this is apparently not working, then the effort should focus on the original composing stage. Perhaps the translator should attend less to Accuracy at this stage, and more to Language. If they focus on composing a good sentence, and don't worry too much about Completeness and Accuracy, then they will have less need to keep looking back at the source text, and hence it is less likely that the source-text wording will negatively influence the translation. In this approach, Accuracy and Completeness can be checked during the post-drafting phase.

If a translator has a problem with speed, it may be that they are wasting time by making many pointless changes during the original drafting of the translation. Suggest that they try Steamrolling through the draft, not stopping to make changes. Checking and correcting/improving will then be concentrated in the post-drafting phase. The translator may also find it easier during the post-drafting phase to identify the weaknesses of the translation, especially in the areas of Logic and Smoothness, because a continuous text is now available in the target language.

If the translator is a student trainee, it is especially important to give advice about self-revision procedure. Since assignments at translation schools are typically rather short, the practicum may be the student's first encounter with the problems of checking a lengthy text.

14.4   Revision of machine translation output

Increasingly, machines are among the 'others' whose work must be revised. MT output differs from human output in that it tends to contain repeated occurrences of linguistic errors of a type human translators would not make. Correcting these errors is an annoying, repetitive task, though one which it may be possible to semi-automate.

Human revision of MT output is called post-editing (human editing of MT *in*put, known as *pre*-editing, is discussed briefly at the end of this section). The European Commission's translation service awards contracts to private-sector translators for post-editing. According to a bulletin for freelances published by the service in 1999, "a post-edited text must be intelligible. Cohesion and read-ability are welcome but not absolutely necessary. ...The client has to weigh up the advantages of a fast service against the possible risk of lower quality." Here lower quality is ethical because the service makes sure clients are aware of what they are getting. Texts produced in this way bear the disclaimer "rapidly revised machine translation".

The work of a post-editor differs from that of a reviser of human transla-tions in that revision most typically aims at publication quality (and frequently at information quality, occasionally at polished quality but hardly ever at mere intelligibility), whereas post-editing typically aims at intelligibility (and frequently at information quality, only occasionally at publication quality, practically never at polished quality)(see Chapter 11.2 on these distinctions).

When I ran the French expression "Habileté à écouter et à comprendre afin de recevoir et répondre aux demandes des traducteurs et des clients" through one online MT program, the output read:

> Skill to listen and include/understand in order to receive and answer at the requests of the translators and the customers.

Here the reviser's task – making the translation intelligible – can be accomplished by deleting the words 'at' and 'include/' (the program was unable to 'decide' which of two common meanings of the French verb 'comprendre' – 'include' and 'understand' – was contextually relevant). A more acceptable translation would read 'ability to... respond to requests from translators and clients', but these ad-ditional changes are not needed to make the text intelligible.

A second MT program offered:

> Ability to listen and understand in order to receive and respond to re-quests for translators and customers

Here the problem is not creating intelligibility but correcting a gross mistransla-tion: it's requests *from* translators and customers. This of course requires looking at the source text, but many of the errors in MT output can be corrected without looking at the source:

> Skill is needed to motivate staff, staff positions, promote the work of team,…

can easily be revised to

> Skill is needed to motivate employees, staff positions, promote team work, …

MT output is of considerable interest for revisers because it poses the twin questions of intelligibility and rapidity in making changes. It suggests the question: How, with the fewest possible keyboard operations, can I achieve at least the low end of the readability/clarity scale? Consider this passage about what happens after a government accidentally overpays or underpays a beneficiary of a social programme:

> Recipients will be notified of any amounts being paid or claimed to them.

The first inclination of a reviser (short of completely retranslating the sentence) will be to fix the sequence 'claimed to'. The reviser will likely analyze the problem in terms of the common error of conjoining two words that require different prepositional complements. The corrected version might then be:

> Recipients will be notified of any amounts being paid to or claimed from them.

This wording could be achieved in two ways: add 'to' after 'paid', then move the cursor to the 'to' following 'claimed', delete it, and add 'from'; or more simply, delete 'or claimed to' and add 'to or claimed from'. However the fastest solution is simple deletion of the last two words in the machine output:

> Recipients will be notified of any amounts being paid or claimed.

Now, depending on how the preceding sentences are worded, it may or may not be immediately obvious that it is the recipients – not some other party – who will either receive more money or be asked to return money. The sentence will probably be correctly understood, albeit with some effort.

In some translation workplaces, the errors in MT output are reduced by pre-editing the input. Generally speaking, MT programs produce better results if the grammatical structures of the source text are clear. For example, many programs will do better with English source texts if all the relative clauses are clearly marked. Thus the pre-editor will change 'the man I saw you with is a translator' to 'the man who(m) I saw you with is a translator'. When I submitted the first of these sentences to the MT system at babelfish.yahoo.com, and requested a French translation, the result was gibberish, whereas when I submitted the second, the result was a correct translation. Similarly, when I asked Google

Translate for a French translation of 'heavy duty oil bath air cleaners', the result was incomprehensible, but when I pre-edited to 'heavy-duty air cleaners of the oil bath type' (inserting a hyphen and explicating the relationship of 'oil bath' to the rest of the expression), the result was intelligible. (If you try this yourself, you may get a different result: by the time you do it, a good translation of 'heavy duty oil bath air cleaners' may have become available to Google Translate, which bases its output on an analysis of what it can find on the Web at the moment you ask for a translation.)

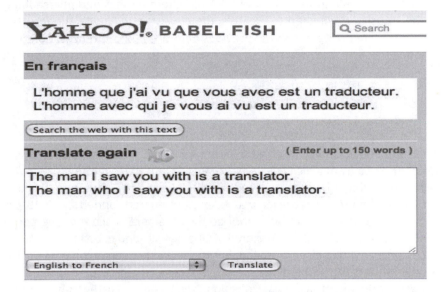

Portion of a machine translation website showing the effects of pre-editing

14.5 Revision of Translation Memory output

Some translators use Translation Memory software, with the result that wordings from other people's translations are inserted into their draft translations. These insertions ought to be checked during self-revision, but in addition, the second translator who is revising the text needs to pay special attention to the wordings that result from the use of Memory technology.

When a text for translation is run through the TM program, each sentence is compared to a database of existing translations, usually by many different translators. If the sentence to be translated matches a sentence in the database to a certain specifiable degree (say an 80% match or better), one of two things happens: (1) the corresponding sentence in the target language is automatically inserted from the database into the text being translated, replacing the source-language sentence, so that the text-to-be-translated becomes a combination of sentences in the source language and sentences in the target language, or (2) the corresponding sentence in the target language appears in a separate box on screen and the translator decides whether or not to insert it in the translation. In either case, inserted wordings need to be examined and often adjusted, either to make the meaning conform to that of the source text or to make the inserted chunk fit into the surrounding target-language text.

Apart from the very real possibility of mistranslations in the database, sentences written by a great many other people, each in a different style, may have been inserted into the translation, and revision may be needed to create an even style from sentence to sentence. Also, as already mentioned in Chapter 7.3, the different people whose sentences have been inserted from Memory into the present translation may not have used the same terminology and phraseology, and the translator will need to create some consistency. Finally, the inserted sentence may not cohere with the previous and following sentences. Consider this sequence:

> At 1403Z, the crew declared an emergency because of an engine problem and requested clearance to return to Montreal. It landed without incident at 1249Z.

The second sentence was inserted by Memory. Doubtless the word 'it' made sense in the text from which this sentence was taken. However now, 'it' has no antecedent and needs to be replaced by 'the aircraft'. In addition, in the text from which the second sentence was taken, the aircraft landed at 12:49 pm Greenwich time. Obviously that cannot be the case here, since the emergency was not declared until 2:03 pm. The time of landing will need to be taken from the source text presently being translated, but this will only happen if the translator or reviser notices the problem.

These problems of accuracy, cohesion, style and consistency have been created by the advent of Memory. Like all technologies, Memory solves some problems but creates others. Because it operates sentence-by-sentence, it has the effect of focusing attention at sentence level. The translator may then neglect problems of inter-sentence coordination (and also may not consider the possibility of splitting or combining sentences).

If the software finds a large number of matches in its database, and these are inserted in place of the source language sentences, then translating becomes a kind of revision task since the translator is mostly examining and adjusting the inserted wordings rather than composing his or her own sentences. Even when there are a smaller number of matches, translating ceases to be a more or less continuous process of reading a bit of source text and then composing a bit of the translation. Instead, one has to keep stopping the read-compose process to revise wordings inserted from the Memory.

In a few translation workplaces, sentences not found in the Memory at the required level of matching (e.g. 80% or better) are run through a Machine Translation program, so that the translator is presented with a text that is entirely in the target language. Translation then ceases to involve any composing work unless the machine output is completely useless; it becomes a pure revision task.

When you are revising other people's Memory-assisted translations, you should bear in mind the psychology that stems from this technology. The translator may have been tempted to use a sentence proposed by the Memory simply because it was there. Using an existence sentence is less time-consuming than creating a new one, and there is some evidence that translators tend to accept wordings inserted by Memory without noticing and correcting errors. Matches which are marked "100%" are especially problematic because they may well look like accurate translations at first glance, but closer inspection (if such an inspection is made!) not infrequently reveals departures from the meaning of the source text.

If a translation is to be published, both the accuracy and the writing quality that results from frequent use of sentences from a Memory may well not be good enough, and more revision effort will be required.

Practice

The texts used for exercises during workshops on revising others should be ones that require no research (except in dictionaries or other wordbooks). That way, participants can focus on the problems of revision and not be distracted by the need to carry out conceptual and terminological research. Workshop leaders should set time limits that will encourage participants to keep moving through a text rather than get fixated on specific points. Also, if they cannot think of a replacement wording, they should simply underline the problem expression.

Exercise 1. Receive from the workshop or course leader a draft translation with handwritten revisions, along with a statement of the brief (the intended user and use), and the source text. Answer the following questions:

(a)   Was each change needed? If so, is the revision a good one?
(b)   If the revision is a good one, how would you justify it? (To justify, participants could refer to general translation principles or to a copy of the parameter list in Chapter 10.)
(b)   Have any errors been missed?
(c)   Have any errors been introduced?

If doing this exercise in a group, half the group could be given one brief (e.g. translation is for publication) and half another (e.g. translation is for the information of a committee).

See Appendix 4 for a sample unilingual re-reading with corrections and commentary.

Exercise 2. Receive a draft translation, the source text and a statement of the brief. Diagnose the *main* problem with the translation in terms of the parameters of Chapter 10. If working in small groups, each group receives a different translation of the same text. The instructor modifies the text ahead of time so that a particular class of problem (e.g. accuracy, idiomaticity, smoothness) is most frequent.

Exercise 3. Receive a draft translation, the source text and a statement of the brief. Revise the draft for training purposes. Using one colour, make changes necessary to achieve the goals of the brief. Using another colour, make changes to show the imagined trainee other or better solutions. Each participant presents a sentence to the group.

Exercise 4. Participants receive the draft translation of a text and the brief, but not the source text. They divide into groups and each group revises for a different set of parameters. For example, one group might revise for Tailoring and Smoothness, another for Idiom and Mechanics, another for Logic and Facts. A representative of each group presents its revision to the other participants.

Exercise 5. Participants receive an overly close translation of a poorly written source text, along with the source text and brief. They work individually at revising the draft for 10 minutes. Then they decide, as a group, whether it is worth continuing. Would it be better to retranslate?

Further reading

(See the References list near the end of the book for details on these publications.)

Sedon-Strutt (1990).
Qualifications of revisers: Hansen (2009a and b).
Translation memory and revision: Christensen and Schjoldager (2010); García (2008).
Post-editing: Guerberof (2009); Guzmán (2007); Vasconcellos (1987).

Appendix 1. Summary of Revision Ideas

Twenty principles for revision

1.   If you find a very large number of mistakes as you begin revising a translation, consider whether the text should be retranslated rather than revised.
2.   Make the fewest possible changes, given the users of the translation and the use they will make of it.
3.   If you cannot understand the translation without reading it twice, or without consulting the source text, then a correction is definitely necessary.
4.   Make small changes to a sentence rather than rewriting it.
5.   Minimize introduction of error by not making changes if in doubt about whether to do so.
6.   Minimize revision time through unilingual re-reading unless the longer comparative procedure is dictated by the likelihood of mistranslation or omission (difficult text, untried translator, etc.) or by the consequences of such errors.
7.   When you make a linguistic correction or stylistic improvement, make sure you have not introduced a mistranslation.
8.   When you make a change, check whether this necessitates a change elsewhere in the sentence or a neighbouring sentence.
9.   Do not let your attention to micro-level features of the text prevent you from seeing macro-level errors, and vice versa.
10.   Do not let your attention to the flow of linguistic forms prevent you from seeing errors in meaning (nonsense, contradiction etc), and vice versa.
11.   Check numbers as well as words; they are part of the message.
12.   Adopt procedures which maximize your opportunity to see the text from the point of view of the first-time reader.
13.   Adopt procedures which allow you to strike a suitable balance between the degree of accuracy of the translation and the degree of readability.
14.   In the final analysis, give preference to the reader's needs over the client's demands.
15.   Avoid creating an immediate bad impression by making sure that there are no spelling or typographical errors on the front page of the translation.
16.   Do not make changes you cannot justify if revising the work of others.
17.   Do not impose your own approach to translating on others.
18.   Do not impose your linguistic idiosyncrasies on others.
19.   Make sure that client and reader receive full benefit from revision work by ensuring that all handwritten changes are properly input and that all changes are saved before the text is sent to the client.
20.   If you have failed to solve a problem, admit it to the client.

Six bad attitudes of revisers

1.   I wonder if this passage can be improved. (Of course it can, but does it need to be?)
2.   There are two ways of saying this ('bear in mind' or 'keep in mind'). Which one is better? (Why does one have to be better?)
3.   I'm revising, so I have to make some changes. (No, you don't.)
4.   This sounds better, so I'll substitute it. ('Sounding better' isn't a valid justification.)
5.   (when revising others) I would have done it this way, so I'll just substitute that. (It's not your translation.)
6.   I've just thought of a better translation, so I'll substitute it. (Is a better translation needed, or will the existing one do?)

Two benefits of other-revision

1.   Revision by a second translator provides a fresh look at the text, somewhat similar to the final user's experience (though not completely, because the final user is interested in the subject matter, not the language).
2.   It's harder to see your own mistakes than for someone else to see them.

Six disadvantages of other-revision

1.   Revision can waste time and money if you make unnecessary changes.
2.   Revision can introduce errors.
3.   Revision can end up as a substitute for proper training and for assigning the right translator to a job.
4.   Revision can make for bad working relationships with other translators.
5.   Revision can create dependency.
6.   Revising the work of others is, for many people, not enjoyable because there is no opportunity for creativity.

A philosophy of revision

1.   Revision is an exercise in reading, not writing.
2.   It is an exercise in spotting significant mistakes.

Appendix 2. Quality Assessment

Quality assessment means a check of selected parts (or perhaps the whole) of a translation, either before or sometimes after delivery to the client, by someone other than the translator, to determine the degree to which professional standards, as well as the standards of the translating organization and the client, have been met with respect to one or more parameters. Quality assessment differs from revision in that no corrections are made.

Assessment may be used for performance appraisal or promotion of employees or for certification of translators. In the case of contracted work, it may be used to select the contractor who will be given a job, or as a point of reference if the translation submitted is rejected and the contractor complains about the financial penalty. Assessments may also be written up as diagnoses of an employee's strengths and weaknesses or to help a freelance improve – a time-consuming exercise which usually cannot be completed before the translation is delivered to the client.

Assessment of a team of translators, or even the whole translation department, may be done in order to report on quality to a senior organization (government or corporation) or in order to determine which if any types of training are required. The results of quality assessment will also tell an organization whether its quality control system is working; if the assessment reveals less than the desired quality, then something is wrong either with the quality control procedures themselves or with their application.

Quantification of error

Often there is a requirement that the assessment system be 'objective', which usually means quantified, that is, the assessment will take the form of a number that is typically obtained by counting errors. Ratings should also be objective in the sense that if two assessors examine the same text, they should usually arrive at more or less the same assessment. For this purpose assessment guidelines are needed, and ideally assessors within an organization will attend workshops during which participants examine two or three texts together, and the workshop leader indicates who is being too severe, and who not severe enough. It would be too expensive and time-consuming to have more than one person assess each translation as a routine practice.

Much of the literature on quality assessment concerns marking the work of translation students. These writings often recommend assessment schemes with an extremely elaborate typology of errors. This is not suitable for professional situations, because it would take too long to assess a translation. Many of the error typologies devised by translation schools are concerned as much with causes of error as with error itself. For example, they may distinguish calque, borrowing and false friends (inappropriate use of source/target cognates), but these are in fact just different causes of the same error, namely, unidiomatic use of the target language. Also, while student work may be marked partly on the basis of process, professional work is assessed solely on the basis of outcome (a good outcome achieved by a wild guess is better than a bad outcome after lengthy systematic research). In this Appendix, we will be concerned with the assessment of work done by professionals for the market.

The simplest error typology has just two types: language errors and transfer (source/target correspondence) errors. Whatever typology is used, it is important to avoid a system in which one is frequently wasting time wondering whether a particular mistake is of type X or type Y.

Quality assessment is performed by randomly selecting one or more passages of the translation, adding up errors of various kinds, and expressing the result as a numerical or alphabetic score or a descriptive ranking (acceptable / unacceptable; or superior / acceptable / borderline / unacceptable), where the ranking is derived from a count of errors; for example, more than X minor mistranslations in a 500 word passage may make it 'unacceptable'.

The rankings are devised in such a way that the result is interpretable in operational terms. For example, a ranking of A (or 90%, or superior) may mean 'deliverable without further revision'; B may mean 'deliverable with just a few minor revisions'; C 'requires major revision work'; and D 'undeliverable; needs retranslation'. The rankings have obvious financial implications: in the case of contracted work, an in-house reviser will have to spend more time on a 'C' text than on a 'B' text; if a staff translator often does 'C' work, that again is going to call for many hours of work by a highly paid reviser.

As more and more texts by a translator or work unit are assessed, a running score can be calculated that will reflect trends in the quality of work produced. In the very simplest approach, where each translation subjected to assessment is rated either acceptable or unacceptable, if four out of five assessed texts are acceptable, the translator or work unit has a score of 80%. Later, if 18 out of 20 have been found acceptable, the score rises to 90%.

It may be desirable to give more than one score to a text – perhaps a score for the quality of the translation itself, a score for deadline-meeting, and a score for physical presentation. That way, one can see that a certain translator produces superior translations but sometimes does not meet deadlines and often submits work with poor physical presentation. This can be important in deciding which of many contractors will be given a certain job in the future: if deadline meeting is extremely important, the job might be given to someone who has less than superior quality but always meets deadlines.

Multiple scores can also be used for the quality of the translation itself. So for example, a translator may be rated superior with respect to accuracy, acceptable with respect to terminology but unacceptable with regard to minor language errors (his submissions are full of typographical errors). This translator will then be easily distinguishable from someone who has perfect spelling but makes many minor mistranslations. Of course the more separate ratings have to be given, the lengthier the work of the assessor.

Major, minor and critical errors

It is important to distinguish major from minor problems when making a quantified assessment. Suppose the translator has translated the word that means 'red' as 'yellow' (perhaps his eye wandered to another place on the page where the word for 'yellow' did indeed appear). Is this a major or minor error? A language teacher would say major, but as an assessor of translations, you are not a language teacher. The question is whether the reader will be misled about an important aspect of the message. If the text is a police report about a stolen car, then its colour is vital, and the error is a major one. But if an in-house employee newsletter mentions that the boss arrived at the staff party in a red car, then the colour probably plays no significant role in the message; it could just as easily have been left out. The error is then either minor, or not counted as an error at all. (Remember that we are talking about assessment here, not quality control. If you are quality controlling a text prior to delivery, naturally you will change 'yellow' to 'red').

This example shows that the major/minor status of an error cannot always be identified at the microstructural level, as a spelling mistake can. To see that 'yellow' is a minor error, you need to consider the genre (in-house newsletter) and the topic of the relevant passage (boss arrived at a party).

An interesting question is what type of negative consequences of error are to be considered. The most common type of consequence which assessors will consider is misunderstanding of the message. The error is 'major' if such misunderstanding bears on some central aspect of the message (a key point in an argument; a key event in a narrative). An out-and-out mistranslation found in a footnote is unlikely to be serious since footnotes rarely contain central aspects of the message. Such a mistranslation would thus probably be a 'minor' error.

Some assessment systems distinguish 'critical' errors from 'major' errors, the former being ones which potentially have negative impacts not just on readers' understanding of the message but on health and safety, the legal liability of the client who publishes the translation, the client's reputation, or the usability of a product.

If the assessor is making a sentence-by-sentence comparison of source text and translation, it is vital not to overlook the linkages in meaning *between* sentences: if the current sentence begins with 'therefore', is its link to the preceding sentence really one of consequence? Inter-sentence errors are a frequent source of serious misunderstanding, and are easily overlooked. More generally, 'macro' issues, such as the flow of an argument, need to be taken into consideration.

As for language errors, these will rarely have a major negative impact (unless they happen to change the meaning or result in nonsense). If I had accidentally left out the word 'to' in the previous sentence, that is minor because the (native or near-native) reader could easily recover the missing word. An example of a major error would be a single spelling mistake on a public sign.

Minor errors are mainly of importance when diagnosing and advising a translator, or writing a performance appraisal. If translators commit many minor errors, that suggests inattentiveness: perhaps they are working too quickly or not self-revising properly. Minor errors do also need to be counted when making a quantitative assessment, but mainly for purposes of reference when selecting a translator for a future job. One might not want to give a closely argued legal text to a translator who is prone to many minor errors. Also, when a fairly large number of minor errors are accompanied by a major error, this suggests that the translator's inattentiveness could sometimes have serious consequences.

Multiple minor language errors may give rise to complaints and political problems in an official multilingual context, where speakers of the language in question could feel that their language, and by implication their nation, is being slighted.

Assessing aspects of a translation

Instead of counting individual errors of each type, an assessor may simply rate the various aspects of a translation taken as whole. A given aspect might be rated as acceptable or not acceptable, or be rated on a descriptive scale. This might be done for such aspects as target-language quality, correspondence of meaning to the source text, handling of specialized content or suitability to future readership. The aspects considered might vary from one text to another. A descriptive scale for correspondence of meaning is provided by Colina (2009: 260):

- The translation reflects or contains important unwarranted deviations from the original. It contains inaccurate renditions and/or important omissions and additions that cannot be justified by the instructions. Very defective comprehension of the original text.
- There have been some changes in meaning, omissions or/and additions that cannot be justified by the translation instructions. Translation shows some misunderstanding of original and/or translation instructions.
- Minor alterations in meaning, additions or omissions.
- The translation accurately reflects the content contained in the original, insofar as it is required by the instructions without unwarranted alterations, omissions or additions. Slight nuances and shades of meaning have been rendered adequately.

Each item on this scale corresponds to a numerical score. If such a scale were applied for each of the four aspects of translation mentioned above, then it would simply be a matter of adding four scores to get a final score for the translation. This approach to assessment is much faster than error counting, though it might turn out to be more subjective. If that proved to be the case, the subjectivity could be reduced by having a translation assessed by several people, but this would be expensive.

Relative assessment

Translations may be far from excellent yet still serve their purpose. The importance of a given feature of the translation (correct terminology, consistency of layout, idiomatic language, even accuracy) varies with the job. If a translation will be used for information only, clients may tolerate considerably less than perfection. For example, a client may have told the translator that she didn't care about correct terminology as along as the meaning was clear. If the translator was aware of such special instructions, and of the use to be made of the text, it would be odd to assess the job as if the translator had been trying to prepare a translation for publication. Failure by assessors to take account of the brief may create a false picture of the quality situation: if all texts are rated as if they were being done for the most demanding clients and the most demanding uses, then it may seem that standards are not being met even when they are.

How can the use factor be incorporated into a formal assessment system? It would not be a good idea for the assessor to sometimes overlook a particular type of error and sometimes not, depending on the use to be made of the translation. Such an approach would make a rating of, say, '90' or 'B' impossible to interpret: sometimes 'B' would mean practically no mistakes, sometimes quite a few. Future users of the organization's quality records would not be able to tell how good a translator is. One solution would be to assign each text to a category (based of course on the use to be made of the translation, not the source text). For example, one category might include prestige publications where even a few minor errors cannot be tolerated; another might include in-house reports, where large numbers of minor errors can be tolerated. A text in the former category might be given a relative rating of 'acceptable' if the score were 90 or more; a text in the latter category would need only 70 to achieve a relative rating of 'acceptable'. Future users of the system would then see, for example, that a certain translator had achieved the following results: in category 1, 75% of texts were acceptable; in category 2, 95% of texts were acceptable, and so on. If users of the records want to know which translators are capable of doing well on the most demanding texts, they look at the percentage acceptable for the corresponding category.

If a relative assessment is to be made some time after the job is completed, or is to be made by someone other than the original quality controller, then a record will have to be kept of the brief from the client, so that the assessor can assign the text to the appropriate category.

One thing the system as so far described does not mention is the field of the text being assessed. A translator may do extremely well on texts in finance or law. It does not follow that they will do well on medical or engineering texts. Anyone using the system to choose a contractor will have to somehow be able to determine the candidates' areas of competence.

Accounting for factors beyond the translator's control

A final issue in assessment is the role of factors beyond the control of the translator or the translation service. For example, a client does not allow nearly enough time to do a proper job, does not provide necessary reference materials or names of resource people, or provides a text that is not fully legible, yet insists on receiving a translation anyway. The question of whether the job ought to be have been refused is now irrelevant; it was not refused, and the issue is now one of assessing a translation which may well be rather bad. Future users of the ratings would be misled if such translations were given poor (absolute or relative) ratings. The contractor would appear less competent than they actually are. One solution might be to leave these jobs out of the reckoning if a running score is being kept. The running score will then reflect only those jobs in which the working conditions were adequate. Meanwhile, a flag could be attached to the rating for that particular job to indicate that the poor result was not the fault of the translator.

The cost of revision as an evaluation measure

If we regard translation as a business, then we could decide to use the cost of revising a text as a way of evaluating it. Now, every text will take a certain amount of time to review even if it turns out to be 'perfect' (does not require any changes). However any additional time taken to make necessary changes could be represented as a monetary value: if one hour, then the reviser's salary for one hour, or some other set amount. It's true that under such a system, a text with five major mistranslations that takes only 15 minutes to correct would be deemed to be four times as a good as a text (of the same length, hence billed the same amount) that has dozens of small language errors and takes 60 minutes to correct. This approach to evaluation tells us nothing about the seriousness or nature of errors. Still, time is a vital consideration in any business; the difference in revision time between the two texts is 45 minutes, and during those 45 minutes, the reviser of the text with five mistranslations had moved on to new texts whereas the other reviser had not.

A further difficulty with evaluation by revision time is that one reviser may take 15 minutes to correct a given draft translation while another may take 30 minutes, perhaps because of a lesser knowledge of the subject matter, or less experience as a reviser. Thus if the text is assessed by the first reviser, it will be deemed to be twice as good as it would have been had the second reviser assessed it. Some corrective factor would have to be devised, based on the organization's knowledge of its revisers' experience and areas of knowledge.

Further reading

(See the References list near the end of the book for details on these publications.)

Mason (1987); Arthern (1983, 1987, 1991); Williams (1989 and 2009); Brunette (2000); O'Brien (2012).
On inter-assessor reliability with non-error-counting assessment, see Colina (2008) and (2009).
For an application of Colina's assessment method to MT output and to translations by students and by professionals: van Rensburg *et al* (2012).

The defects (inapplicability to professional situations) of theoretical writings on quality assessment are discussed in Lauscher (2000), Drugan (2013) and Hajmo-hammadi (2005).

On the cost of poor quality, European Union (2012).

Appendix 3. Quantitative Grading Scheme for Editing Assignments

This grading scheme for copyediting and style-editing exercises not only yields a numerical mark but also serves to indicate to students their areas of weakness and strength. It's a somewhat complicated scheme that separately assesses each change made in the text, so it will not suit all instructors. The scheme can also be applied to revision exercises if so desired.

For each change the student has made, assign two independent evaluations – one to the original text and one to the edited text. Use the mark 'v' to indicate that the text is fine, the mark 'o' to indicate that it is so-so, and the mark 'x' to indicate that it is bad. Thus:

√
thin
~~narrow~~
x

means that the original text, with 'narrow', was bad, but the edited text, with 'thin', is fine, whereas

o
tight
~~thin~~
√

means that the original text, with 'thin', was fine whereas the edited text, with 'tight', is so-so.

There are nine possible annotations:

1 √	2 o	3 x
√	√	√
4 √	5 o	6 x
o	o	o
7 √	8 o	9 x
x	x	x

Draw an oval around each pair of symbols to make it clear that they go together, as shown in the sample text toward the end of this Appendix.

If you find this too complicated, you could try eliminating the 'so-so' category. You will then have just four combinations (1, 3, 7 and 9). The difficulty with this approach is that you will often find yourself wondering whether to assign a case to 'fine' or 'bad'. The 'so-so' category drastically reduces the amount of such hesitation.

You also need to annotate cases where you think a change ought to have been made but wasn't, using either an 'o' or an 'x' under the original text. Finally, place a circled 'x' above a change to indicate the introduction of a language error during a correction. For example:

√

people ⊗

the ~~man~~ is here

    x

√ ⊗

tihgt

~~thin~~

    o

The student rightly changed 'man' to 'people', but forgot to change the verb to plural. Then the student rightly changed 'thin' to 'tight' (the lexical choice was good) but introduced a typographical error.

This gives three more cases to add to the above nine:

10   original text was so-so and no change was made

o

11   original text was bad and no change was made

x

12   language error was introduced during change

⊗

In the margin, place one of six letters to indicate an area of strength or weakness (or let the students place the letters themselves):

B: made the text <u>better</u> (cases 4, 7 and 8)
W: made the text <u>worse</u> (cases 2, 3 and 6)
N: failed to <u>notice</u> a problem in the text (cases 10 and 11)
S: noticed a problem but failed to <u>solve</u> it (cases 5 and 9)
U: made an <u>unnecessary</u> change (case 1)
C: <u>careless</u> when making changes (case 12)

Count up the number of instances of each letter to yield a diagnosis (e.g. "Often makes the text better, but too many unnecessary changes and too many failures to make needed improvements").

Of course, this system does not diagnose strengths and weaknesses with respect to particular types of change: a student may be strong on mechanical changes but weak on non-mechanical matters such as level of language, or information focus. If you wish, you could add independent annotations above the relevant word or phrase; these will obviously differ for each assignment, depending on what type of editing students have been asked to do.

The last step is to assign marks to the various cases. The amounts shown below are for use when an assignment is given a mark out of 100.

Case 7:	+ 2 marks (depending on the focus of a particular assignment, you may decide to give spelling, grammar and punctuation corrections just + 1 mark)
Case 8:	+ 1 mark
Case 4:	neither + nor -
Case 1:	- 1 mark (after the first five of these unnecessary changes)
Cases 5 &10:	- 1 mark
Cases 2 & 9:	- 2 marks
Cases 3, 6 &12:	- 3 marks (when the mistake introduced in case 12 is a matter of grammar, punctuation or spelling, you may want to subtract just 1 or 2 marks)
Case 11:	- 4 marks (or less, depending on the type of mistake)

Bonuses: If only a few students in the class make a change of type 7 or 8, give these observant editors an extra mark or two.

With regard to Case 1, if you find that students are having difficulty with the notion of unnecessary changes, you could try a different approach: whenever a student has replaced an acceptable wording with another acceptable wording, decide whether the second wording is an improvement (even if an unneeded one). If it is, add a mark; otherwise, ignore it.

Add up the + marks; add up the - marks. The difference will almost always be a negative amount, which you can then subtract from 100 to arrive at a numerical score. So a student who has 20 + marks and 40 - marks ends up with (100+20-40=) 80. If necessary, assign a letter grade depending on the score.

The first time you mark an editing assignment using a detailed scheme like the one above, you may find that your students' marks are on average far too high or far too low. There could be two reasons for this. First, the assignment may be too easy or too difficult. Second, given the mathematics of the scheme, the text may be too short (not enough opportunities for error) or too long (too many opportunities). It may not be obvious which of these two factors (length or difficulty) is at work.

After some experimenting, I settled on the scheme set out above because, on a series of assignments, it usually yielded an average mark in the 65-70 range with a text about 400 words long. So if the text was 800 words long, I would simply divide by 2 before subtracting the student's score from 100. Since I found that it was hard to predict what students would find difficult, I simply defined difficulty in terms of the marking scheme itself: if the average mark was 58, that meant the assignment was much too difficult, and I gave each student 10 additional marks.

Here is a sample paragraph. The students have been given the text on a page organized in three columns. They have edited the text in the wide central column in black. Then in this central column the instructor has written assessments of editing quality in red (shown here as grey). Error-type annotations are seen in the left column, and +/- marks in the right column.

If you have time, write in explanations in red:

- Line 4: Write 'research centres', to indicate why 'centres of research' has a so-so mark under it.
- Line 4: Cross out the comma after 'becoming' to indicate that the editor forgot to remove this comma when moving the phrase 'with increasing rapidity'.
- Line 6: Cross out 'itself', to indicate that words like 'very' and 'itself' make it harder rather than easier for the reader to relate this sentence to the previous one.

Appendix 4. Sample Unilingual Re-reading

In a static object like a book, it's impractical to illustrate the actual process of revision; all that can be shown is a sample outcome. The following illustration concerns unilingual re-reading, since a sample comparative re-reading would require reference to a text in a language which many readers of this book would not know. A draft translation with a fairly large number of defects is used so that several problems can be illustrated in a short space. The example is a segment of a draft English translation of a French text that introduces a series of articles on environmental ethics. It was done by a student trainee on a work placement. The brief was to prepare a translation for publication in a ministry magazine that would be distributed mainly within the civil service. One of the magazine's functions is to make employees aware of the ministry's outlook on various issues; the editor of the magazine has therefore emphasized, in the brief, the importance of readability. In order to focus on language and style matters, the reviser began with a unilingual re-reading, that is, checked the translation without looking at the source text unless a passage seemed odd.

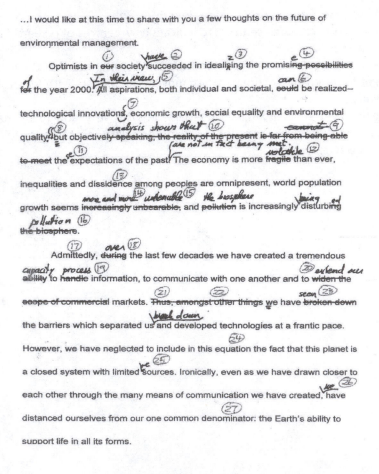

The revisions can be seen in handwriting. The number next to each revision refers to the commentary which follows the passage.

Note that the text shown here could be used in a class or workshop as an exercise in justification of changes. Simply ask participants to mark up the text as follows:

X	the change made a good translation bad or a bad translation worse
√	a change was needed and the change improved the quality
Single underline	a change was needed but the change did not improve the quality
Double underline	a change was needed but no change was made
Circle	no change was needed

Commentary

1. Deletion of 'our' is an unnecessary change. Note that it doesn't much matter what the source text says. If the passage went on to contrast 'our' society with other societies, eliminating 'our' would create a minor omission, but in fact this is not the case.
2. The perfective is needed because (as the subsequent text makes clear) there is present relevance. This is a common mistake in translating from Romance languages. It would be tempting to further revise to 'have idealized', but a glance at the source text removes the temptation: the wording suggests that the optimists did in fact have to overcome some opposition, and this is reflected in 'succeeded'.
3. The style sheet requires –ize rather than –ise in all words where both spellings are possible.
4. The draft is verbose. In a translation for information only, the draft could have been left as is. Given the brief, it is not necessary to have the highest level of writing quality, but some of the verbosity should be removed.
5. Without this introductory phrase, it is not immediately clear who is speaking, the author or the 'optimists'. A problem of intersentence flow. (As it happens, there is no such phrase in the French, but the grammatical structure makes it clear that it is the optimists who are speaking.)
6. Sequence of tense problem here: the present is required to match the perfective in the previous sentence. This type of change is easily missed if you are focusing entirely on the current sentence.
7. The aspiration would be to innovation in general, not specific innovations.
8. This is the key point of the paragraph, so it merits a sentence of its own (regardless of what the source text has).
9. 'is far from being able to' is unidiomatic. Revision to 'the reality of the present cannot meet' seems close enough to the same meaning. This fails to capture 'far from' but that is a minor omission of no importance.
10. 'reality...cannot meet' is obscure. One possibility would have been for

the reviser to guess that this sentence simply contradicts the view of the optimists as stated in the previous sentence; this could be expressed by 'objectively speaking, the present cannot meet the expectations of the past'. In fact, the reviser looked at the source text and decided on something more elaborate, which unfortunately required structural change of the sentence. However, looking at the source text was a good idea because the point being made in it is not that the present *cannot* meet the expectations of the past, but that it *is* not meeting them. Whereas *cannot* suggests that if we made changes we might be able to meet the expectations, *is* better suits the argument which will be made, namely that there is something wrong with the expectations themselves. Literal translation of the source text: 'in all objectivity, the balance-sheet one can draw from the present is far from meeting these expectations of the past'.

11. Changing 'the' to 'these' creates a better link to the previous sentence, making it clear that the expectations are for innovation, growth and so on. It doesn't matter whether the source text has such a linking word.

12. 'fragile economy' is an odd word combination to express what the reviser correctly guessed is just a cliché in the source text.

13. The reviser missed 'dissidence'. Once again, a more ordinary word combination (perhaps 'conflicts among peoples') is required, because the thought is a commonplace.

14. Perhaps after reading 'increasingly' in the next phrase, the reviser decided to eliminate the repetition. Is this a needed improvement? One could argue that the repetition of the word is effective. If in doubt, make no change.

15. 'Unbearable' does not go with 'population growth'.

16. The reviser has placed the key word 'pollution' in focus position, but the effort required does not seem worth it. The draft was readable. And unfortunately, after moving 'pollution', the reviser forgot to put 'by' in front of it.

17. Is 'admittedly' really the right word to introduce this paragraph? The argument in favour is perhaps that the previous sentence described some negative features of the current scene, and the writer is now 'admitting' that the picture has positive features as well. However, while the second sentence of the paragraph continues with the positive features, the third sentence takes us back to the negatives. The argument of a text can be hard to follow if it contains too many 'but'-like words, and 'admittedly' is just such a word. If we delete it, then the first two paragraphs will have simple and parallel structural signals: positives – however – negatives; positives – however – negatives. There is no need for a linking expression at the beginning of a paragraph in English. Indeed, if the entire segment shown here had been a single paragraph in the source text, it would have been a good idea to create a paragraph break in the translation at this point, precisely in order to avoid having to use a 'but' word.

18. Changing 'during' to 'over' is an unnecessary improvement.

19. Changing 'ability to handle' to 'capacity to process' introduces words which fit better with 'information'. It's on the borderline of being a necessary change, given the brief.
20. 'widen the scope of commercial markets' is verbose, slightly unidiomatic (scope of a market?) and contains a redundancy (commercial market). A worthwhile change.
21. 'Thus': a pointless linking word, probably present in the draft only because the source text has a linking word. French is much less friendly than English to sentences with no linking word.
22. 'Amongst other things': French frequently specifies that the items being mentioned do not constitute an exhaustive list. In English, this is much less common; the non-exhaustivity of lists is usually left implicit.
23. Changing 'we have broken down...' to 'we have seen...break down' is pointless. A glance at the source text confirms that it does not improve the accuracy of the translation.
24. What equation? Nothing equation-like has been mentioned. This is an empty buzzword, which should be removed.
25. 'Sources': fast typing or a brief lapse in attention resulted in a wrong word in the draft. Spellcheck would not catch it.
26. The reviser spotted the missing 'we'. It may have disappeared when the translator pressed the delete key once too often while re-arranging the sentence. The reviser could easily have missed it through over-attention to the immediate context, since the structure 'we have created, have distanced...[and...]' is a perfectly good one.
27. This writer seems to like mathematical metaphors. Is Earth's ability to support life a 'common denominator'? But there is a bigger problem: what is the connection between the two aspects of the 'irony'? A look at the source text does not help: the thought, whatever it is, is just as poorly expressed in French. There seem to be three ideas: (a) we are now more closely linked than ever with each other, but (b) we have lost touch with the one thing we were all previously close to, namely the planet which (c) supports life in all its forms. Should the reviser have intervened to help the writer? Probably not, since it might take quite a while to rewrite the sentence, and anyway these are only opening remarks. Readers will be more interested in the next part of the text (which specifically concerns the ministry they work for).

Appendix 5. Revising and Editing Vocabulary

The following list defines terms as they are used in this book. It does not report on the meanings given to these terms by other writers. Some of these other meanings are indicated in terminology notes in the body of the book. Words in a definition are italicized if they are themselves defined (with the exception of a few words such as *revise*).

There does not appear to be any prospect of a terminology that would be accepted even within one country, let alone throughout the English-speaking world. Perhaps this state of affairs does not matter much, because what is important is that everyone who revises and edits *within* an organization knows what is meant by 'copyedit' or 'proofread' in that particular workplace. Organizations that contract editing and revision work to outsiders must of course explain in some detail (perhaps with examples) what exactly they expect when they ask for 'revision' or 'editing'.

There is a copious literature on editing, but the terminology is far from standardized: terms like *copyedit, proofread* and *rewrite* are used in a variety of overlapping or contradictory ways. There is only a small published literature on revision in English, but in what does exist, as well as in spoken usage, terms such as *re-read, quality control, proofread, review* and *check* are, again, not used in any consistent way.

The terminology of revision is discussed in Chapter 9.2.

adapting
> Composing a new text that re-expresses, in the same language, the content of an existing text in order to make it suitable for a readership differing from the intended readership of the existing text.

amending, amendment
> Rewording a text to either *correct* or *improve* it.

architect strategy
> A drafting strategy in which the translator reads a source sentence, ponders possible target-language wordings at length, then writes down one of them and moves on to the next sentence without making any changes.

authentic
> Quality of a translation which reads like a target-language original not only in its grammar, *idiom* and terminology, but also in its use of phrasing and rhetoric typical of target-language texts of that genre. The *brief* may or may not call for authenticity.

brief
> The client's explicit and implicit specifications for a translation job. Sometimes called the commission.

check
> Read to identify *errors*.

clarity, clear
> Characteristic of a text whose ideas are *logical*. Compare: *readability*.

client

> The purchaser of the translator's services, or the agent of an institution who asks for the translation. Sometimes called the commissioner.

coherence, coherent

> See *Logic*.

cohesion, cohesive

> See *Smoothness*.

comparative re-reading

> Type of *revision* in which sentences of the translation are compared to sentences of the source text. The main purpose is to detect inaccuracies and omissions, and make suitable changes. Often accompanied by a check of one or more *Content, Language* or *Presentation parameters*. Also called bilingual re-reading and *cross-reading*. Compare: *unilingual re-reading*.

completeness

> Characteristic of a translation in which no source-text information has been omitted in such a way that it cannot be recovered from context, and in which no information has been added that is not even implicit in the source text. One of the *Transfer parameters* of revision.

consistent

> Characteristic of a translation or set of translations in which (i) any given word, term or phrasing in the source text is always translated in the same way (assuming the concept is the same), and possibly also (ii) two different words, terms or phrasings in the source text are always translated in different ways (i.e. they are never treated as synonyms).

content editing

> Checking a text for its ideas. At the macro-level, includes changes in the coverage of the topic. At the micro-level, includes correction of factual, logical and mathematical errors.

Content parameters

> The following two revision parameters: Logic, Facts.

copyediting

> Checking a text to bring it into conformance with pre-set rules, including the publisher's house style, rules of *correct usage*, and the grammar, punctuation and spelling rules of the language.

correct usage

> Rules explicitly stated by some authority that prescribe certain ways of using a language while proscribing others.

correction, correcting

> (1) An amendment that is required by a rule, such as a rule of spelling, punctuation or grammar, an instruction in a *style sheet* or *style manual*, or a widely accepted rhetorical or genre-related principle of the target language.
>
> (2) Rectification of a straightforward terminology mistake, mistranslation or gross translationese.
>
> (3) Rectification of a factual or mathematical error.

(4)   The process of making a change once an *error* has been identified.
Compare: *improvement, check*

cross-reading
Used by some to mean *comparative re-reading,* by others to mean *unilingual re-reading* (perhaps because it may involve occasional reference to the source text).

draft translation
In *self-revision*, a translation, or passage of a translation, which has not yet been through the *post-drafting phase*. Otherwise, a translation which has not yet been checked by the revising translator.

drafting phase
The period of time when the wording of a translation is first put down. It may or may not include *self-revision* work.

editing
The process of reading a text that is not a translation (or is not being treated as a translation) to spot *errors*, and making appropriate *amendments.* Editing a sentence is to be distinguishing from *rewriting* it. There are four types of editing: *copyediting, stylistic editing, structural editing* and *content editing.*
Used by some translators to refer to *unilingual re-reading* of a translation, or to *revision* in general.

error
Any feature of a text which requires *correction* or *improvement*.

flow
Synonymous with *smoothness*.

full revision
(1)   Check of the entire translation rather than just selected portions. Also called a full reading.
(2)   Check of all *parameters* rather than just selected ones.
A revision can be full in one or both senses.

gatekeeping
A function of editors and revisers, who must *correct* the text so that it conforms to society's linguistic and textual rules and achieves the client's goals.

glancing
Revising a translation by reading only the title or cover page, and the first paragraph.

house style
A list of rules, issued by a publishing organization, which writers are to follow when preparing a manuscript. Takes the form of a brief style sheet or a longer style manual.

Idiom, idiomatic, idiomaticity
A passage is unidiomatic if it contains a combination of words that is not in use by the speakers of the language, or if a word is used in a meaning it does not have. In a broader sense, a translated passage is unidiomatic

if it fails to observe the stylistic and rhetorical preferences of the target language. One of the *Language parameters* of revision.

improvement, improving
>The process of making an amendment other than a *correction*. Improvements enable a text to serve its purpose, most notably through *tailoring* and *smoothing*.

information quality
>Level of quality in which the aim is to achieve a translation which avoids misleading the reader about primary or secondary aspects of the message of the source text, but is only fairly *readable* and fairly *clear*. This is the level of quality needed for a translation to be used for information only. Compare: *intelligible, publication quality* and *polished*.

intelligible
>(1) Characteristic of a text which has a bare minimum of *readability* and *clarity*. Important in post-editing of machine translation output.
>
>(2) Level of quality in which the aim is to achieve a translation that has a bare minimum of *readability* and *clarity* and is roughly accurate (it will not seriously mislead the reader about primary aspects of the message of the source text). Compare: *information quality, publication quality* and *polished*.

internationalization
>Removing from a text all those features which will create comprehension problems for an international audience, including notably non-native readers of the language.

Language parameters
>The following five revision parameters: Tailoring, Smoothing, Sub-language, Idiom and Mechanics.

level of language
>The degree of formality or technicality of the language. Formality must suit the relationship between author and audience, and the occasion and purpose of the document. Technicality must suit the readers' knowledge of the subject matter.

localization
>Adding to a text features that will mark it as being for a particular local readership, and subtracting features that would mark it as being for some other local readership.

Logic, logical
>Characteristic of a text in which the sequence of ideas makes sense. A logical text is free of nonsense, tautology and contradiction. One of the *Content parameters* of revision. Also called *clear* or 'coherent'. Compare: *smooth*.

macro-level checking
>Checking a text for *errors* in matters concerning units larger than a pair of consecutive sentences. This would include things such as the logic of an argument or the level of formality of language used across an entire text.

Mechanics
> Linguistic features subject to relatively strict rules such as those of spelling and grammar, as well as house style requirements.

mental editing
> Correcting or improving the writing quality of a text while translating it. Also called *transediting*.

micro-level checking
> Checking a text for *errors* in matters concerning individual words, phrases or sentences, or the relationship between a sentence and the one that precedes it.

norm of translation
> The approach to translation generally accepted by a society as a whole, or a subculture of it, including that of professional translators.

oil painter strategy
> A drafting strategy in which the translator reads a source sentence, quickly writes down a wording, amends that wording (with or without reference to the source text), possibly several times, and then moves on to the next sentence.

other-revision
> Revising a translation prepared by another translator.

parameter
> One of the twelve text features which may be checked during revision.

partial revision
> (1)   Check of selected portions of a translation rather than the entire translation. Includes *scanning*, *spot-checking* and *glancing*.
> (2)   Check of selected parameters rather than all parameters.
> A revision can be partial in one or both senses.

polished
> Finely crafted writing quality that makes the reading experience enjoyable in itself. Suitable for literary and some commercial translation. Compare: *intelligible*, *publication quality* and *information quality*.

post-drafting phase
> The period of time after the draft translation is complete. It includes *unilingual re-reading* and possibly *comparative re-reading*, corrections and improvements.

post-editing
> Revising the output of a machine translation program.

pre-drafting phase
> The period of time before the translator begins to set down the wording of the translation, during which the translator may read all or part of the source text, conduct research or jot down translation ideas.

pre-editing
> Amending a text to make it suitable for machine translation.

Presentation parameters
> The following three revision parameters: Layout, Typography, Organization.

procedure

A pre-determined sequence of steps used in editing or revision.

proofreading

(1)   In the publishing industry, checking an edited text for any *errors* remaining after page design and typesetting.

(2)   In the translation industry, checking of a text for *Mechanics* and the *Presentation parameters,* often by a non-translator.

(3)   In the translation industry, sometimes used as a synonym of *unilingual re-reading* or *revision*.

publication quality

Level of quality in which the aim is to achieve a translation that is very *clear* and *readable* and avoids misleading the reader about primary or secondary aspects of the message of the source text. Compare: *intelligible, information quality* and *polished*.

quality

In general, the quality of something is the totality of its characteristics that bear on its ability to satisfy stated and implied needs.

With regard to a translation,

(1)   the set of characteristics that make it fit or unfit for its future readers and the use they will make of it.

(2)   the set of characteristics required by an employer, client or translation agency.

quality control

Synonymous with *revision*. Quality control may involve checking either all or part of a translation, and either all or just some of the *parameters*. It may or may not include comparison with the source text.

quality assessment

A check of selected parts of a translation, often after delivery to the client, by someone other than the translator, to determine the degree to which professional standards, as well as the standards of the translating organization and the client, were met with respect to one or more *parameters*. No corrections are made. The result of the assessment may be quantified for such purposes as employee performance assessment and selection of contractors. Also called 'quality evaluation'.

quality assurance

The whole set of procedures applied before, during and after the translation production process, by all members of a translating organization, to ensure that quality objectives important to clients are being met. Objectives may pertain to quality of service (deadlines met, interaction with translation unit pleasant), quality of the physical product (layout, electronic form), and quality of the text (style suited to user and use, proper terminology, correct language).

readability, readable

Characteristic of a text which is *tailored* to readers and has a *smooth* sequence of sentences and paragraphs. Compare: *clarity*.

re-reading

See *comparative re-reading*; *unilingual re-reading*.

repurposing

Making changes in a text so that it can be used in a different medium.

reviewer, review

A subject-matter expert who examines a manuscript to determine whether it makes a contribution to its field, to suggest additions or subtractions from coverage of the topic, or to identify conceptual or terminological errors.

revising, revision

The process of reading a *draft translation* to spot *errors,* and making appropriate *amendments*. Revising is to be distinguished from retranslating.

rewriting

Composing a new text (or sentence or passage of a text) that re-expresses, within the same language, and for the originally intended readership, the content of a manuscript. May be necessary, if the manuscript is uneditable, or unnecessary, if the manuscript was editable. Compare: *adapting.*

retranslating

Composing a new translation (of an entire text or, more frequently, a sentence), starting from the source text. May be necessary, if the draft is unrevisable, or unnecessary, if the draft was revisable.

scanning

Revising a translation by focused reading for just one or two *parameters*.

self-revision

An integral part of the translation production process in which one checks and amends one's own translation.

Smoothness, smoothing

The quality of a text in which sentences are well focused and have an easily perceptible syntactic structure, and in which paragraphs have easily perceptible connections between sentences. A contribution, along with *tailoring*, to *readability*. One of the *Language parameters* of revision. Other terms for a smooth text are 'cohesive' and 'flowing'. Compare: *logical*.

spot-checking

Revising a translation by checking either regularly spaced or randomly selected paragraphs or pages spread over a text.

steamroller strategy

A drafting strategy in which the translator reads a source sentence, quickly writes down a translation and then moves on immediately to the next sentence without making any changes.

strategy of translation

A general approach used for a translation job in order to comply with the brief, such as giving preference to accuracy over readability, writing in a conversational style, summarizing verbose sentences, or retaining source-language terms for cultural references with bracketed explanations.

strategic error

An error in the approach to drafting a translation which has multiple negative consequences that require a large amount of time to correct, such as
writing the draft in too formal a style.

structural editing

Checking the physical structure of a text to help readers follow its conceptual structure.

stylistic editing

Checking and improving a text to ensure it reads *smoothly* and is *tailored*
to its readers.

style manual

See *house style*.

style sheet

See *house style*.

Sub-language

Subset of the lexical, syntactic and rhetorical resources of a language
which are typically used in a given genre and field. One of the *Language
parameters* of revision.

Tailoring, tailored

Adjusting the wording of a text to make it more suitable for its particular
readership. One of the *Language parameters* of revision. A contribution,
along with *smoothing,* to *readability.*

training revision

Revision of a translation in which two types of change are made (and
distinguished): changes needed to prepare the translation for delivery to
the client and changes designed to show a trainee translator other (and
possibly better) solutions to translation problems.

transediting, trediting

See *mental editing*. Transediting may also be used to refer to *adapting*
the source while translating.

Transfer parameters

The two revision parameters: Accuracy and Completeness.

unilingual re-reading

Type of *revision* in which the translation alone is read unless a passage is
nonsensical or there is some other reason for the reviser to look at the
source text. Also known as *cross-reading*, monolingual reading or just
plain re-reading. Compare: *comparative re-reading.*

Further reading

(See the References list near the end of the book for details on these publications.)

Shuttleworth and Cowie (1997): see the definitions of adaptation, rewriting, norms,
post-editing, pre-editing, verifiability, sub-language, rewording, idiomatic, nat-
uralness, commission.

Delisle et al (1999). Brunette *et al* (2000).

Appendix 6. Empirical research on revision

Revision needs to be not merely done, but also studied, in order to improve revision practices. There is now a considerable, and expanding, literature that describes, analyzes and interprets observations of translators engaged in revising translations. These studies are worth reading because they will enable you to compare your own methods with those of others, but they are not yet sufficiently advanced to demonstrate that some particular approach is better than others, in the sense that it results in a higher quality translation or in greater speed or both.

Most studies concern self-revision rather than other-revision, and combine discussion of self-revision with other aspects of translation. These studies confirm that different people take different approaches. There is some evidence that as people gain experience, they become able to do most of the needed self-revisions during the drafting phase, whereas less experienced translators tend to rely more on the post-drafting phase. For pedagogical purposes, however, it is not a good idea to teach students the approaches that have been observed with very experienced translators. There are probably natural stages people go through as they learn to translate, and there is no point in trying to skip to the final stages. Much of what experienced translators do arises from confidence – something which can only be acquired through lengthy experience.

Four observing methods are used in empirical studies, sometimes in combination: (i) Think-aloud studies ask translators to speak aloud their thoughts while they are revising. The translators' comments are recorded and analyzed. (ii) Keystroke logging studies rely on software that records all keyboard actions by the translator, including of course changes made to the text; the record can be played back or printed out and analyzed. (iii) Video recording studies (and more recently, screen logging studies) show how translators move from window to window (as they do research for example) or consult paper reference works. (iv) Eye-tracking studies record translators' eye movements, making it possible to know what wordings of source and translation they were looking at and for how long. All these methods can be combined with each other and with the older method of comparing revised and unrevised versions of a translation, or successive revisions.

Some aspects of the translator's work process can be directly observed (for example, the translator switches from a Word window to a Web browser window); others have to be inferred (for example, mental processes inferred from the self-reports produced in think-aloud studies).

In addition to empirical studies proper, there are interview and questionnaire studies. One type of interview study takes a retrospective look at translations, asking the translators interviewed why they did what they did, including perhaps questions about revision. There are also several questionnaire studies which ask individual translators about their revising habits, or ask translation services about their revision policies.

Some of the results of the studies are expected and some unexpected, and many are rather alarming: if their results are confirmed, then all is not well in the world of revision. Two subjects revising the same text make changes at quite different locations; a reviser thinking aloud states the need to avoid unnecessary changes but then makes such changes; errors are overlooked or introduced.

Early studies, in the 1980s and 90s, mostly used translation or language students as subjects. Later there was a transition to using professional translators, sometimes with comparison to students. Most studies have been conducted at university facilities rather than in translators' workplaces, and the researchers may have given their subjects texts of an unfamiliar type, or asked them to perform tasks which they have rarely or never performed. Thus a question of realism arises: Do translators revise in the same way in a 'laboratory' setting as they do when working in their normal surroundings with familiar text types and with a paying client's deadline looming?

Keep in mind that almost none of the findings have been confirmed through repetition by other researchers and that most studies have very few subjects (typically fewer than 10, because it takes so long to process and analyze the data). Also, some studies may have methodological problems; with one exception, I have not included studies that are focused on methodological issues. Finally, researchers usually have a panel of revisers or specialized translators to assess the revisions produced by subjects, but different studies are most often not comparable because the panel members in one study were not given the same instructions as those in another study.

List of studies

Overview
Mossop (2007)

Observational Methods
Göpferich and Jääskeläinen (2009)

Interview and questionnaire studies
Morin-Hernández (2009); Rasmussen and Schjoldager (2011); Robert (2008); Shih (2006)

Observational studies of self-revision
Alves and Couto Vale (2011); Asadi and Seguinot (2005); Dragsted and Carl (2013); Englund-Dimitrova (2005); Jakobsen (2002); Lorenzo (2002); Pavlović and Antunović (2011); Toury (1995)

Observational studies of other-revision
Brunette *et al* (2005); Krings (2001); Künzli (2005, 2006a, b, c; 2007a, b; 2009); Lorenzo (2002); Robert (2012 and 2013)

References and Readings

This list contains items referred to at the ends of chapters as well as other readings on revision, editing and related matters. I have attempted to give complete coverage of published (print or online) material in English up to mid 2013 that deals solely or mainly with revising other people's translations; these items are marked (R). On self-revision and MT post-editing, as well as revision pedagogy and translation quality assessment and quality assurance, I have given only a small selection from the literature. Items preceded by an * concern editing or language in general rather than translation revision in particular. For this third edition, I have included a few items in languages other than English, including two doctoral dissertations available online.

Several of the items in the list can be viewed free of charge on the Internet, sometimes in Google Books or Google Scholar: to find out, simply enter the title in your search engine, or enter the author's name to reach their personal sites, from where you may be able to download articles. Items listed with only author and title will be found online.

Be sure to look at the references list at the ends of articles to find other materials of interest.

Note that at the translators' site ProZ.com, there is a forum called Proofreading/Editing/ Reviewing which covers revision. Some of the topics discussed in this book are also dealt with in the Translation Techniques forum at translatorscafe. com. You will also find one or two articles about revision at both these sites.

(R) Allman, Spencer (2008) 'Negotiating Translation Revision Assignments', in Ian Kemble (ed.) *Translation and Negotiation. Proceedings of the Conference held on 10th November 2007 in Portsmouth*, Portsmouth: University of Portsmouth, School of Languages and Area Studies, 35-47.

Alves, Fabio and Daniel Couto Vale (2011) 'On Drafting and Revision in Translation: A corpus linguistic oriented analysis of translation process data', *Translation: Computation, Corpora, Cognition* 1(1):105-122.

ASTM (2006) *Standard Guide for Quality Assurance in Translation* (ASTM F2575-06).

(R) Arthern, Peter J. (1983) 'Judging the Quality of Revision', *Lebende Sprachen* 28(2): 53-57.

(R) Arthern, Peter (1987) 'Four Eyes are Better than Two', in Catriona Picken (ed.) *Translating and the Computer 8: A profession on the move*, London: Aslib, The Association for Information Management, 14-26.

(R) Arthern, Peter J. (1991) 'Quality by Numbers: Assessing revision and translation', in Catriona Picken (ed.) *Proceedings of the Fifth Conference of the Institute of Translation and Interpreting*, London: Aslib, 85-91.

Asadi, Paula and Candace Séguinot (2005) 'Shortcuts, Strategies and General Patterns in a Process Study of Nine Professionals', *Meta* 50(2): 522-547.

Austermühl, Frank (2001) *Electronic Tools for Translators*, Manchester: St Jerome.

*Baron, Naomi (2000) *From Alphabet to Email*, London & New York: Routledge.

*Bell, Allan (1991) *The Language of News Media*, Oxford UK & Cambridge MA: Blackwell.

*Benson, Morton, Evelyn Benson and Robert F. Ilson (2010) *BBI Combinatory Dictionary of English*, Amsterdam: Benjamins.

(R) Bertaccini, Franco and Sara Di Nisio (2011) 'Il traduttore e il revisore nei diversi ambiti professionali' [the translator and the reviser in various professional environments], in Danio Maldussi and Eva Wiesmann (eds), *Specialised Translation II*, Special Issue of *Intralinea*, http://www.intralinea.org/specials/article/il_traduttore_e_il_revisore_nei_diversi_ambiti_professionali [last accessed 8 August 2013].

Biel, Łucja (2011) 'Training Translators or Translation Service Providers? EN 15038:2006 standard of translation services and its training implications', *Journal of Specialised Translation* 16, http://www.jostrans.org/issue16/art_biel.php [last accessed 8 August 2013].

*Bisaillon, Jocelyne (2007) 'Professional Editing Strategies used by Six Editors', *Written Communication* 24(4): 295-322.

*Bodine, Anne (1974) 'Androcentrism in Prescriptive Grammar: Singular 'they', sex indefinite 'he', and 'he or she'', *Language in Society* 3(4): 129-146.

Bowker, Lynne (2002) *Computer-Aided Translation Technology: A practical introduction,* Ottawa: University of Ottawa Press.

Bowker, Lynne and J. Pearson (2002) *Working with Specialized Language: A practical guide to using corpora*, London & New York: Routledge. Chapter 11.

Bowker, Lynne and Michael Barlow (2008) 'A Comparative Evaluation of Bilingual Concordancers and Translation Memory Systems' in Elia Yuste-Rodrigo (ed.) *Topics in language resources for translation and localisation*, Amsterdam: Benjamins, 1-22.

Brunette, Louise (2000) 'Toward a Terminology for Translation Quality Assessment: A comparison of TQA practices', *The Translator* 6(3): 169-182.

(R) Brunette, Louise, Chantal Gagnon and Jonathon Hine (2005) 'The GREVIS Project: Revise or court calamity', *Across Languages and Cultures* 6(1): 29-45.

*Burrough-Boenisch, Joy (2003) 'Shapers of Published NNS Research Articles', *Journal of Second Language Writing* 12: 223-243.

*Burrough-Boenisch, Joy (2013a) 'The Authors' Editor: Working with authors to make drafts fit for purpose', in Valerie Matarese (ed.) *Supporting Research Writing*, Oxford: Chandos Publishing, 173-189.

*Burrough-Boenisch, Joy (2013b) *Righting English That's Gone Dutch* (3rd edition), Voorburg: Kemper Conseil Publishing.

*Butcher, Judith, Caroline Drake and Maureen Leach (2009) *Butcher's Copy-editing: The Cambridge handbook for editors, copy-editors and proofreaders* (4th edition), Cambridge: Cambridge University Press.

Canadian General Standards Board (2008) *Translation services* (CAN/CGSB-131.10).

(R) Chakhachiro, Raymond (2005) 'Revision for Quality', *Perspectives: Studies in Translatology* 13(3): 225-238.

*Chandler, Daniel (1993) 'Writing Strategies and Writers' Tools', *English Today* 9(2): 32-38.

Chesterman, Andrew (1997) *Memes of Translation*, Amsterdam & Philadelphia: Benjamins.

Christensen, Tina Paulsen and Anne Schjoldager (2010) 'Translation-Memory (TM) Research: What do we know and how do we know it?', *Hermes – Journal of Language and Communication Studies* 44: 1-13.

Colina, Sonia (2008) 'Translation Quality Evaluation: Empirical evidence for a functionalist approach', *The Translator* 14(1): 97-134.

Colina, Sonia (2009) 'Further Evidence for a Functionalist Approach to Translation Quality Evaluation', *Target* 21(2): 235-264.

Cowie, Anthony Paul, and Ronald Mackin (1975) *Oxford Dictionary of Current Idiomatic English Vol 1: Verbs with prepositions and particles*, Oxford: Oxford University Press.

*Crystal, David (2007) *The Fight for English: How language pundits ate, shot and left,* Oxford: Oxford University Press.

*Dayton, David (2003) 'Electronic Editing in Technical Communication: A survey of practices and attitudes', *Technical Communication* 50(2): 192-205.

*Dayton, David (2004a) 'Electronic Editing in Technical Communication: The compelling logics of local contexts', *Technical Communication* 51(1): 86-101.

*Dayton, David (2004b) 'Electronic Editing in Technical Communication: A model of user-centered technology adoption', *Technical Communication* 51(2): 207-223.

*Dayton, David (2011) 'Electronic editing', chapter 6 of Rude and Eaton 2011.

Delisle, Jean, Hanna Lee-Jahnke, Monique Catherine Cormier and Jörn Albrecht (eds) (1999) *Translation Terminology,* Amsterdam & Philadelphia: Benjamins.

*Dragga, Sam and Gwendolyn Gong (1989) *Editing: The design of rhetoric,* Amityville NY: Baywood.

Dragsted, Barbara and Michael Carl (2013) 'Towards a classification of translation styles based on eye-tracking and keylogging data', *Journal of Writing Research* 5(1): 133-158.

Drugan, Joanna (2013) *Quality in Professional Translation: Assessment and improvement,* London: Bloomsbury.

Englund Dimitrova, Birgitta (2005) *Expertise and Explicitation in the Translation Process*, Amsterdam: Benjamins. Sections 2.3.5, 4.5, 4.6.4 and 6.2.2.

European Committee for Standardization (2006) *Translation Services – Service Requirements* (EN 15038).

(R) European Commission, Directorate General for Translation (2010) *Revision Manual.*

European Union (2012) 'Quantifying Quality Costs and the Cost of Poor Quality in Translation'.

García, Ignacio (2008) 'Translating and Revising for Localisation: What do we know? What do we need to know?', *Perspectives: Studies in Translatology* 16(1-2): 49-60.

General Administration of Quality Supervision, Inspection and Quarantine of People's Republic of China, Standardization Administration of the PRC (2003; revised 2008) *Specification for Translation Service – Part 1 Translation* (GB/T 19363).

General Administration of Quality Supervision, Inspection and Quarantine of People's Republic of China, Standardization Administration of the PRC (2005) *Target text quality requirements for translation services* (GB/T 19682).

*Gopen, George and Judith Swan (1990) 'The Science of Scientific Writing', *American Scientist* 78(6): 550-558.

Göpferich, Susanne and Riitta Jääskeläinen (2009) 'Process Research into the Development of Translation Competence: Where are we, and where do we need to go?', *Across Languages and Cultures* 10(2): 169-191.

*Gowers, Ernest (revised by Sidney Greenbaum & Janet Whitcut) (1987) *The Complete Plain Words*, London: Penguin.

Greenbaum, Sidney (1996) *The Oxford English Grammar*, Oxford: Oxford University Press.

Guerberof, Ana (2009) 'Productivity and Quality in MT Post-editing', www.mt-archive.info/MTS-2009-Guerberof.pdf   [last accessed 11 August 2013].

Guzmán, Rafael (2007) 'Manual MT Post-editing: If it's not broken, don't fix it!', *Translation Journal* 11(4), http://www.bokorlang.com/journal/42mt.htm [last accessed 8 August 2013].

Hajmohammadi, Ali (2005) 'Translation Evaluation in a News Agency', *Perspectives: Studies in Translatology* 13(3): 215-224.

*Halliday, M.A.K. (1989) *Spoken and Written Language*, Oxford: Oxford University Press.

*Halliday, M.A.K. and Ruqaiya Hasan (1976) *Cohesion in English*, London: Longman.

(R) Hansen, Gyde (2009a) 'The Speck in your Brother's Eye – the beam in your own: Quality management in translation and revision', in Gyde Hansen, Andrew Chesterman and Heidrun. Gerzymisch-Arbogast (eds) *Efforts and Models in Interpreting and Translation Research*, Amsterdam: Benjamins, 255-280.

Hansen, Gyde (2009b) 'A Classification of Errors in Translation and Revision', in Martin Forstner, Hannelore Lee-Jahnke and Peter A. Schmitt (eds) *CIUTI Forum 2008: Enhancing Translation Quality: Ways, means, methods,* Bern: Peter Lang, 313-326.

Hine, Jonathan (2003) 'Teaching Text Revision in a Multilingual Environment', in Brian James Baer and Geoffrey S. Koby (eds) *Beyond the ivory tower: Rethinking translation pedagogy,* Amsterdam: Benjamins, 135-156.

*Hirsch, Eric Donald (1977) *The Philosophy of Composition,* Chicago: University of Chicago Press.

(R) Horguelin, Paul and Michelle Pharand (2009) *Pratique de la révision* [practising revision], 4e édition, Montréal: Linguatech.

International Organization for Standardization (2012) *Translation projects – General guidance* (ISO/TS 11669).

Jakobsen, Arnt Lykke (2002) 'Translation Drafting by Professional Translators and by Translation Students', in Gyde Hansen (ed.) *Empirical Translation Studies: Process and Product*, Copenhagen Studies in Language 27, Copenhagen: Samfundslitteratur, 191-204.

*Judd, Karen (2001) *Copyediting: A Practical Guide*, 3rd edition, Menlo Park, California: Crip Learning.

*Kirkman, John (2006) *Good Style: Writing for science and technology*, 2nd edition, London: Routledge.

Klaudy, Kinga (1995) 'Quality assessment in School vs Professional Translation', in Cay Dollerup and Vibeke Appel (eds) *Teaching Translation and Interpreting 3*, Amsterdam & Philadelphia: Benjamins, 197-204.

(R) Ko, Leong (2011) 'Translation Checking: A view from the translation market', *Perspectives: Studies in Translatology* 19(2): 123-134.

Krings, Hans (2001) *Repairing Texts: Empirical investigations of machine translation post-editing processes* [edited by Geoffrey S. Koby, translated from German by Geoffrey S. Koby, Gregory. Shreve, Katjz Mischerikow and Sarah Litzer], Kent, Ohio: Kent State University Press.

*Kruger, Haidee (2008) 'Training Editors in Universities: Considerations, challenges and strategies', in J. Kearns (ed.) *Translator and Interpreter Training,* London: Continuum, 39-65.

(R) Künzli, Alexander (2005). 'What Principles Guide Translation Revision? A combined product and process study', in Ian Kemble (ed.) *Translation Norms: What is 'normal' in the translation profession? Proceedings of the Conference held on 13th November 2004 in Portsmouth*, Portsmouth: University of Portsmouth, School of Languages and Area Studies, 31-44.

(R) Künzli, Alexander (2006a) 'Teaching and Learning Translation Revision: Some suggestions based on evidence from a think-aloud protocol study', in Mike Garant (ed.) *Current trends in translation teaching and learning*, Helsinki Department of Translation Studies Publication III. Helsinki: Helsinki University, 9-24.

(R) Künzli, Alexander (2006b) 'Translation Revision - A study of the performance of ten professional translators revising a technical text', in Maurizio Gotti and Susan Sarcevic (eds), *Insights into specialized translation,* Bern/Frankfurt: Peter Lang, 195-214.

(R) Künzli, Alexander (2006c) 'Die Loyalitätsbeziehungen der Übersetzungsrevisorin' [the loyalty relationships of the translation reviser] in Michaela Wolf (ed.) *Übersetzen – Translating – Traduire: Towards a 'social turn'?* Münster/Hamburg/Berlin/Wien/London: LIT-Verlag, 89-98.

(R) Künzli, Alexander (2007a) 'Translation Revision: A study of the performance of ten professional translators revising a legal text', in Yves Gambier, Miriam Shlesinger and Radegundis Stolze (eds), *Translation Studies: Doubts and directions*, Amsterdam: Benjamins, 115-126.

(R) Künzli, Alexander (2007b) 'The ethical dimension of translation revision. An empirical study', *Journal of Specialised Translation 8.*

(R) Künzli, Alexander (2009) 'Qualität in der Übersetzungsrevision' [quality in translation revision] in Larisa Schippel and Hartwig Kalverkämper (eds) *Translation zwischen Text und Welt,* Berlin: Frank & Timme, 291-305.

Lauscher, Susanne (2000) 'Translation Quality Assessment: Where can theory and practice meet?', *The Translator* 6(2): 149-68.

(R) Lorenzo, María Pilar (2002) 'Competencia revisora y traducción inversa' [revision competence and translation into the second language], *Cadernos de Tradução* 10: 133-166.

Lu, Guang-hui and Ya-mei Chen (2011) 'The Mediation of Reader Involvement in Soft News Transediting', *Translation and Interpreting* 3(2): 48-66.

(R) Martin, Timothy (2007) 'Managing Risks and Resources: A down-to-earth view of revision' *Journal of Specialised Translation* 8: 57-63, http://www.jostrans.org/issue08/art_martin.pdf   [last accessed 8 August 2013].

Mason, Ian (1987) 'A text Linguistic Approach to Translation Assessment', in Hugh Keith and Ian Mason (eds) *Translation in the Modern Languages Degree*, London: Centre for Information on Language Teaching and Research, 79-87.

Matis, Nancy (2011) 'Quality Assurance in the Translation Workflow – A professional's testimony' in Ilse Depraetere (ed.), *Perspectives on Translation Quality,* Berlin/Boston: de Gruyter, 147-159.

*McArthur, Tom (1998) *The English Languages*, Cambridge: Cambridge University Press.

Merkel, Magnus (1998) 'Consistency and Variation in Technical Translation: A study of translators' attitudes', in Lynne Bowker, Michael Cronin, Dorothy Kenny and Jennifer Pearson (eds), *Unity in Diversity? Current Trends in Translation Studies*, Manchester: St. Jerome Publishing, 137-149.

*Milroy, James and Lesley Milroy (1999) *Authority in Language: Investigating standard English* (3rd edition), London & New York: Routledge.

(R) Morin-Hernández, Katell (2009) 'La révision comme clé de la gestion de la qualité des traductions en contexte professionnel' [revision as key to managing translation quality in a professional environment], Ph.D. Thesis. Université Rennes: France.

Mossop, Brian (1982) 'A Procedure for Self-Revision', *Terminology Update* 15(3): 6-9.

Mossop, Brian (1992) 'Goals of a Revision Course', in Cay Dollerup and Anne Loddegaard (eds) *Teaching Translation and Interpreting*, Amsterdam & Philadelphia: Benjamins, 81-90.

Mossop, Brian (2006) 'From Culture to Business: Federal government translation in Canada', *The Translator* 12(1), 1-27. Section 3.1.

(R) Mossop, Brian (2007) 'Empirical Studies of Revision: What we know and need to know', *Journal of Specialised Translation* 8: 5-20, http://www.jostrans.org/issue08/art_mossop.pdf [last accessed 8 August 2013].

(R) Mossop, Brian (2011) 'Revision', in Yves Gambier and Luc van Doorslaer (eds), *Handbook of Translation Studies: Volume 2,* Amsterdam: Benjamins, 135–139.

Nord, Christiane (1997) *Translating as a Purposeful Activity,* Manchester: St Jerome.

Nordman, Lieselott (2003) 'From Draft to Law - Studying the translation process of legal bills in Finland', in Heidrun Gerzymisch-Arbogast, Eva Hajičová, Petr Sgall, Zuzana Jettmarová, Annely Rothkegel and Dorothee Rothfuß-Bastian (eds) *Textologie und Translation,* Tübingen, Gunter Narr, 203-217.

O'Brien, Sharon (2012) 'Towards a Dynamic Quality Evaluation Model for Translation', *Journal of Specialised Translation* 17, http://www.jostrans.org/issue17/art_obrien.pdf [last accessed 12 August 2013].

*O'Connor, Maeve (1986) *How to Copyedit Scientific Books and Journals*, Philadelphia: ISI Press.

Olohan, Maeve (2004) *Introducing Corpora in Translation Studies*, London & New York: Routledge. Chapter 10.

(R) Parra Galiano, Silvia (2011) 'La Revisión en la Norma Europea EN-15038' [revision in the European standard EN-15038], *Entreculturas* 3: 165-187, http://www.entreculturas.uma.es/n3pdf/articulo09.pdf [last accessed 8 August 2013].

Pavlović, Nataša and Goranka Antunović (2011) 'Here and Now: Self-revision in student translation processes from L2 and L3', *Across Languages and Cultures* 12(2): 213-234.

Payne, Jerry (1987) 'Revision as a Teaching Method on Translating Courses', in Hugh Keith and Ian Mason (eds) *Translation in the Modern Languages Degree*, London: Centre for Information on Language Teaching and Research, 43-51.

Picken, Catriona (ed.) (1994) *Quality-assurance, Management & Control.* Proceedings of the Seventh Annual Conference of the Institute of Translation and Interpreting, London: ITI Publications.

(R) Prioux, René and Michel Rochard (2007) 'Économie de la révision dans une organisation internationale : le cas de l'OCDE' [revision at an international organization: the case of the OECD], *Journal of Specialised Translation* 8, http://www.jostrans. org/issue08/art_prioux_rochard.php [last accessed 8 August 2013].

(R) Rasmussen, Kirsten and Anne Schjoldager (2011) 'Revising Translations: A survey of revision policies in Danish translation companies', *Journal of Specialised Translation* 15, http://www.jostrans.org/issue15/art_rasmussen.php [last accessed 8 August 2013].

Risku, Hanna (2004) *Translationsmanagement. Interkulturelle Fachkommunikation im Informationszeitalter* [translation management – intercultural specialized communication in the information age], Tübingen: Narr. Sections 9.2.2.3 and 9.3.1.4.

(R) Robert, Isabelle (2008) 'Translation Revision Procedures: An explorative study' in Pieter Boulogne (ed.) *Translation and its Others. Selected Papers of the CETRA Research Seminar in Translation Studies 2007,* 1-25.

(R) Robert, Isabelle (2012) 'La révision en traduction : les procédures de révision et leur impact sur le produit et le processus de révision' [revision procedures and their impact on the product and process of revision], http://www.alineremael. be/data/These_ISBN_20120425_BW.pdf [last accessed 8 August 2013].

(R) Robert, Isabelle (2013) "Translation revision: Does the revision procedure matter?" in *Tracks and Treks in Translation Studies: Selected papers from the EST Congress, Leuven 2010,* Amsterdam: Benjamins, 87-102.

*Rodale, Jerome Irving (1947) *The Word Finder*, Emmaus PA: Rodale Books.

*Rude, Carolyn and Angela Eaton (2011) *Technical Editing* (5th edition), New York: Longman.

*Samson, Donald (1993) *Editing Technical Writing*, Oxford & New York: Oxford University Press.

Samuelsson-Brown, Geoffrey (1996) 'Working Procedures, Quality and Quality Assurance', in Rachel Owens (ed.) *The Translator's Handbook* (3rd edition), London: Aslib, 103-135.

Samuelsson-Brown, Geoffrey (2010) *A Practical Guide for Translators* (5th revised edition), Clevedon: Multilingual Matters.

Schjoldager, Anne, Kirsten Rasmussen and Christa Thomsen (2008) 'Précis-writing, Revision and Editing: Piloting the European Master in Translation', *Meta* 53(4): 798-813.

Schopp, Jürgen, (2007) 'Korrekturlesen - ein translatorisches Stiefkind?' [revision – a poor cousin of translation?] in *Lebende Sprachen* 52(2): 69-74.

Sedon-Strutt, Hugh (1990) 'The Revision of Translation Work', *Language International* 2(3): 28-30.

*Sellen, Abigail and Richard Harper (2001) *The Myth of the Paperless Office*, Cambridge MA: MIT Press.

Shih, Claire Yi-yi (2003) 'A Cognitive Approach to Three Trainee Translators' Overnight Revision Processes', *Translation Quarterly* 28, 1-17.

Shih, Claire Yi-yi (2006) "Revision from Translators' Point of View: An interview study", *Target* 18(2): 295-312.

Shuttleworth, Mark and Moira Cowie (1997) *Dictionary of Translation Studies*, Manchester: St Jerome.

*Steinberg, Erwin R. (ed) (1991) *Plain Language: Principles and practice,* Detroit: Wayne State University Press.

Stetting, Karen (1989) 'Transediting – A new term for coping with the grey area between editing and translating', in Graham Caie (ed.) *Proceedings from the Fourth Nordic Conference for English Studies*, Copenhagen: University of Copenhagen, 371-382.

Toury, Gideon (1995) 'Studying Interim Solutions', in *Descriptive Translation Studies and Beyond*, Benjamins: Amsterdam, 181-192.

(R) United Nations (2003) 'Inter-agency Meeting on Language Arrangements, Documentation and Publications, Working Group on Translation' (see especially Annexes 4 to 8). http://www.ilo.org/public/english/standards/relm/interagency/pdf/rep-wg-tran.pdf

(R) United Nations (2004) 'Inter-agency Meeting on Language Arrangements, Documentation and Publications, Report to IAMLADP 2004 Quality Management. http://uncti.net/pages/essays/quality_mngt.pdf

*Van de Poel, Kris, Wannie Carstens and John Linnegar (2012) *Text editing: A handbook for students and practitioners,* Antwerp: Uitgeverij UPA University Press.

Van Rensburg, Alta, Cobus Snyman and Susan Lotz (2012) 'Applying Google Translate in a Higher Education Environment: Translation products assessed', *Southern African Linguistics and Applied Language Studies,* 30(4): 511-524.

Vasconcellos, Muriel (1987) 'A Comparison of MT Postediting and Traditional Revision', in Karl Kummer (ed.) *Proceedings of the 28th Annual Conference of the American Translators Association*, Medford, NJ: Learned Information, 409-416.

*Ventola, Eija and Anna Mauranen (1991) 'Non-native Writing and Native Revising of Scientific Articles', in Eija Ventola (ed.), *Functional and Systemic Linguistics*, Berlin & New York: Mouton de Gruyter, 457-492.

Vuorinen, Erkka (1997) 'News translation as Gatekeeping', in Mary Snell-Hornby, Zuzana Jettmarová and Klaus Kaindl (eds) *Translation as Intercultural Communication: Selected papers from the EST Congress, Prague 1995,* Amsterdam & Philadelphia: Benjamins, 161-171.

*Wagner, Emma (2005) 'Translation and/or Editing: The way forward?', in Gunilla Anderman and Margaret Rogers (eds) *In and Out of English: For better, for worse?*, Clevedon: Multilingual Matters, 214-226.

*Westley, Bruce H. (1972) *News Editing*, New York: Houghton Miflin.

Williams, Malcolm (1989) 'The Assessment of Professional Translation Quality', *TTR* 2(2): 13-33.

Williams, Malcolm (2009) 'Translation Quality Assessment', *Mutatis Mutandis* 2(1): 3-23.

*Wood, Frederick T. (1967) *English Prepositional Idioms*, London: Macmillan.

Index